Let's Brew!

Mini Book Series

VOLUME XXX

By

Ronald Pattinson

Mini Book Series volume XXX: Let's Brew!

Copyright © 2017 Ronald Pattinson

The right of Ronald Pattinson to be identified as the author of his work has been asserted by him in accordance with the

COPYRIGHT, DESIGNS AND PATENTS ACT OF 1988

All rights reserved. No part of this publication may be reproduced, stored in a retrieval system, or transmitted, in any form or by any means without the prior written permission of the publisher, nor be otherwise circulated in any form other than that in which it is published and without a similar condition being imposed upon the subsequent purchaser.

1st edition

Published in August 2017 by

Kilderkin
171 hs Warmondstraat, Amsterdam, Noord- Holland

ISBN 978-94-90270-31-5

Mini Book Series volume XXX: Let's Brew!

Contents

Let's Brew!..1
Foreword...10
   Introduction to recipes 11
      Making invert sugar 12
I Mild Ale 13
   1914 Adnams XX Mild...14
   1950 Adnams XX Mild...15
   1904 Amsdell XX...16
   1838 Barclay Perkins X Ale 18
   1839 Barclay Perkins XX Ale 19
   1839 Barclay Perkins XXX Ale..20
   1857 Barclay Perkins X Ale 21
   1862 Barclay Perkins XX 22
   1862 Barclay Perkins XXX 23
   1880 Barclay Perkins XX 24
   1880 Barclay Perkins X 25
   1887 Barclay Perkins X 26
   1899 Barclay Perkins X 28
   1914 Barclay Perkins X 30
   1916 Barclay Perkins X 31
   1917 Barclay Perkins X 32
   1917 (April) Barclay Perkins Government Ale 34
   1917 (November) Barclay Perkins Government Ale.................................36
   1939 Boddington Mild..38
   1955 Flowers XXX...40
   1946 Fullers X 42
   1937 Greene King XX 43
   1950 Lees Best Mild...45
   1958 Lees Best Mild...46
   1963 Lees Mild 47
   1947 Shepherd Neame MB 49
   1916 Tetley X3 51
   1919 Tetley F 52
   1946 Tetley Mild 54
   1956 Shepherd Neame MB 55
   1952 Strong XXX Mild 56
   1969 Truman LM...58
   1917 Wadworth XXXX...60
   1837 Whitbread X..61
   1905 Whitbread XK...63
   1954 Whitbread Best Ale...64
II Pale Ale...65
   1913 Adnams BLB...66
   1950 Adnams PA 68
   1959 Adnams LBA 69

3

Mini Book Series volume XXX: Let's Brew!

1946 Fullers PA	70
1958 Fullers London Pride	72
1955 Flowers PX	73
1955 Flowers GL	75
1955 Flowers BX	78
1955 Flowers IPA	80
1955 Flowers OB	82
1955 Flowers Stout	84
1937 Greene King AK	86
1937 Greene King IPA	87
1950 Lees Bitter	88
1984 Maclay PA 6d	90
1984 Maclay Export	92
1984 Maclay SPA	93
1933 Perry IPA	94
1966 Perry Phoenix Ale	95
1838 Reid IPA	96
1947 Shepherd Neame LDA	98
1947 Shepherd Neame BB	100
1947 Shepherd Neame BA	101
1956 Shepherd Neame SXX	102
1956 Shepherd Neame Abbey Ale	103
1956 Shepherd Neame PA	105
1869 Simonds XXX Pale	106
1952 Strong SAK	107
1952 Strong Golden Ale	109
1952 Strong SPA	111
1885 Thomas Usher 80/-	114
1855 Truman EI Contract IPA	115
1877 Truman P1	116
1883 Truman P2	117
1883 Truman P1 S	118
1887 Truman LB	119
1963 Watneys Keg Red Barrel	120
1972 Watneys Red	121
1909 Whitbread IPA	122
1909 Whitbread PA	123
1957 Whitbread IPA	124
1959 Whitbread PA	125
Whitbread Session IPA	126
1962 Whitbread Ex PA	128
1957 Robert Younger Export	129
1879 William Younger 80/-	131
III Porter and Stout	132
1950 Adnams DS Stout	133
1933 Barclay Perkins Milk Stout	135

4

1901 Boddington Stout 137
1915 Courage Porter 139
1915 Courage Double Stout 140
1915 Courage Imperial Stout 141
1946 Fullers P 142
1956 Lees Stout 144
1962 Lees Archer Stout 145
1935 Perry Special Stout 147
1937 Perry XX Stout 148
1837 Reid DBSt 149
1837 Reid P 151
1837 Reid BS 153
1838 Reid EBSt 155
1838 Reid KBSt 156
1845 Reid SS 157
1877 Reid Rg 158
1877 Reid Crs 159
1877 Reid S 160
1877 Reid SS 161
1877 Reid SSS 163
1947 Shepherd Neame SS 164
1952 Strong Black Bess Stout 166
1858 Tetley SP 168
1858 Tetley X2P 169
1858 Tetley X1P 170
1868 Tetley X3P 171
1868 Tetley X1P 172
1850 Truman Export Keeping 173
1850 Truman Imperial Stout 175
1856 Truman Crimea Porter 176
1943 Whitbread Mackeson Stout 177
1947 Whitbread Stout 179
1948 Whitbread Extra Stout 181
1954 Whitbread Mackeson Stout 183
1973 Whitbread Mackeson Stout 185
1868 William Younger DBS 186
1939 William Younger Btlg DBS 188
IV Strong Ale 190
  1949 Adnams XXXX 191
  1953 Adnams Tally Ho 193
  1891 Barclay Perkins KK 195
  1891 Barclay Perkins KKK 197
  1909 Barclay Perkins KK 198
  1913 Boddington CC 200
  1939 Boddington CC 202
  1914 Courage XX 204

1955 Flowers SA 205
1946 Fullers BO 206
1958 Fullers Old Burton Extra 207
1958 Fullers Strong Ale 208
1951 Lees "C" Ale 209
1954 Lees Golden Brew 211
1992 Maclay Scotch Ale 212
1952 Strong SSB 214
1853 Reid KK 216
1853 Reid KKK 217
1853 Reid KKKK 218
1954 Tennant's Gold Label 219
1877 Truman K4 221
1883 Truman S4 x 222
1887 Truman S3 223
1887 Truman S5 224
1914 Truman S3 225
V Lager 226
   Notes on Lager recipes 227
      Munich method 227
      The Bohemian method 228
      Triple Decoction 229
      The Kulmbach method of decoction 229
      Double decoction 230
      Bohemian double decoction 231
   1866 Munich Bock 232
   1896 Munich Lagerbier 233
   1869 Vienna Märzen 234
   1870 Bohemian Summer Beer 235
   1888 Bohemian Export 236
   1929 Bohemian Lagerbier 237
   1929 Bohemian Schankbier 238
   1929 Bohemian Doppelbier 239
   1879 Kulmbacher Export 240
   1911 Heineken Bok 241
   1911 Heineken Gerste 242
   1911 Heineken Beiersch 243
   1911 Heineken Pils 244
   1911 Heineken Lagerbier 245
   1933 Oranjeboom Pils 247
   1933 Oranjeboom Munchener 248
   1933 Oranjeboom Licht Gerste 249
   1933 Oranjeboom Gerste 250
   1933 Oranjeboom Stout 251
   1933 Oranjeboom Bok 252
   1956 Amstel Gold 253

1956 Amstel Pils	254
1956 Amstel Oud Bruin	255
1927 Barclay Perkins Export	256
1925 Barclay Perkins Dark Lager	258
1932 Barclay Perkins Draught Lager	259
1939 Barclay Perkins Sparkling Beer	260
1942 Barclay Perkins Export	261
1942 Barclay Perkins Draught Lager	262
1941 Barclay Perkins Dark Lager	264
1953 Barclay Perkins Export	265
1953 Barclay Perkins Sparkling Beer	266
1953 Barclay Perkins Dark Lager	267
1953 Barclay Perkins Draught Lager	268
1959 Lees Lager	269
1964 Eldridge Pope Konig Lager	270
1888 Tennent's Lager Beer	271
1940 Whitbread Lager	272
1969 Truman LL	273
VI Brown Ale	**276**
1955 Fullers Old Harry	277
1963 Manns Brown Ale	279
1956 Shepherd Neame DB	280
1959 Watneys Brown Ale	281
1954 Whitbread Double Brown	283
1954 Whitbread Forest Brown	285
1968 Whitbread Forest Brown	287
VII North America	**290**
1833 Vassar Double Ale	291
1833 Vassar Single Ale	292
1834 Vassar Pale Double Stock Ale	293
1893 Labbatt Pale Ale	294
1893 Labatt IPA	295
1893 Labatt Brown Stout	296
1904 Amsdell Burton	297
1905 Amsdell India Pale Ale	299
1900 Amsdell Winter Stock	300
1900 Amsdell Winter XX	301
1900 Amsdell Export Scotch	302
1900 Amsdell Special Still	303
1900 Amsdell Light XXX Stock Ale	304
1901 Amsdell Polar	305
1901 Amsdell XX	306
1901 Amsdell Diamond Stock	307
1901 Amsdell Sth Porter	308
1904 Amsdell XX	309
Index	310

Mini Book Series volume XXX: Let's Brew!

Mini Book Series volume XXX: Let's Brew!

Mini Book Series

What started out as a way of collecting together my blog posts into a series of small books. Mostly for my own convenience, but with the thought in the back of my mind that I might be able to shift a few.

As I wrote more and more blog posts – which I added to the initially quite small volumes – I soon ended up with books which weren't very mini at all. And as I thought of more themes to assemble my posts under, the number of books began to grow, too. The initial set of eleven had soon doubled in number. I'm now up to volume XXX. Even I struggle to remember all the titles.

Doubtless – unless I'm hit by a tram next week – there will be more volumes to come. There's just so much I want to write about. And my list of beery obsessions grows ever longer. Feel free to buy them all. Then I might be able to retire early. Which has been my dream since, er, I started working.

Amsterdam, July 29th 2017.

Mini Book Series volume XXX: Let's Brew!

Foreword

This started as such a simple project. But it all got a bit out of hand.

The original idea was to produce a compilation of my Let's Brew recipes from the past two years. I've been writing a lot of recipes and it would be handy (for me, if no-one else) to have them handily in one spot rather than scattered about the blog.

But when I looked at what I'd assembled, I realised it was unbalanced. Lots of Mild recipe, but not many Stout ones. Lots from the 1940s and 1950s, but little from the 19th century. So I started working on some extra recipes to fill in the gaps.

It made sense to try to use some of the brewing records I'd never done much with. Like Reid, for example. Then I thought, wouldn't it be nice to finally publish some more North American recipes. Especially as that might tempt people to buy the book. Then I started thinking about all the Lager stuff I'd accumulated. Why not include some of that, too?

Hopefully this book contains a set of recipes that will entice and delight you. And remember, I'm always happy to receive bottles, should a beer turn out particularly nice. After all, the main point of me publishing these recipes is so I can get to drink the beers. Thirsty work, burrowing away in dusty archives.

Amsterdam, July 29th 2017.

Mini Book Series volume XXX: Let's Brew!

Introduction to recipes

A couple of remarks before you dive into the recipes.

First, I'm not going to try to explain how to brew in this book. I'm assuming that you already know that. If you don't, this isn't a good place to start. The one exception is a description of various methods of decoction mashing to accompany the Lager recipes.

These recipes have been written using original brewing records as the source. The level of detail on old brewing logs varies greatly. Some, especially the older ones, are a bit vague. Many miss out completely vital pieces of information.

How have I coped with missing information? I'll be honest: I've guessed. Not just random guesses, but ones based on other sources, such as brewing manuals. Or later brewing records from the same brewery. It's not perfect, but it's the best that can be done.

Virtually no logs have any record of the hop additions. With the exception of some 20th-century Barclay Perkins logs. All the other hop additions listed in these recipes are a guesstimate. Feel free to tinker with them as suits you.

The ingredients, mashing details, OG and FG are always taken from the original brewing records.

It should be noted, however, that before 1880 I assume the quarters used to measure malt are volume rather than weight. I've assumed a quarter of pale malt to be 324 pounds and black or brown malt to be 244 pounds. These weights are based on figures given in brewing records of the period. After 1880, I assume all quarters of grain to be 336 pounds and a quarter of sugar as 224 pounds.

Care should be taken with the quantity of hops used. I've used the original quantities, with no attempt to take into account the age of the hops. For authenticity, you might want to reduce the amount of hops, especially when those used in the original were two or more years old.

Getting a perfect match for 19th-century malts is likely to be tricky. Especially for brown and amber malt, which varied over time and from one maltster to another. In particular the brown malt used before the introduction of black malt was quite different from modern versions. Mild malt is probably the best modern match for lower-quality 19th-century pale malt, used in beers such as Mild and Porter. For Pale Ales, I'd stick to pale malt.

In the 20th-century recipes, the sugars are the problem. Brewers used a whole range of different sugars, many of them proprietary brands. I'm not sure if exact equivalents are available at all today, let alone to home brewers.

Numbered invert sugars are a bit easier. I know exactly what they are and they're still produced commercially. Except it's almost impossible for the home brewer to buy them.

Which is why I've included below instructions on how to make them.

Hops are rather simpler. Where it says EK or MK, you can't go far wrong with Goldings for early 19th century beers. After 1870 or so a combination of Fuggles and Goldings would be a good approximation. Cluster is best for anything called American, Oregon, Californian or Pacific.

Making invert sugar

As brewers' invert sugars aren't easily available, making them yourself is probably the best option. It doesn't take a huge amount of ingredients or equipment. You'll need:

- cane sugar (not table sugar)
- citric acid
- water
- a candy thermometer
- a saucepan

This is what you do:

- For each pound (455 g) of sugar you use, bring 1 pint (473 ml) of water to the boil.
- Switch off the heat and add the sugar slowly, dissolving it.
- Add 1/4 teaspoon (1 g) of citric acid per pound of sugar.
- Turn on the heat again (not too high) and set the alarm on the candy thermometer to 230°F (110°C).
- Stir frequently while it starts to simmer.
- When the temperature hits 230°F (110, reset the alarm for 240°F (115.6°C).
- Heat slowly (the slower the better) until the temperature gets to 240°F (115.6°C).
- Lower the heat to keep at 240°F–250°F (115.6°C –121.1°C).
- For No. 1 maintain at heat for 20–30 minutes.
- For No. 2 maintain at heat for 90–120 minutes.
- For No. 3 maintain at heat for 150–210 minutes.
- For No. 4 maintain at heat for 240–300 minutes.

The colours you're aiming for are:

- No. 1, 12-16 SRM
- No. 2, 30-35 SRM
- No. 3, 60-70 SRM
- No. 4, 275-325 SRM

Mini Book Series volume XXX: Let's Brew!

I Mild Ale

Mini Book Series volume XXX: Let's Brew!

1914 Adnams XX Mild

While it's still May I suppose I should come up with some more Mild recipes. Like this slight oddity.

Why is it odd? Because of its strength. Or maybe I'm just too used to looking at London beers. This beer was originally brewed just as WW I was breaking out. At the time, a standard London X Ale had and OG of around 1055° and an ABV of 5.5%. With a gravity of just 1042°, Adnams XX looks more like a 1920's Mild.

But maybe I shouldn't be do surprised. Before WW I, breweries didn't really compete on price. The cost of a barrel of beer of a certain type was the same whichever brewery you bought it from. Large, efficient breweries, such as those in London, instead of discounting the price simply made their beer stronger. As quite a small, rural brewery, Adnams wouldn't have been able to brew as efficiently as Whitbread or Truman.

The grist is pretty simple, though there are three types of malt: pale, crystal and "medium". For the latter I've substituted mild malt. Other than that, there's a bit of flaked maize and sugar. The latter mostly in the form of "cane blocks", but also a little tintose, which was presumably a type of caramel used for colour corrections. Not sure what colour that was 5000 SRM is a guess on the dark side.

The hops I only know to have been from Oregon and East Kent. I've interpreted those as Cluster and Goldings, respectively. You could replace the Goldings with Fuggles or some other appropriate English hop.

1914 Adnams XX		
pale malt	2.75 lb	30.32%
mild malt	4.00 lb	44.10%
crystal malt 80 L	0.50 lb	5.51%
flaked maize	0.50 lb	5.51%
cane sugar	1.25 lb	13.78%
caramel 5000 SRM	0.07 lb	0.77%
Cluster 105 mins	0.50 oz	
Goldings 60 mins	0.50 oz	
Goldings 30 mins	0.50 oz	
OG	1042	
FG	1008	
ABV	4.50	
Apparent attenuation	80.95%	
IBU	23	
SRM	25	
Mash at	152° F	
Sparge at	170° F	
Boil time	105 minutes	
pitching temp	60° F	
Yeast	WLP025 Southwold	

Mini Book Series volume XXX: Let's Brew!

1950 Adnams XX Mild

Time to look at Adnams other draught beer from 1950, their XX Mild.

Do you know what's really, really weird about this beer? It's stronger than it was in 1939. I can't think of another beer where that statement is true. Why should that be? Because Adnams didn't brew what I would call a full-strength Mild before WW II. They brewed what I would call a 4d Ale. A low-gravity type of Mild that was the bastard son of WW I's Government Ale. Adnams had gravity of 1029°, while a standard Mild would have been around 1036° and a strong Mild over 1040°. XX spent most of the war at 1027° before rising to 1030° in 1950.

I quite like the look if the grist. I've come across a couple of interesting Mild recipes from the 1950's. Ones that include some coloured malts like this does. Lees Mild springs to mind. This, with both amber and crystal malts, probably drank above its gravity. Obviously, there was also No.3 invert sugar and caramel to add extra colour and depth of flavour. Plus little bitterness. I'd order a pint if I saw it on the bar.

This was surely also the basis of Adnams Nut Brown Ale. There's no separate brew of Nut Brown Ale so I assume it was a bottled version of this. It may have been primed differently before bottling, but the basic recipe would have been identical.

1950 Adnams XX		
mild malt	5.00 lb	78.43%
amber malt	0.50 lb	7.84%
crystal malt 80L	0.50 lb	7.84%
no. 3 sugar	0.25 lb	3.92%
caramel	0.13 lb	1.96%
Fuggles 90 min	0.75 oz	
Fuggles 30 min	0.50 oz	
OG	1030	
FG	1005.5	
ABV	3.24	
Apparent attenuation	81.67%	
IBU	20	
SRM	27	
Mash at	148° F	
Sparge at	170° F	
Boil time	120 minutes	
pitching temp	61° F	
Yeast	WLP025 Southwold	

1904 Amsdell XX

Now here's one for the historians – a genuine Albany Ale.

The New York state capital was long famed for its brewing industry, starting with the Dutch settlers. They swapped over to brewing English styles in the 19th century, but by the end of the century German techniques were starting to take over.

Which is what makes these records so fascinating. English-style beer being brewed using German techniques like kräusening. And measuring gravity in Balling rather than pounds per barrel, even though there's still a place for what they call "long" gravity on the brewing log.

One of the mainstays of American Ale brewing was something called XX or XXX. Obviously a descendent of English Mild Ales, unlike its ancestor across the Atlantic, it didn't turn dark at the start of the 20th century.

I've drunk an example of a XXX Ale myself – Ballantine's. It was still available when I lived in New York in the mid-1980's. At the time, I didn't realise that I was drinking the US equivalent of Mild.

As for the Amsdell beer, it's not a million miles away from an English X Ale of the period. It's about the same gravity. And the grist of pale malt, sugar and flaked maize is similar, too. Though the percentage of flaked maize wasn't usually higher than 15% in the UK. With their more diastatic malt, American brewers could get away with using more adjuncts.

This beer comes out pretty hoppy. The IBUs are, in fact, higher than most UK X Ales of the time. Now there's a surprise.

Mini Book Series volume XXX: Let's Brew!

1904 Amsdell XX		
pale malt 6 row	8.50 lb	70.10%
Black malt	0.125 lb	1.03%
Glucose	0.75 lb	6.19%
Syrup	0.25 lb	2.06%
Flaked maize	2.50 lb	20.62%
Cluster 90 min	2.00 oz	
Cluster 30 min	1.00 oz	
OG	1055	
FG	1016	
ABV	5.16	
Apparent attenuation	70.91%	
IBU	58	
SRM	9	
Mash at	158° F	
Sparge at	160° F	
Boil time	90 minutes	
pitching temp	60° F	
Yeast	Wyeast 1099 Whitbread Ale	

Mini Book Series volume XXX: Let's Brew!

1838 Barclay Perkins X Ale

Pretty sure that it's still May. Got to keep those Mild recipes coming.

I was rather shocked to see how few Barclay Perkins recipes there are in my book "Mild! plus". Just a couple from the 1930's and 1940's.

I'll admit to ulterior motives. And not just trying to slip in as many Barclay Perkins references as possible. Though that's always good, too. No, my aims are far more noble. I want to remind everyone that Mild Ale wasn't always a low-gravity beer. That it's a piss simple recipe for me to write is by the by.

The original recipe was slightly more complicated than mine, the grist being about a 50-50 split of Herts. pale and Herts. white malt. I suppose you could use half mild malt and half pale malt to emulate this.

The hops in the original were half 1837 EK and half 1838 MK. So all pretty fresh hops (it was brewed on 22nd November). Usually to interpret MK as Fuggles and EK as Goldings. But this is a few decades too early for Fuggles, leaving me no option but to go for all Goldings. You may have noticed that there are rather a lot of them. Which brings me onto another point: Mild Ale wasn't always lightly hopped.

The mashing scheme is pretty complicated: and infusion mash with a strike heat of 170° F, flowed by an underlet at 190° F, then a third mash at 200° F. There were two further mashes for return worts. This is pretty typical of the multi-mash schemes favoured in London in the first half of the 19th century.

Not much else really to say. Other than: drink Mild!

1838 Barclay Perkins X Ale		
pale malt	16.25 lb	100.00%
Goldings 300 mins	2.50 oz	
Goldings 90 mins	2.50 oz	
Goldings 30 mins	2.50 oz	
OG	1071.5	
FG	1012.4	
ABV	7.82	
Apparent attenuation	82.66%	
IBU	89	
SRM	7	
Mash at	151° F	
Sparge at	170° F	
Boil time	300 minutes	
pitching temp	59° F	
Yeast	Wyeast 1099 Whitbread Ale	

Mini Book Series volume XXX: Let's Brew!

1839 Barclay Perkins XX Ale

Another Mild for May. This time a lightly beefier one from the 1830's.

It's as uncomplicated as an early 19th-century recipe can be. The original only had two ingredients (other than yeast and water): Herts white malt and MK hops. So not only two ingredients, but also ones that were relatively locally-sourced. This would be the case for much longer. After 1840 foreign hops and foreign barley were imported in increasingly large quantities. The UK wouldn't be self-sufficient in brewing materials again until the 1940's.

I've actually reduced the hopping a little – it actually worked out to 9 oz. in total. But as they were all from the 1838 harvest and this beer was brewed in September 1839, it seems logical to knock it down a bit to take into account their age.

Probably not most people's idea of a Mild: pale, 9.5% ABV and 90 IBU. It just shows how much a style can change over time.

1839 Barclay Perkins XX Ale		
pale malt	19.75 lb	100.00%
Goldings 150 mins	2.75 oz	
Goldings 90 mins	2.75 oz	
Goldings 30 mins	2.75 oz	
OG	1087.3	
FG	1015.5	
ABV	9.50	
Apparent attenuation	82.25%	
IBU	90	
SRM	8	
Mash at	149° F	
Sparge at	168° F	
Boil time	150 minutes	
pitching temp	58° F	
Yeast	Wyeast 1099 Whitbread Ale	

Mini Book Series volume XXX: Let's Brew!

1839 Barclay Perkins XXX Ale

One final Mild for May. A rather beefy beer.

I can guess what you're thinking: that isn't a Mild, it's a Double IPA. Or a Barley Wine. Anything but a Mild. But that's definitely what this is.

The recipe is very much like the XX. There's just a bit more of everything. All of Barclay Perkins beers were pretty strong at this point. The only one under 6% ABV was their Table Beer, which was a sort of low-gravity Porter. Though even that was 3.5% ABV. And that was for the kiddies.

You may have noticed that some of Barclay's Ales of this period had very long boils, as much as 5 hours in some cases. It would be nice to compare and contrast Ale boil times with those for Porter and Stout. Unfortunately, even though they're in the same brewing book, there are no details of boil times for the Porters.

What's odd is that the Ale and Porter records are in different formats, too. No idea why that should be. They didn't have a dedicated Ale brewery at this point.

Barclay Perkins only started brewing Ales in the 1830's. As did all the other big Porter breweries. It's undoubtedly related to the 1830 Beer Act. This introduced a new type of the pub, the beer house, which couldn't sell spirits. These seem to have greatly boosted the popularity of Ales, prompting the Porter brewers to get in on the action.

Until then they had only tied their pubs for Porter and Stout, letting them buy in Ales from wherever they liked. By the 1870s Ale had outstripped Porter in sales, even in London. Ale, in the form of Mild Ale, was to retain its dominance for almost a century.

1839 Barclay Perkins XXX Ale		
pale malt	23.50 lb	100.00%
Goldings 240 mins	3.50 oz	
Goldings 90 mins	3.50 oz	
Goldings 30 mins	3.50 oz	
OG	1104	
FG	1018	
ABV	11.38	
Apparent attenuation	82.69%	
IBU	114	
SRM	9	
Mash at	147° F	
Sparge at	165° F	
Boil time	240 minutes	
pitching temp	58° F	
Yeast	Wyeast 1099 Whitbread Ale	

Mini Book Series volume XXX: Let's Brew!

1857 Barclay Perkins X Ale

I know. May is over. But I can't help myself. Plus I've published so few Barclay Perkins Mild Ale recipes from the 19th century.

Nearly 20 years on and not much has changed. OK, the OG has dropped by six points. But the hopping has remained identical. And all fresh English hops. This was brewed in May 1857 and the hops were all MK (Mid Kent) from the 1856 harvest. Basically as fresh as was possible.

The grist 100% HW (Hertfordshire while malt). Meaning the ingredients were all pretty local. About as local as you could get, it your brewery was in London.

It's interesting to not how different the fermentation profile is compared to the Porters and Stouts in the same brewing book. The Ales fermented much cooler. This beer was pitched at 59.5° F and reached a maximum of 75.23° F. The Porters were pitched at 66-67° F and peaked around 80° F.

I'll be fascinated to see how soon the foreign ingredients kick as we track Barclay Perkins Mild Ales through the 19th century.

1857 Barclay Perkins X Ale		
pale malt	14.75 lb	100.00%
Goldings 150 mins	2.50 oz	
Goldings 90 mins	2.50 oz	
Goldings 30 mins	2.50 oz	
OG	1065.4	
FG	1011.4	
ABV	7.14	
Apparent attenuation	82.57%	
IBU	94	
SRM	6	
Mash at	150° F	
Sparge at	172° F	
Boil time	150 minutes	
pitching temp	59.5° F	
Yeast	Wyeast 1099 Whitbread Ale	

Mini Book Series volume XXX: Let's Brew!

1862 Barclay Perkins XX

These Barclay Perkins early Mild recipes are such fun, I just have to keep on going. Plus they're a handy addition to the new edition of "Mild! Plus" I'm working.

Working on along with several other projects. "Victory!" – have I ever published that? (I've just checked.) Nope, not published that yet. And it could be a little tricky to release, seeing as it weighs in at almost 900 pages. Considerably more than the maximum Lulu book length. Looks like it will need to be a two volume job.

But I digress like a politician asked a tricky question. Back to Mild Ale, in particular the 1862 XX of my favourite London brewery Barclay Perkins.

As you can see, this is another typical Victorian Mild Ale, pale in colour, high in alcohol and packed full of hops. Just about everything a modern Mild isn't. But what would be the fun if this was exactly like modern interpretations of the style? Plus I'd be out of a job.

Once again, the recipe is dead simple. Just white malt and Kent hops. The brewing record doesn't even specify which bit of Kent. Goldings are always a safe bet. I'm slightly surprised that no foreign ingredients have shown up in these recipes yet. A lot of US hops were being imported in the 1860's.

You'll note that the boil has become much shorter, down from 3 hours or more to just 75 minutes. I've absolutely no idea why the earlier boils were so long nor why they were suddenly cut so much.

1862 Barclay Perkins XX Ale		
pale malt	18.00 lb	100.00%
Goldings 75 mins	3.00 oz	
Goldings 60 mins	3.00 oz	
Goldings 30 mins	3.00 oz	
OG	1079.2	
FG	1020	
ABV	7.83	
Apparent attenuation	74.75%	
IBU	92	
SRM	7	
Mash at	148° F	
Sparge at	163° F	
Boil time	75 minutes	
pitching temp	64° F	
Yeast	Wyeast 1099 Whitbread Ale	

Mini Book Series volume XXX: Let's Brew!

1862 Barclay Perkins XXX

You know what I can never get too much of? Crazy old Mild recipes. This is another good one.

And proof – should you have doubted my word – that the term "Mild" had nothing to do with low ABV or a low hopping rate.

By the 1860s, XXX was Barclay Perkins top of the range Mild Ale. Though it wasn't around for that much. My last spotting of it was in 1869. I'm not sure why, but, despite the style's huge popularity, London brewers had dropped all but X Ale by 1900. Super strong Mild had, perhaps, simply gone out of fashion.

A majority of the hops were pretty fresh, but I've still reduced the hopping rate. Nevertheless, it ends up with well over 100 calculated IBUs. Not exactly typical for a Mild today. I've just guessed the hop varieties. All I know for certain is that they were English.

As for the malt, the original contained 20 of pale and 100 of white malt. So I'm sure it would have been a pretty pale beer. Probably around what BeerSmith calculated.

Not sure that there's much else I can tell you.

1862 Barclay Perkins XXX Ale		
mild malt	22.50 lb	100.00%
Goldings 75 mins	5.00 oz	
Goldings 60 mins	5.00 oz	
Goldings 30 mins	5.00 oz	
OG	1098.6	
FG	1030	
ABV	9.08	
Apparent attenuation	69.57%	
IBU	132	
SRM	9	
Mash at	151° F	
Sparge at	165° F	
Boil time	75 minutes	
pitching temp	60° F	
Yeast	Wyeast 1099 Whitbread Ale	

Mini Book Series volume XXX: Let's Brew!

1880 Barclay Perkins XX

This will be exciting for you. An old Mild recipe with more than just mild malt and Goldings. Yes, a truly thrilling change of pace.

The OG is the same as in the 1860's, but there have been changes elsewhere. There's sugar in addition to malt and American hops as well as English ones. Despite the use of higher alpha hops, the calculated IBUs are down. So quite a different beer.

I'm not sure exactly when the 1880 Free Mash Tun Act came into effect, but I suspect it was later than March, which is when this beer was brewed. Which would explain the absence of unmalted grain. Sugar, remember, had been allowed since 1847.

Talking of sugar, No. 1 invert is a guess. The only description of it in the log simply says: "Scotch". Feel free to use any type you fancy. It could have been just straight sucrose, for all we know.

The hops are described as MK and American. I think my choice of varieties is about right. Though you could substitute Goldings for the Fuggles.

1880 Barclay Perkins XX Ale		
pale malt	14.00 lb	86.15%
No. 1 invert sugar	2.25 lb	13.85%
Cluster 90 min	4.00 oz	
Fuggles 60 mins	2.25 oz	
Fuggles 30 mins	2.25 oz	
OG	1079.5	
FG	1027.7	
ABV	6.85	
Apparent attenuation	65.16%	
IBU	106	
SRM	9	
Mash at	160° F	
Sparge at	170° F	
Boil time	90 minutes	
pitching temp	59° F	
Yeast	Wyeast 1099 Whitbread Ale	

Mini Book Series volume XXX: Let's Brew!

1880 Barclay Perkins X

And here's the X Ale to go with the XX Ale. They really do go together, as they were the two parts of a parti-gyle.

Which is going to make my life easy. Everything I said about the XX in terms of grist and hopping also applies to this beer.

Despite being the smaller sibling, this beer still packs a fair punch. It's well north of 5% ABV, but it's the IBUs that most intrigued me. They're exactly the same as for XX, even though I've scaled the quantity down perfectly correctly. It interested me, at least.

Not really much more to say. Just enjoy the recipe. And drink Mild!

1880 Barclay Perkins X Ale		
pale malt	10.75 lb	86.00%
No. 1 invert sugar	1.75 lb	14.00%
Cluster 90 min	3.50 oz	
Fuggles 60 mins	2.00 oz	
Fuggles 30 mins	2.00 oz	
OG	1060.4	
FG	1018	
ABV	5.61	
Apparent attenuation	70.20%	
IBU	106	
SRM	7.5	
Mash at	160° F	
Sparge at	170° F	
Boil time	90 minutes	
pitching temp	59° F	
Yeast	Wyeast 1099 Whitbread Ale	

1887 Barclay Perkins X

There's a reason why I'm publishing a Barclay Perkins X recipe that's just a few years later than the last one. There had been a couple of significant changes to the recipe in the intervening years.

This is when Mild recipes started to take on their modern form. The 1880 Free Mash Tun act allowed brewers much greater freedom in their choice of ingredients and they were soon taking advantage. In this case, by using flaked rice.

That's a slightly unusual choice of adjunct. Usually flaked maize was preferred, but in the early years a few breweries played around with rice. My guess is that the reason they eventually plumped for maize was cost.

The other big change to the grist is the addition of crystal malt. In the 19th century crystal malt was mostly used in Mild Ales and Porter, the styles for which it was originally designed. Its use in Pale Ales was much later, mostly after WW II.

Another big change from the 1880 version is the hopping rate, which has been greatly reduced. The calculated IBUs have fallen from over 100 to just 34. I wish I had records for all the intervening years so I could see if this was a gradual process or more abrupt.

The hops now include some "Bavarians" which I've interpreted as Spalt. While I've substituted No. 1 invert for the unspecified sugar in the brewing log.

Quite big changes in a short space of time. The next significant transformation for Mild Ale was going dark. Or at least darker.

Mini Book Series volume XXX: Let's Brew!

1887 Barclay Perkins X Ale		
pale malt	8.50 lb	70.83%
crystal malt 60L	0.50 lb	4.17%
flaked rice	1.50 lb	12.50%
No. 1 invert sugar	1.50 lb	12.50%
Fuggles 75 mins	1.00 oz	
Spalt 60 min	1.00 oz	
Goldings 30 mins	1.00 oz	
OG	1057.7	
FG	1015	
ABV	5.65	
Apparent attenuation	74.00%	
IBU	34	
SRM	9	
Mash at	150° F	
Sparge at	180° F	
Boil time	75 minutes	
pitching temp	63° F	
Yeast	Wyeast 1099 Whitbread Ale	

Mini Book Series volume XXX: Let's Brew!

1899 Barclay Perkins X

You're probably thinking: why is he still publishing Mild recipes when it's almost the end of June? Because I can.

That's the great thing about being your own man, without any editor or publisher to oblige. I can do what the hell I want, when I want to do it.be continuing to roll through Barclay Perkins X Ale recipes until I get to the 1930's.

At first glance, this looks pretty similar to the 1887 recipe. Though on closer inspection there have been some significant changes. The most obvious being that the flaked rice has been replaced by flaked maize. Presumably on cost grounds.

The sugar content has increased from 12.5% to 18.45%. If only I knew for certain what type of sugar it was. Whereas in the last recipe I was fairly confident about my guess of No. 1 invert, this time I'm not so sure. The brewing record is no more specific than "Sacch.". But I know this is about when Mild started turning darker. So it's possible that the sugar was No. 3. Though it could also have been something else. There's no way of knowing for sure.

I'm 100% sure that the Goldings in this recipe are Goldings, because it specifically says so in the brewing record. The other two hops don't get more specific than MK and American.

Note that the boil time has increased again. It's most confusing, this jumping around in the length of the boil. Absolutely no idea why they kept changing it.

1899 Barclay Perkins X Ale		
pale malt	7.75 lb	70.45%
crystal malt	0.25 lb	2.27%
flaked maize	1.00 lb	9.09%
No. 3 invert sugar	2.00 lb	18.18%
Cluster 120 mins	1.00 oz	
Fuggles 120 mins	0.25 oz	
Fuggles 60 mins	1.25 oz	
Goldings 30 mins	1.25 oz	
OG	1054.7	
FG	1009.4	
ABV	5.99	
Apparent attenuation	82.82%	
IBU	52	
SRM	14	
Mash at	150° F	
Sparge at	168° F	
Boil time	120 minutes	
pitching temp	61° F	
Yeast	Wyeast 1099 Whitbread Ale	

Mini Book Series volume XXX: Let's Brew!

1914 Barclay Perkins X

I hope you've been paying attention to all these X Ale recipes. Because they're telling a tale. About how a beer changes over time.

Despite only 15 years having elapsed since the last recipe, there have been considerable changes. Crystal malt has been dropped and amber malt added. I know for certain that this one contained No. 3 invert sugar. As well as something called "dark sacc." Which I've replaced with more No. 3.

But the biggest change is the hopping rate which has almost halved. As have the calculated IBUs. There are no American hops, either, this time. Just Mid Kent and East Kent hops, which I've interpreted as Fuggles and Goldings respectively.

Almost forgot. There's also some caramel in this recipe. Add that to the dark sugar and amber malt and the result is: a significantly darker beer. We've caught Mild turning dark. I'm not totally sure of the finished colour, as I don't know how dark the caramel was. The 20 SRM in the recipe is a guess. Based on the other ingredients, BeerSmith calculated the colour at 14 SRM.

Note that, despite all the other changes, the boil time has remained constant at 2 hours. Though due to everything else, I'm sure the finished beer looked and tasted quite different.

What's next? Some nice watery recipes from WW I.

1914 Barclay Perkins X Ale		
pale malt	6.50 lb	61.90%
amber malt	0.75 lb	7.14%
flaked maize	1.25 lb	11.90%
no. 3 sugar	2.00 lb	19.05%
Fuggles 120 mins	0.75 oz	
Fuggles 60 mins	0.75 oz	
Goldings 30 mins	0.75 oz	
OG	1051.3	
FG	1013.6	
ABV	4.99	
Apparent attenuation	73.49%	
IBU	27	
SRM	20	
Mash at	153° F	
Sparge at	170° F	
Boil time	120 minutes	
pitching temp	61° F	
Yeast	Wyeast 1099 Whitbread Ale	

1916 Barclay Perkins X

Now we've got to WW I we're going to be going through the years rather more slowly than before. There was just so much happening.

Though not in the early years of the war. Apart from gravities falling a small amount, there wasn't much change in the first three years of the war. As you'll see from the recipe below. The gravity is a bit lower, but the recipe is essentially the same. The only difference is a sugar I've substituted. In the previous recipe it was "dark sacc." In this one BS. Pretty sure both of them were dark in colour, so I've just bumped up the No. 3 content.

Oddly, this beer was slightly more heavily hopped than the 1914 version. Not sure why that was. There was a glut of hops after 1917, when beer production was drastically cut, but that didn't mean prices fell. In 1914 a hundredweight of hops cost £4 3s 9d, in 1916 £6 14s and in 1918 £18 15s.[1]

I've not really anything else to say. This recipe is really just for comparison purposes so you can see how quickly and drastically things changed over the next couple of years.

1916 Barclay Perkins X Ale		
pale malt	5.75 lb	58.90%
amber malt	0.75 lb	7.68%
flaked maize	1.25 lb	12.80%
no. 3 sugar	2.00 lb	20.49%
caramel 500 SRM	0.01 lb	0.12%
Fuggles 120 mins	1.00 oz	
Fuggles 60 mins	0.75 oz	
Fuggles 30 mins	0.75 oz	
OG	1048.6	
FG	1012.2	
ABV	4.82	
Apparent attenuation	74.90%	
IBU	30	
SRM	17	
Mash at	152° F	
Sparge at	170° F	
Boil time	120 minutes	
pitching temp	61° F	
Yeast	Wyeast 1099 Whitbread Ale	

---

[1] Brewers' Almanack 1955, page 63.

Mini Book Series volume XXX: Let's Brew!

1917 Barclay Perkins X

Not knowing when to stop. That's one of my most endearing traits. Which is why I'm stumbling on with Barclay Perkins X Ale.

We're now getting close to beer Armageddon, when British beer was changed forever. This beer was brewed on 6th July 1917. Just a few days earlier, on July 1st the first restrictions on gravity were introduced. Half the beer a brewery made had to be no more than 1036º[2]. And guess what? Parti-gyled with this beer was the very first batch of Government Ale, at a gravity of 1036.4°.

There have also been changed to the recipe. Out goes the flaked maize, the sugar content is halved and in comes crystal malt. And the percentage of amber malt has increased by 50%. Flaked maize disappeared from Barclay Perkins' recipes in May 1917, presumably because it was no longer available. Maize wasn't grown in the UK at the time and had to be imported, usually from the USA. I assume shortages also explain the reduction in sugar content. Only the hopping has remained unchanged.

All the changes in ingredients must have had an impact on the character of the beer. You could argue that the enforced changes have improved the recipe, as it now contains to adjuncts and a higher percentage of malt. But, as we'll see in a few recipes' time, as soon as it was available, Barclay Perkins went back to using flaked maize.

The OG has fallen, but only by a couple of points. However, that's deceptive. Because after this date most of the Mild Barclay Perkins brewed was GA. For example, the batch of X Ale brewed on 2nd July was 859 barrels. This batch was just 242 barrels with 438 barrels of GA. Most drinkers would have been on GA. Though I'm sure some unscrupulous publicans sold GA as X Ale.

Next time we'll take a look at that GA.

---

[2] "The Brewers' Almanack 1928" page 100.

Mini Book Series volume XXX: Let's Brew!

1917 Barclay Perkins X Ale		
pale malt	7.50 lb	74.96%
amber malt	1.00 lb	10.00%
crystal malt	0.50 lb	5.00%
no. 3 sugar	1.00 lb	10.00%
caramel	0.01 lb	0.05%
Fuggles 120 mins	1.00 oz	
Fuggles 60 mins	0.75 oz	
Fuggles 30 mins	0.75 oz	
OG	1046.7	
FG	1012.7	
ABV	4.50	
Apparent attenuation	72.81%	
IBU	31	
SRM	17	
Mash at	152° F	
Sparge at	170° F	
Boil time	120 minutes	
pitching temp	61° F	
Yeast	Wyeast 1099 Whitbread Ale	

1917 (April) Barclay Perkins Government Ale

As promised, here's the new member of X Ale's family, new-born younger sibling Government Ale.

This is the very first brew of GA, something Barclay Perkins would churn out in large quantities in the second half of 1917 and the beginning of 1918. Most batches were between 900 and 1,200 barrels. Meaning it was the bulk of what they brewed. X Ale brews were around 200 barrels, those of XLK, the only Bitter they brewed at this point, were 300-400 barrels.

But everything changed in April 1918, when permitted output was cut again and average gravity reduced to 1030° (everywhere except Ireland, where it was 1045°). The first price controls were also introduced: <1030° 4d per pint, 1030 – 1034° 5d per pint.[3]

The rule changes had an immediate impact at Barclay Perkins. Both X Ale and GA were discontinued and replaced by a new, even weaker Mild: Ale 4d, at 1027°. For the next year this was the only Mild they brewed, until April 1919 when average gravity was increased to 1040° and Barclay's brought back X Ale (at a gravity of 1036°)[4]. Though they continued to brew Ale 4d at the lower gravity. Amazingly, it survived right through to the next war, only being discontinued in 1941.

There's not much really to say about GA. It's literally a scaled down version of X Ale, having been parti-gyled with it. All the same ingredients, just slightly smaller quantities. In many ways, WW I saw the birth of modern Mild. Beers of just 3 and a bit percentage ABV and reasonably dark in colour.

Now I've told you all about Ale 4d, guess what recipe will come next? That's right, a lovely watery Mild.

---

[3] "The Brewers' Almanack 1928" pages 100 - 101.
[4] "The Brewers' Almanack 1928" pages 100 - 101.

1917 Barclay Perkins GA		
pale malt	5.75 lb	75.76%
amber malt	0.75 lb	9.88%
crystal malt	0.33 lb	4.35%
no. 3 sugar	0.75 lb	9.88%
caramel	0.01 lb	0.13%
Fuggles 120 mins	0.75 oz	
Fuggles 60 mins	0.50 oz	
Fuggles 30 mins	0.50 oz	
OG	1036.4	
FG	1008.3	
ABV	3.72	
Apparent attenuation	77.20%	
IBU	23	
SRM	12	
Mash at	152° F	
Sparge at	170° F	
Boil time	120 minutes	
pitching temp	61° F	
Yeast	Wyeast 1099 Whitbread Ale	

Mini Book Series volume XXX: Let's Brew!

1917 (November) Barclay Perkins Government Ale

This beer shows the direct relationship between government rules and changes to recipes during WW I.

The initial version of Barclay Perkins' GA was the result of rules introduced in April 1917. These were changed in October of the same year:

> **Oct. 1 1917**: Rate and conditions of previous quarter continued but gravity for one-half of the output raised to 1042°. Prices also fixed at 4d. per pint under 1036°, 5d. per pint under 1042°.
> **Source**: "The Brewers' Almanack 1928" pages 100 - 101.

The result? Barclay Perkins increased the gravity of their GA to 1041.9°. There's no way that was a coincidence. I've even got the letter telling the brewery to raise the gravity. It's pinned inside the front cover of the brewing book.

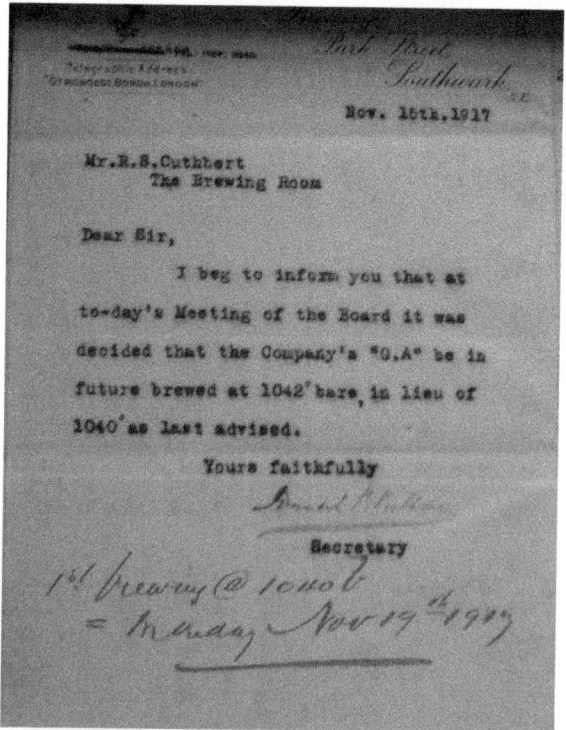

The recipe is that beer from the 10th November.

As for the recipe, there's been a very significant change to the grist: out goes crystal malt and in comes brown malt. And, at over 11%, a considerable amount of brown malt. With the No. invert sugar dropping from over 9% to 3.5%, too. I'm sure that latter change was dictated by a shortage of sugar for brewing. Being something that could be easily used for food, unlike malt, supplies were mostly allocated for that purpose.

I reckon that the addition of brown malt is at least partly to add colour to make up for the reduction in no. 3 invert. There's an intriguing note in the front of the brewing book which reads:

> "For color
> Roasted 1 sack (1/2 Qtr.) = 70 lbs caramel"

That says to me that they were short of caramel and using roasted malt as a substitute. It's also dead useful for me because it means I can work out the exact colour of the caramel they were using: approximately twice as dark as roasted malt. (Or barley, it isn't quite specific.)

If I'm being honest, this looks like a more interesting beer than pre-war X Ale. I like the look of that pale, brown and amber malt combination.

1917 Barclay Perkins GA		
pale malt	7.25 lb	76.00%
brown malt	1.00 lb	10.48%
amber malt	1.00 lb	10.48%
no. 3 invert sugar	0.25 lb	2.62%
caramel 1000 SRM	0.04 lb	0.42%
Fuggles 120 mins	0.75 oz	
Fuggles 60 mins	0.50 oz	
Fuggles 30 mins	0.50 oz	
OG	1041.9	
FG	1011.1	
ABV	4.07	
Apparent attenuation	73.51%	
IBU	22	
SRM	14	
Mash at	152° F	
Sparge at	170° F	
Boil time	120 minutes	
pitching temp	61° F	
Yeast	Wyeast 1099 Whitbread Ale	

Mini Book Series volume XXX: Let's Brew!

1939 Boddington Mild

I'd almost forgotten that it was Mild month. What better excuse for some lovely Mild recipes?

I'm so pleased that I got my hands on some more Boddington's records. Especially ones from before WW II. Like this one. A beer brewed 9 months or so before the war started.

The biggest surprise about this beer is its strength. With an OG in the low 1030°'s, it looks much more like a post-war Mild. Standard Mild gravities were usually a bit higher before the war.

In the 1930's Boddington had some unusual ingredients in their grists. Like wheat malt. And enzymic malt. The latter seems to have been very popular before and after the war. I'm not 100% sure how it differed from normal malt or what it's purpose was. I suppose to help mash efficiency by ensuring there were plenty of enzymes.

It's another example of a darkish beer with no darker malt than crystal in it. The colour coming from sugar. There's the usual problem with proprietary sugars, in this case DMS and FL, plus an unspecified invert. I've simplified it to all No. 3 invert.

The log isn't very informative when it comes to hops. For the English hops, it only identifies the grower or dealer, not the region where they were grown nor the variety. I've guessed Fuggles. I've assumed the Oregon hops listed were Cluster.

It looks like a nice straightforward drinking beer. Which I guess was the point

1939 Boddington XX Mild			
pale malt		4.50 lb	63.16%
crystal malt 60L		0.625 lb	8.77%
flaked maize		0.75 lb	10.53%
wheat malt		0.25 lb	3.51%
enzymic malt		0.20 lb	2.81%
caramel		0.05 lb	0.70%
No. 3 invert sugar		0.75 lb	10.53%
Cluster 90 mins		1.25 oz	
Fuggles 30 mins		1.25 oz	
OG		1033.8	
FG		1007	
ABV		3.55	
Apparent attenuation		79.29%	
IBU		46	
SRM		21	
Mash at		150º F	
Sparge at		162º F	
Boil time	90 minutes		
pitching temp		62º F	
Yeast	Wyeast 1318 London ale III (Boddingtons)		

Mini Book Series volume XXX: Let's Brew!

1955 Flowers XXX

We're approaching the finishing line with Flowers. With what was undoubtedly one of their biggest sellers.

Mild was still wildly popular in the mid-1950's. Though that was already beginning to change. Younger drinkers were switching to Bitter. And there was a swing from draught to bottled beer, which also didn't help Mild.

It was during the post-war period that Mild's status as exclusively a low-gravity beer evolved. Before WW II there had still been Milds with gravities over 1040°, about the same as Ordinary Bitter. Barclay Perkins had three Milds, at 1043°. 1035° and 1031°. After the war, few breweries had more than one Mild. Some had a Best Mild, but this was usually only a couple of degrees stronger than standard Mild. Ones with gravities over 1036° were extremely rare.

Looking at lots of 1950's Milds recently, I've notices a big variation in the degree of attenuation. The gravities are all much of a muchness: 1030-1033°, mostly. But because the attenuation varies from the low 60's to high 80's, the ABV goes from 2.7% to 3.7%. Which much have entailed very different drinking experiences. And not just in terms of intoxication.

Flowers XXX is towards the low end of the attention scale, not quite managing 3% ABV. Though, looking at the ingredients, that isn't such a surprise. You're never going to get a 85% attenuation with 7% lactose in the grist. The brewers was obviously aiming for body and a degree of sweetness in the finished beer.

Lactose aside, it's an unspectacular grist. Just pale malt, No. 3 invert sugar and a touch of malt extract. Still not totally sure why malt extract was so common in the 1950's. Especially in such small amounts.

Not much to say about the hopping. The variety is a guess. But Fuggles were the standard hop of the day. The chances are that was what was used in the original. Goldings were generally reserved for more delicate hop-oriented beers.

Almost forgot. You'll need to add caramel to get the right colour. It won't get anywhere close without it.

Mini Book Series volume XXX: Let's Brew!

1955 Flowers XXX		
pale malt	5.75 lb	82.14%
No. 3 invert	0.50 lb	7.14%
lactose	0.50 lb	7.14%
malt extract	0.25 lb	3.57%
Fuggles 90 min	0.50 oz	
Fuggles 60 min	0.50 oz	
Fuggles 30 min	0.50 oz	
OG	1032.4	
FG	1010	
ABV	2.96	
Apparent attenuation	69.14%	
IBU	22	
SRM	24	
Mash at	150° F	
Sparge at	160° F	
Boil time	90 minutes	
pitching temp	59° F	
Yeast	WLP007 Dry English Ale	

1946 Fullers X

Another of Fullers brews from the immediate post-war years. This time what would have been their top seller: X Ale. Or ordinary Mild. Or Hock, as it was also called.

I had some wonderful pints of Hock in the 1970's. A lovely beer when looked after well. And there was the problem. In most pubs it didn't sell well enough to be in good condition. Inevitably, it was discontinued as a regular beer. Sadly, I can't ever see it being in Fullers regular line up again.

Typically, this beer contains no dark malt at all, just pale malt, flaked barley and sugar. And not really that much of the latter. Why? Sugar was still rationed in 1946. Brewers couldn't use as much as they would have wished. About 7% of the grist is made up of sugar. In normal times it would have been double that.

While we're on the topic of sugar, I've had to make substitutions again. The original has something called PEX and another called intense. I've substituted No. 2 and No. 3 invert respectively. But you'll also need to add caramel to get the right colour.

I've simplified the mashing scheme. The original had an initial mash temperature of 147° F which was held for 25 minutes, then raised to 155° F by water added through the underlet and stood for another two hours. It's a really typical London mashing method, used for most of the 20th century.

The hopping, as you would expect, is quite light. It's not a beer intended to challenge the drinker, but to be slurped back by the gallon. Did I mention I once managed to drink 5 pints of Hock in a half-hour lunch break? I think I did the beer justice.

1946 Fullers X		
pale malt	5.50 lb	78.57%
flaked barley	1.00 lb	14.29%
glucose	0.25 lb	3.57%
No. 2 invert	0.125 lb	1.79%
No. 3 invert	0.125 lb	1.79%
Fuggles 90 min	0.75 oz	
Fuggles 30 min	0.50 oz	
OG	1030.7	
FG	1009	
ABV	2.87	
Apparent attenuation	70.68%	
IBU	15	
SRM	20	
Mash at	155° F	
Sparge at	165° F	
Boil time	90 minutes	
pitching temp	62° F	
Yeast	WLP002 English Ale	

Mini Book Series volume XXX: Let's Brew!

1937 Greene King XX

Just time to squeeze in one last Mild recipe in May. And a special one.

As this is a brand that still exists. Sort of. Greene King still produce a Mild called XX, but, other than the name, it has no connection with this beer. Greene King rationalised their Milds a while back and in order to decide which recipe to keep, they did a taste off. Hardy & Hanson's won and was renamed XX.

Thinking about it, it's strange that they picked Kimberley Mild. Unless they've changed the recipe a lot since the 1980's. It was far too sweet. Very unlike the other Nottingham Milds. One of the few cask Milds I really didn't care for.

Wondering how come I have a Greene King recipe? I've Ed to thank. He visited Greene King recently and in a blog post about it included a photo of a brewing record. I'll take brewing records wherever I find them. I'm starting to get quite a collection.

The beer itself is a classic 4d Mild. Amongst London brewers, the standard Mild Ale was a 5d or 6d beer of 1037° and 1043°, respectively. But out in the sticks, the standard version was often weaker. I can still remember a few breweries well away from the big cities having Milds of a little under 1030° in the 1970's. Most bumped up the gravities a degree or two when CAMRA published OGs.

Just looked through my analysis spreadsheet and I see that in 1968 XX had an OG of 1026.8°. Which really is taking the piss. If XX was already under 1030°, I wonder what the hell they did during WW II? It couldn't have got much weaker. Literally. Because of the way the tax system worked there was no point dropping the gravity below 1027°. However weak a beer was, you always paid a minimum of the tax for one of 1027°.

The grist is what I would expect: base malt, crystal malt, flaked maize and sugar. With Kent and Mid-Kent hops.

Nothing more for me to say really.

Mini Book Series volume XXX: Let's Brew!

1937 Greene King XX		
pale malt	4.75 lb	79.17%
crystal malt 60L	0.25 lb	4.17%
flaked maize	0.50 lb	8.33%
table sugar	0.25 lb	4.17%
No. 3 invert sugar	0.25 lb	4.17%
Fuggles 90 mins	0.50 oz	
Fuggles 60 mins	0.50 oz	
Goldings 30 mins	0.25 oz	
Goldings dry hops	0.25 oz	
OG	1028.8	
FG	1005.5	
ABV	3.08	
Apparent attenuation	80.90%	
IBU	20	
SRM	10	
Mash at	151° F	
Sparge at	165° F	
Boil time	90 minutes	
pitching temp	61° F	
Yeast	WLP025 Southwold	

Mini Book Series volume XXX: Let's Brew!

1950 Lees Best Mild

I suppose I should do Lees Best Mild to go with their Bitter. Then you'll be able to recreate that 1950 Manchester pub experience more completely.

Lees had an interesting range in 1950: Bitter, Mild, Best Mild, Stout and "C" Ale. I was particularly pleased in finding the last one. I'd seen references to "C" Ale from several breweries in the Manchester area, but had no idea what sort of beer it was.

Lees Best Mild has a slightly more complicated recipe than their Bitter. There's a little crystal malt, for starters. And some glucose. As well as a pretty tiny amount of black. Even so, there's nothing like enough dark malt to get the finished colour of the beer. You'll need to add caramel to hit the number.

I've simplified the sugar again. The original included a couple of types of proprietary sugar.

This is quite a strong beer for a Mild, even a Best Mild at this date. Some brewers had Mild at 1027° and Best Mild at 1032°. This was about as strong as Mild got in 1950.

I can't think of anything else to say. Except: here's the recipe.

1950 Lees Best Mild		
pale malt	6.50 lb	81.81%
black malt	0.07 lb	0.88%
crystal malt 60 L	0.25 lb	3.15%
enzymic malt	0.125 lb	1.57%
glucose	0.25 lb	3.15%
No. 3 Invert	0.75 lb	9.44%
Fuggles 90 min	1.00 oz	
Goldings 30 min	0.75 oz	
Goldings dry hops	0.125 oz	
OG	1035	
FG	1008	
ABV	3.57	
Apparent attenuation	77.14%	
IBU	28	
SRM	25	
Mash at	149° F	
Sparge at	170° F	
Boil time	90 minutes	
pitching temp	60° F	
Yeast	Wyeast 1318 London ale III (Boddingtons)	

Mini Book Series volume XXX: Let's Brew!

1958 Lees Best Mild

Many breweries are dead boring, bashing out the same basic recipe for decades with only occasional minor tweaks. Not so Lees. They liked to swap their Mild recipe around.

That's my excuse for publishing recipes just a few years apart. Without any war inbetween causing upheaval.

While some earlier iterations were all about the malts, this version is a symphony of sugar, with a total of seven in the original. Several different proprietary sugars, a couple of inverts and lactose. And both flaked maize and flaked barley. And 7% brown malt just to add to the confusion.

Leaving a dead complicated recipe. Even in my slightly rationalised version. Almost a full set of the numbered inverts and lactose, too. They were very keen on their lactose in the post-war period. It popped up in more than just Milk Stout.

As befits a Best Mild, it has a decent gravity. The ABV is a guess, Lees not bothering to enter the FG in this period.

1958 Lees Best Mild		
pale malt	3.50 lb	51.06%
brown malt	0.50 lb	7.29%
flaked maize	0.33 lb	4.81%
flaked oats	0.15 lb	2.19%
lactose	0.25 lb	3.65%
No. 2 invert sugar	0.75 lb	10.94%
No. 3 invert sugar	1.00 lb	14.59%
No. 4 invert sugar	0.38 lb	5.47%
Northern Brewer 90 mins	0.50 oz	
Fuggles 60 mins	0.50 oz	
Fuggles 30 mins	0.50 oz	
OG	1035	
FG	1007	
ABV	3.70	
Apparent attenuation	80.00%	
IBU	28	
SRM	20	
Mash at	148° F	
Sparge at	170° F	
Boil time	90 minutes	
pitching temp	60° F	
Yeast	Wyeast 1318 London ale III (Boddingtons)	

Mini Book Series volume XXX: Let's Brew!

1963 Lees Mild

It being Mild month once more, it seems a good time for another Mild recipe.

The 1950's version of Lees Best Mild has been a big hit with home brewers. Mostly, I think, because of its complex malt bill. This time, though, we're looking at its younger brother: simple Mild. What's most surprising to me, is that not only wasn't it parti-gyled with Best Mild, but it has a totally different grist.

There's one good reason for that: the two beers were different in colour. The usual convention was Ordinary Mild dark, Best Mild pale. For some reason, Lees did it the other way around. And with all the dark malt and dark sugar in Best Mild, there's no way they could parti-gyle Ordinary Mild with it.

I sometimes wonder why pubs sell several Bitters of only slightly differing gravities. This case is even crazier – Best Mild, at 1035°, was only 2 gravity points higher than this beer. It does make you wonder why they bothered. Though I suppose, at least, the different grists left beers with distinct characters.

Speaking of grists, Ordinary Mild contained crystal malt, which Best didn't. While Ordinary lacked the oak smoked and flaked oats that were in Best.

There's an even bigger difference when it comes to the sugars. Best: Invert, Black Invert, PS Crystals, D.C.S., HX and C.D.M. Ordinary: Invert, C.M.E., Stacons, Laverna, D.C.S, HX and a tiny amount of C.D.M. I won't even try to guess what all that lot were. I've substituted No. 1 and No. 2 invert.

Oddly, Ordinary Mild has a slightly higher hopping rate than Best. I've guessed Fuggles, but all I know for sure is that they were English. Around 10% of the hops were Styrian Goldings. But as that would only amount to 0.15 oz. at this scale, I didn't bother with it. Feel free to throw a few in if you feel like it.

Before I forget, the FG is also a guess. Lees didn't bother filling it in.

1963 Lees Mild		
pale malt	5.25 lb	76.98%
crystal malt 60 L	0.25 lb	3.67%
flaked maize	0.33 lb	4.84%
No. 1 invert sugar	0.33 lb	4.84%
No. 2 invert sugar	0.66 lb	9.68%
Fuggles 90 min	0.75 oz	
Fuggles 30 min	0.75 oz	
OG	1033	
FG	1007	
ABV	3.44	
Apparent attenuation	78.79%	
IBU	21	
SRM	6.5	
Mash at	148° F	
Sparge at	170° F	
Boil time	90 minutes	
pitching temp	60° F	
Yeast	Wyeast 1318 London ale III (Boddingtons)	

1947 Shepherd Neame MB

It's a special day. As is every day I get my hands on a new set of brewing records. Especially when it's a brewery whose beers I've supped.

And when I can combine the records with my post-war austerity obsession, I'm like a pig on a spit. No, pig in shit, that's what I meant. (That image of me roasting a spit will now live with me forever.) Throw in a lovely watery Mild recipe and paradise is adjacent.

For the day, it's a pretty honest recipe. Just pale malt, brewing sugar and malt extract. Plus the obligatory flaked barley of the late war years.

The sugar bill is slightly simplified. There was a bit of something that looked like WWCS. I just bumped up the No. 3.

Mini Book Series volume XXX: Let's Brew!

1947 Shepherd Neame MB		
pale malt	3.25 lb	59.09%
flaked barley	0.75 lb	13.64%
no. 3 sugar	0.75 lb	13.64%
malt extract	0.75 lb	13.64%
Fuggles 120 mins	0.50 oz	
Goldings 30 mins	0.50 oz	
OG	1027.1	
FG	1005.5	
ABV	2.86	
Apparent attenuation	79.70%	
IBU	15	
SRM	9	
Mash at	156° F	
Sparge at	170° F	
Boil time	120 minutes	
pitching temp	63° F	
Yeast	Go to a Shepherd Neame pub, buy a pint of cask beer. If it's nice and fresh, buy another pint and surreptitiously pour it into a bottle, add a half teaspoon of sugar and wait 3 days. Carefully decant most of the beer into a glass and drink. Add malt extract and leave in a warm place for a few days.	
	Or just use a Southern English Ale yeast	

1916 Tetley X3

I couldn't let Mild month pass without a Tetley's Mild recipe.

And an unusual one. Because it's a late example of a pretty strong Mild. It's from Tetley, too. You know how obsessed I am with them and their Mild. The impressionability of youth.

The happy memories I have of that beer. Discovering it handpulled in the Sheepscar. When Sheepscar was a clearance wasteland, with only a couple of lonely pubs still standing. A sad time for Britain's cities. Bulldozed and bullied.

Tetley, unlike those soft Southern brewers in London, continued to brew stronger versions of Mild. Like this one. Which has double the ABV of their Mild I adored.

I lived for a while in a back to back in Cross Green. Mostly uncleansed and with its pubs intact. One was a former Hemmingway's pub, that still had their windows and Mild just the way I liked it. I think a day or two more in the cellar before sale.

One pub I drank in had electric pumps. You couldn't be sure if it was cask of bright beer. I was convinced the beer was bright. Until the landlord went on holiday and a relief manager took over. Then it tasted like cask. My conclusion? The regular gaffer was selling the beer as soon as it dropped bright. While the good ones left it to condition for a few days.

A simple enough recipe. Which doesn't need any explanation from me.

1916 Tetley X3		
pale malt	5.25 lb	42.86%
mild malt	5.50 lb	44.90%
demerera sugar	1.50 lb	12.24%
Cluster 90 mins	1.00 oz	
Fuggles 90 mins	1.00 oz	
Fuggles 30 mins	2.00 oz	
OG	1059	
FG	1011.6	
ABV	6.27	
Apparent attenuation	80.34%	
IBU	54	
SRM	5	
Mash at	150° F	
Sparge at	165° F	
Boil time	90 minutes	
pitching temp	62° F	
Yeast	Wyeast 1469 West Yorkshire Ale Timothy Taylor	

1919 Tetley F

A final Mild recipe for Mild Month. OK, it's one day into June, but I couldn't resist.

Especially as it's another Tetley recipe. F, which I'm pretty sure stands for Family Ale. A bottled beer I remember from my time living in Leeds. In those days it looked very much like a bottled version of their Mild.

This one is an, er, interesting recipe. With grits making up 25% of the fermentables. Plus a tiny little bit of chocolate malt. And South American sugar. "Peru" is how it's described. That's another 18% of the grist. Making it pretty low on malt. Sure it tastes lovely, mind. It is a Tetley beer, after all.

When this was brewed, 30th October 1919, it would have counted as a 5d beer:

Price control 1917-1921					
	Oct 1917	Apr 1918	Feb 1919	Jul 1919	Apr 1920
2d				<1019	
3d			<1023	1020-1026	<1019
4d	<1036	<1030	1023-1028	1027-1032	1020-1026
5d	1036-1042	1030-1034	1029-1034	1033-1038	1027-1032
6d			1035-1041	1039-1045	1033-1038
7d			1042-1049	1045-1053	1039-1045
8d			>1050	>1054	1045-1053
9d					>1054
Sources: The Brewers' Almanack 1928 pages 100 - 101. "The British Brewing Industry 1830-1980"					

F was parti-gyled with X at 1027.1 and X1 at 1041.3, meaning they were 4d and 6d beers, respectively.

Tetley continued to brew F up to 1940. It always had a gravity of around 1034.

Mini Book Series volume XXX: Let's Brew!

1919 Tetley F			
pale malt		1.50 lb	21.74%
mild malt		2.25 lb	32.61%
chocolate Malt		0.15 lb	2.17%
grits		1.75 lb	25.36%
demerera sugar		1.25 lb	18.12%
Cluster 90 mins		0.50 oz	
Fuggles 30 mins		0.75 oz	
OG		1033.8	
FG		1010.2	
ABV		3.12	
Apparent attenuation		69.82%	
IBU		21	
SRM		7	
Mash at		151º F	
Sparge at		165º F	
Boil time		90 minutes	
pitching temp		65º F	
Yeast	Wyeast 1469 West Yorkshire Ale Timothy Taylor		

Mini Book Series volume XXX: Let's Brew!

1946 Tetley Mild

Here's a beer with a very special place in my heart. Something which for seven years was about the only beer I drank.

It's typical of a type of Mild brewed in Yorkshire, lying somewhere between pale and dark. Weirdly, all those years I drank it, I never realised that it wasn't really that dark. More of a dark red than brown.

The effect of the war is plain to see in the grist. Flaked barley was forced on brewers as a replacement for flaked maize during hostilities. It's interesting to see how Tetley's adjunct usage changed over time. In 1939 it was grits, in 1941 flaked rice, in 1943 flaked oats, in 1944 flaked barley and flaked oats and in 1945 flaked barley. All mostly out of the brewer's hands.

What I've interpreted as brown sugar was listed as Barbados in the brewing record. While what I've put down as No. 3 invert was mostly ERC with a touch of G & S. No idea what either of those were but No. 3 is probably the best substitute.

The hops were a combination of Kent and Worcester, with no mention of variety. Chances were that they were Fuggles.

Though there's not much difference in the OG compared the version I drank, the high degree of attenuation leaves this beer about 0.6% ABV stronger. The gravity is quite high for a Mild of this period. 1027-1030° was more typical.

1946 Tetley Mild		
pale malt	4.00 lb	59.26%
flaked barley	1.00 lb	14.81%
brown sugar	0.75 lb	11.11%
No. 3 invert sugar	1.00 lb	14.81%
Fuggles 120 mins	0.25 oz	
Fuggles 60 mins	0.25 oz	
Fuggles 30 mins	0.25 oz	
OG	1034.3	
FG	1005.3	
ABV	3.84	
Apparent attenuation	84.55%	
IBU	10	
SRM	9	
Mash at	148° F	
Sparge at	165° F	
Boil time	120 minutes	
pitching temp	63.75° F	
Yeast	Wyeast 1469 West Yorkshire Ale	

Mini Book Series volume XXX: Let's Brew!

1956 Shepherd Neame MB

It's a very special beer for a very special day.

For two reasons. Today is my 60th birthday and this beer was brewed on the day that I was born, October 19th 1956. That it's a Mild just makes it even more appropriate.

In most other respects, it's not that special a beer. It isn't particularly strong, though the gravity had increased a tad since 1947. Just about enough to tip it over into intoxicating land. It just manages to scrape in over 3% ABV, usually my bottom limit for bothering.

Shepherd Neame didn't go for complicated recipes. This one just has a single type of pale malt, a dash of malt extract, No. 3 invert sugar and something called UKCS which must be some type of proprietary sugar. I've just bumped up the No. 3 content to allow for this.

At this point Shep's seem to have only been using hops from their own gardens. At least that's all that turns up in the photos I have. It makes perfect sense, the brewery being located in Kentish hop country. I am surprised by the modest level of their hopping. I've always imagined breweries in Kent being enthusiastic hoppers.

I quite like the fact that it's such an ordinary beer. One meant for supping by the gallon down the pub with your mates. It seems appropriate for a beer born on the same day as me.

1956 Shepherd Neame MB		
pale malt	5.50 lb	84.49%
no. 3 sugar	1.00 lb	15.36%
malt extract	0.01 lb	0.15%
Fuggles 120 mins	0.75 oz	
Goldings 30 mins	0.50 oz	
OG	1030.2	
FG	1007.2	
ABV	3.04	
Apparent attenuation	76.16%	
IBU	19	
SRM	9	
Mash at	152° F	
Sparge at	170° F	
Boil time	120 minutes	
pitching temp	62.25° F	
Yeast	a Southern English Ale yeast	

Mini Book Series volume XXX: Let's Brew!

1952 Strong XXX Mild

The final Mild recipe for May is one of mine. From one of the many breweries gobbled up and spat out by Whitbread. Good news for me, because Whitbread were very good at preserving the brewing records of the breweries they bought.

I could have drunk Strong's beers as they didn't close until 1981. Except I've never been to that bit of the country (Hampshire) and Strong's beers never travelled far. Whitbread had bought them in 1965, along with 950 pubs.[5] They were still brewing a cask Mild at time of closure. It was probably the descendant of this beer, though the gravity was a little lower.

Speaking of which, 1033.5 is a little high for a 1950's Mild gravity. I've just averaged the OG for the hundred Milds I have from the period and it came to 1032.5. What does that tell us? What I already knew. That British beer strength haven't changed much in the last 60 years. At least not the established, traditional styles.

The recipe itself is unspectacular: base malt and sugar. No maize and no slops in this one. Note the complete lack of dark malts despite the reasonably dark shade of the finished beer. The colour all comes from the No. 3 invert and caramel colouring.

I realise that back in my home brewing days I got Mild recipes totally wrong, using black or chocolate malt for the colour. I now realise few Milds were ever brewed that way. Had Dark Mild developed a couple of decades earlier, that might not have been the case. Then again, it's probably only because simple ways of obtaining were available after 1880 when the use of sugar exploded. It had been legal in beer since 1847, but the Free Mash Tun Act of 1880 seems to have boosted sugar use. Especially specialist brewing sugars.

The hops are a total guess. But, knowing as I now do that 75% of the British crop was Fuggles in the early 1950's, it seems a reasonable assumption. Especially as most of the other 25% consisted of Golding types. And you wouldn't usually throw Goldings into Mild. You'd save those for classier, more hop-focused beers like Bitter.

I like the fact that there's a full fermentation record in Strong's logs. Which means that not only am I pretty confident about the FG, I also know that Strong used the dropping system. The fermenting beer was dropped 2 days into a 7 day primary.

Right that's me done. I need to write a stack of posts to cover my California trip.

---

[5] "The Brewing Industry a Guide to Historical Records" by Lesley Richmond and Alison Turton, 1990, page 317.

Mini Book Series volume XXX: Let's Brew!

1952 Strong XXX Mild		
MA malt	3.75 lb	57.69%
PA malt	1.25 lb	19.23%
no. 3 sugar	0.50 lb	7.69%
candy sugar	0.75 lb	11.54%
malt extract	0.25 lb	3.85%
Fuggles 90 min	0.75 oz	
Fuggles 30 min	0.75 oz	
OG	1033.5	
FG	1007	
ABV	3.51	
Apparent attenuation	79.10%	
IBU	21	
SRM	23	
Mash at	151° F	
Sparge at	160° F	
Boil time	90 minutes	
pitching temp	61° F	
Yeast	WLP007 Dry English Ale	

Mini Book Series volume XXX: Let's Brew!

1969 Truman LM

Ah, the happy hours I spent drinking this type of beer in the 1970's. Ordinary, watery Mild. It's sad that it's become such a rarity.

Mild – especially cask Mild – is a cracking long drink. A beer to accompany, rather than dominate, an evening down the pub with your mates. I was reminded just how much I missed that sort of beer and that sort of session when I spent a Saturday evening with Jeff Bell in The Royal Oak in Southwark a couple of weeks ago. Sometimes you need to down at least half a gallon.

Earlier that same Saturday, appropriately enough, is when I collected this recipe. From a Truman's Ale brewing book in Derek Prentice's possession. It was great going through the book with him. He could explain exactly what all the Brewhouse names stood for.

I can't help wondering how close this beer is to the cask Mild Truman introduced in the early 1980's. The two have similar gravities: 1032° for this, 1034° for the 1980's version. It's strange. The 1969 Mild feels way in the past to me, as it's before my drinking time. While the 1980's version feels like an old friend, as I drank it reasonably often. Yet just 13 years separate the two. Perspective is everything.

Let's crack on with the recipe. It's quite an odd one in several ways. For a start, it's coloured with roast barley, which isn't a very common ingredient in Mild. In fact, it's not a very common ingredient in English beer at all. Nor are roast malts that common in Mild. Not unheard of, but not that common. A spot of black or chocolate malt occasionally.

Impressively, the recipe boasts three types of unmalted barley. In addition to roast barley, there's also flaked barley and – this is a first – pearl barley. Again, I was glad to have Derek at my shoulder. I'd have missed it, as it's listed as "P. Brights". In all, unmalted barley makes up 15% of the grist.

You may have assumed that brown sugar is a substitute for some other type of sugar. It isn't. The original really did contain Tate & Lyle brown sugar. Though it did make up slightly less than half of the total sugar. Most of the rest was liquid cane sugar. There was also a touch of something called B.C.L., which I'm guessing is some sort of dark sugar. I've substituted No. 4 invert.

More sugar, in the form of primings, was added to the fermenting vessels just before the end of primary fermentation. It would have upped the gravity by a degree or two. Not sure if Truman were still brewing cask at this point. If they were, the FG would have fallen a few more points before being sold. So don't worry if your attenuation is a bit more than I've listed.

I know nothing about the hops, other than that they were English. Fuggles, which were the commonest hop grown in England, probably isn't far wrong. They probably wouldn't have wasted Goldings in a Mild. Feel free to use any traditional English hop variety.

Mini Book Series volume XXX: Let's Brew!

1969 Truman LM		
pale malt	4.50 lb	64.84%
crystal malt	0.75 lb	10.81%
roast barley	0.25 lb	3.60%
flaked barley	0.33 lb	4.76%
pearl barley	0.33 lb	4.76%
cane sugar	0.50 lb	7.20%
brown sugar	0.25 lb	3.60%
No. 4 invert	0.03 lb	0.43%
Fuggles 90 mins	0.50 oz	
Fuggles 60 mins	0.50 oz	
Fuggles 30 mins	0.25 oz	
OG	1031.9	
FG	1011.6	
ABV	2.69	
Apparent attenuation	63.64%	
IBU	17	
SRM	22	
Mash at	150° F	
Sparge at	165° F	
Boil time	90 minutes	
pitching temp	62° F	
Yeast	Wyeast 1099 Whitbread ale	

Mini Book Series volume XXX: Let's Brew!

1917 Wadworth XXXX

I get all sorts of bits and bobs. Brewing records and other stuff. It's been a great help as there's a limit to how many archives and breweries I can get to.

This recipe is derived from a materials sheet. That shows each brew in a particular month and the materials used in it. I think Boak and Bailey sent me it. There are a few details missing: mashing temperatures, boil times, pitching temperature. All of those, I've guessed. Plus the hops are only defined as English and foreign.

Wadworth were still brewing three Milds at this point. More than London brewers were, who'd mostly slimmed down to just X Ale. While Wadworth had X, XX and XXXX. Odd the way XXX was missing.

The grist is typical 20th century: base malt, flaked maize and sugar. As I've often told you before, getting the colour from sugar is typical of British beers. This is quite dark, making it an unusual combination. A Mild that is both quite strong and dark. By the time Mild had gone properly dark, there were few strong ones left.

I'm less garrulous than usual. Here's the recipe.

1917 Wadworth XXXX		
pale malt	7.25 lb	70.53%
flaked maize	1.75 lb	17.02%
No. 3 invert sugar	1.25 lb	12.16%
caramel	0.03 lb	0.29%
Cluster 90 mins	0.75 oz	
Fuggles 60 mins	0.75 oz	
Fuggles 30 mins	0.75 oz	
OG	1049.6	
FG	1016.6	
ABV	4.37	
Apparent attenuation	66.53%	
IBU	35	
SRM	18	
Mash at	152° F	
Sparge at	165° F	
Boil time	90 minutes	
pitching temp	60° F	
Yeast	Wyeast 1275 Thames Valley ale (Brakspear)	

Mini Book Series volume XXX: Let's Brew!

1837 Whitbread X

I love early Mild recipes for a reason. No, not that they're dead strong. (Though I certainly don't hold that against them.) It's that they're really, really simple.

They're pretty much all SMASH recipes. Just base malt and hops. That's it. Which doesn't leave me a huge amount to talk about.

This recipe comes from Whitbread's first Ale brewing book. As a Porter brewer, Whitbread had exclusively brewed Beer until 1836. Porter and Stout, if you recall, being types of Brown Beer. All the big London Porter brewers took up Ale brewing in the 1830's. Possibly in reaction to the 1830 Beer Act, which had seen the establishment of a new class of pubs which sold beer but no spirits. Ale seems to have been very popular in this class of establishment.

It's not very much like a modern Mild. The OG is way higher. The colour much paler. The attenuation much lower. The hopping much heavier.

Not sure which style-Nazi cubbyhole it could be forced into. Not dark enough for a Scotch Ale or an Old Ale. Not strong enough for a Barley Wine. Maybe some sort of IPA. There are so many of those it must sort of fit the specs for one. Or maybe I can think up my own new IPA substyle. Mild IPA – how about that. Don't think it's been done yet.

Not really much more that I can say than that. Oh yes, I remember. Drink Mild!

1837 Whitbread X		
mild malt	16.50 lb	100.00%
Goldings 90 mins	2.50 oz	
Goldings 30 mins	2.50 oz	
OG	1072.6	
FG	1033.8	
ABV	5.13	
Apparent attenuation	53.44%	
IBU	59	
SRM	7	
Mash at	154° F	
Sparge at	165° F	
Boil time	90 minutes	
pitching temp	64° F	
Yeast	Wyeast 1099 Whitbread Ale	

Mini Book Series volume XXX: Let's Brew!

1905 Whitbread XK

It's been another busy week. Loads more recipes written. Including this intriguing little devil.

One of the biggest remaining mysteries in beer history is when Mild became dark. And why. It seems to have been around 1890 to 1900 that the process started. It's hard to pin down exactly, because that's also when sugar was starting to be used in a big way. But brewing records aren't often that specific about the type of sugar.

Often it will just say sugar or invert. The exact type of sugar will have a big impact on the colour of the finished beer. No. 3 invert is pretty dark and a reasonable amount will considerably darken a beer. While other types of sugar will add no colour at all.

Sugar use may be one of the reasons of the reasons for Mild getting darker. Dark sugars and caramel give the brewer complete control over the colour of his finished beer. It's much easier to brew a beer with a more subtle shade, that is, not really pale or really dark.

With both brown malt and No.3 in the grist, this is darker for sure that Whitbread's Milds in the 1870's. Though somewhere between those dates, when they were vaguer about the type of sugar, the process could already have started.

Brown malt is pretty rare in Mild recipes. Barclay Perkins did occasionally use it in wartime. Why did Whitbread use it? Probably because it was something they were already using. Their Porter and Stout always contained brown malt.

Looks like an interesting recipe to me. I'd love to know how it tasted.

1905 Whitbread XK		
pale malt	11.25 lb	88.24%
brown malt	0.375 lb	2.94%
no. 3 invert sugar	1.125 lb	8.82%
Cluster 90 mins	0.75 oz	
Fuggles 90 mins	0.75 oz	
Fuggles 30 mins	1.50 oz	
OG	1059.8	
FG	1014	
ABV	6.06	
Apparent attenuation	76.59%	
IBU	40	
SRM	13	
Mash at	150° F	
Sparge at	175° F	
Boil time	90 minutes	
pitching temp	61.5° F	
Yeast	Wyeast 1099 Whitbread Ale	

Mini Book Series volume XXX: Let's Brew!

1954 Whitbread Best Ale

We complete this trilogy of Whitbread dark Ales with their standard-strength draught Mild, Best Ale.

It's a beer with a long history, having its origins in their X Ale of the 1830's. Though obviously there were a few little changes over the years. Most notably a slow but steady knocking of the stuffing out of it strength-wise. Back in 1836, it was 1077°. By 1854 it was down to 1068°, by 1868 to 1059°. In 1901, it fell to 1052°, where it remained until the start of WW I. After WW I, it stabilised around 1042°, before dropping in 1931 to 1036°. WW II knocked of a few more gravity points leaving the beer you'll see below.

This is one Whitbread that I know 100% certain that I drank. Though, as it was in the late 1970's, it probably came from Luton. It was only keg, but I was so desperate to drink Mild, I didn't let that put me off. What was it like? Dark, a bit watery, a bit sweet and overall rather dull. I'm sure cask conditioning would have improved it considerably.

I think Best Ale has been discontinued. But not all that long ago. Which shows quite some resilience for a beer that's been as fashionable as a mullet for the last 50 years.

I'm struggling for much else to say. The recipe is basically the same as Forest Brown. Just a little weaker and a little more heavily hopped.

1954 Whitbread Best Ale		
mild malt	5.25 lb	80.77%
crystal malt	0.50 lb	7.69%
no. 3 invert sugar	0.75 lb	11.54%
Fuggles 60 min	0.75 oz	
Fuggles 40 min	0.50 oz	
Goldings 20 min	0.50 oz	
OG	1030.9	
FG	1010	
ABV	2.76	
Apparent attenuation	67.64%	
IBU	23	
SRM	25	
Mash at	147° F	
Sparge at	168° F	
Boil time	60 minutes	
pitching temp	65° F	
Yeast	Wyeast 1099 Whitbread ale	

Mini Book Series volume XXX: Let's Brew!

Il Pale Ale

Mini Book Series volume XXX: Let's Brew!

1913 Adnams BLB

I just realised that I've published very few Adnams recipes, despite having a very long run of their records.

This is a little number from the eve of WW I. Looking at Adnams beers of this period, it becomes obvious that wartime restrictions on beer gravity had a much bigger impact on London brewers. Gravities in London were significantly high than in more rural areas like Southwold. Whitbread's weakest Pale Ale in 1913 had an OG of 1050°, its strongest 1061°.

Though the difference in Mild Ale gravities is even greater. Adnams had two Milds, X at 1033° and XX at 1039°. While Whitbread's only Mild, X Ale was 1055°. When gravities began to be limited in 1917, Whitbread needed to make far bigger cuts than Adnams.

The grist is both uncomplicated and typical: pale malt, flaked maize and invert sugar. Which is about as complex as Pale Ale recipes got back then. As you're no doubt bored of hearing, crystal malt was pretty much unknown in Pale ales before WW I and fairly rare after it. Only after WW II did it become pretty much standard.

The original beer was made using an underlet mash. The initial heat was 151°, rising to 152.5° after the underlet (hot water added to the mash tun from the bottom). In most examples, the heats were 150°, rising to 152°. Not sure if I'd bother with such a small temperature change, but if you want 100% authenticity, feel free to give it a go.

The hops are more interesting. The log lists Worcester, Kent and Saaz. The first two I've interpreted as Fuggles and Goldings, respectively. The Saaz is, well, obviously Saaz. They were also used as dry hops, in quite a large quantity. In a beer of this gravity about half that amount would be normal.

The rate of attenuation is pretty high, leaving the beer about 0.5% ABV higher than you would expect. With modern malts, that probably won't be much of a problem.

BLB didn't survive the war. My last sighting of it is in December 1916, when it still had a respectable OG of 1042°. In 1917 its replacement, simply called PA, was just 1032°. PA survived its wartime experience, only to be replaced by BB in 1961, a beer with a slightly higher OG.

1913 Adnams BLB		
pale malt	7.00 lb	77.78%
flaked maize	0.50 lb	5.56%
No. 1 invert sugar	1.50 lb	16.67%
Fuggles 120 min	0.75 oz	
Goldings 60 min	0.75 oz	
Saaz 30 min	1.00 oz	
Saaz dry hop	1.00 oz	
OG	1044	
FG	1007	
ABV	4.89	
Apparent attenuation	84.09%	
IBU	30	
SRM	6	
Mash at	151° F	
Sparge at	165° F	
Boil time	120 minutes	
pitching temp	60.5° F	
Yeast	WLP025 Southwold	

Mini Book Series volume XXX: Let's Brew!

1950 Adnams PA

The 1950's – what a wonderful decade. I sort of feel at home there, seeing it's the era when I was born. Odd thought that.

But the usual images – teddy boys, rock and roll, rising living standards – all come from much later in the decade. The early years were much tougher. Rationing and shortages of almost everything were the order of the day. Beer output was falling and gravities were only just starting to creep back up a little.

Yet this beer from that time is very recognisable. It looks much like the Ordinary Bitters I remember from my youth. OG of 1036, 3.6% ABV. Glancing at the 1977 Good Beer Guide there are dozens of Bitters with similar gravities. Including Adnams. Their Bitter is listed with exactly the same gravity as this version.

It would be difficult to have a much simpler beer than this: pale malt, No. 1 invert and English hops. It looks to me like a classic drinking Bitter. Especially as it has fairly robust hopping. In short, a beer built for a session. The eight pints in two hours kind of session.

It's so simple, I'm struggling to think of anything more to say. Other than brew this beer. I'm sure you won't regret it.

1950 Adnams PA		
pale malt	7.50 lb	93.75%
no. 1 sugar	0.50 lb	6.25%
Fuggles 90 min	0.75 oz	
Goldings 60 min	0.75 oz	
Goldings 30 min	0.75 oz	
OG	1036	
FG	1008.9	
ABV	3.59	
Apparent attenuation	75.28%	
IBU	34	
SRM	5	
Mash at	149° F	
Sparge at	170° F	
Boil time	120 minutes	
pitching temp	61° F	
Yeast	WLP025 Southwold	

Mini Book Series volume XXX: Let's Brew!

1959 Adnams LBA

This is an odd beer. It's sort of the reverse of what most breweries did in the mid-1950's.

When restrictions were removed on the strength of beer in the early 1950's, many breweries took the opportunity to introduce a new, stronger Bitter. Something closer in strength to pre-war beers. Young's Special is a good example. It was a way of offering drinkers a stronger beer but without generally raising the gravity of their standard beers.

Adnams did the exact opposite. In 1956 they introduced a weaker Bitter. Which is very odd as their existing Bitter wasn't all that strong. Even before WW II it was only 1039° compared to 1048-1050° in London. That just seems to make less reasonable to start brewing a weaker beer. But that's exactly what they did.

At just 1031°, it looks very much like a West Country Boy's Bitter. These were Bitters with a gravity similar to Ordinary Mild and when Mild went into serious decline, they often took its place. Maybe that's why this beer existed, too. Something cheap and cheerful for drinkers who didn't want to sup Mild.

It's another very simple recipe, consisting of just pale malt and sugar. And I've made it even simpler. The original contained three sugars: No. 1 invert, Hydrol and a tiny amount (7 lbs) of something called sucramel. I've just upped the No. 1 invert amount. The original also contained a small amount of enzymatic malt.

It looks like a nice light, easy-drinking Bitter. The stuff you're meant to drink by the gallon.

1959 Adnams LBA		
pale malt	5.50 lb	84.62%
no. 1 sugar	1.00 lb	15.38%
Fuggles 90 min	0.75 oz	
Fuggles 60 min	0.75 oz	
Goldings 30 min	0.75 oz	
OG	1031	
FG	1009.4	
ABV	2.86	
Apparent attenuation	69.68%	
IBU	33	
SRM	4	
Mash at	150° F	
Sparge at	180° F	
Boil time	90 minutes	
pitching temp	60.5° F	
Yeast	WLP025 Southwold	

1946 Fullers PA

I thought I'd go for a full-on austerity Bitter. And what better beer than Fullers PA. Because it demonstrates nicely the arc of Pale Ales.

Let's go back in time a little. To 1887. When Fullers PA was still called IPA. Then it was the strongest of Fullers Pale Ales at 1060°. They brewed four Pale Ales is in all, with quite small differences in gravity between them, just 10 points between the strongest and weakest. A bit like some cask breweries today, it looks.

By the 1950's, PA and X Ale were the only Fullers beers still around that had been brewed in the 19th century. But PA paid a price for its longevity. Its gravity was greatly reduced. As its gravity dropped, it gradually squeezed out all the Pale Ales below it.

But when gravity restrictions were relaxed in the early 1950's, some breweries grasped the chance to brew a stronger Bitter again. Fullers was one. But instead of restoring some of PA's strength they introduced a new Bitter, SPA (presumably standing for "Special Pale Ale"). A beer whose name was later changed to something more familiar: London Pride.

PA had been downgraded from top dog to second fiddle. When An even stronger Bitter, ESB, was introduced, poor old PA was down to third in the pecking order.

Here are the 19th-century Pale Ales:

Fullers Pale Ales in 1887 - 1888					
Beer	OG	FG	ABV	App. Atten-uation	hops lb/brl
IPA	1059.6	1018.0	5.50	69.77%	3.28
XK	1057.1	1016.1	5.42	71.84%	2.84
AK	1053.5	1014.7	5.13	72.54%	2.66
AKK	1049.9	1014.7	4.65	70.56%	2.53
Source: Fullers brewing records held at the brewery,					

And the 1950's ones.

Fullers Pale Ales in 1959					
Beer	OG	FG	ABV	App. Atten-uation	hops lb/brl
LP	1043.2	1011.6	4.17	73.06%	1.10
PA	1032.2	1008.9	3.09	72.48%	0.82
Source: Fullers brewing records held at the brewery,					

You've probably already noticed the simplicity of post-war recipes. This is no exception. Just pale malt, sugar and flaked barley. In normal times the latter would have been replaced by flaked maize. But that was unavailable during the war. And in a wartime attempt to save some of the energy used in malting, brewers had been ordered to use flaked barley. It turns up in pretty much every recipe in this period. Even those of brewers like Whitbread who used no adjuncts pre-war.

That's about all I have to say. So here's the recipe:

1946 Fullers PA		
pale malt	6.00 lb	77.42%
flaked barley	1.25 lb	16.13%
no. 2 sugar	0.25 lb	3.23%
glucose	0.25 lb	3.23%
Fuggles 90 min	0.75 oz	
Fuggles 60 min	0.75 oz	
Fuggles 30 min	0.75 oz	
OG	1034.6	
FG	1010.8	
ABV	3.15	
Apparent attenuation	68.79%	
IBU	32	
SRM	12	
Mash at	154° F	
Sparge at	168° F	
Boil time	90 minutes	
pitching temp	62° F	
Yeast	WLP002 English Ale	

Mini Book Series volume XXX: Let's Brew!

1958 Fullers London Pride

This is a beer you may possibly have heard of. I've heard it's quite popular.

It certainly is with Dolores. Pride is her preferred drink, when in London. Though you'll notice that the brewhouse name wasn't LP, as in later logs, but SPA. Which presumably stands for Special Pale Ale. I'm not sure exactly when it was introduced, but it seems to have been sometime in the early 1950's. Something called Best PA appears in the Whitbread Gravity Book in 1951. It looks very similar to Pride in gravity. The first mention of London Pride in the Gravity Book is in 1953.

Many brewers took the opportunity to introduce a stronger Bitter in the 1950's. Wartime restrictions had killed forced Bitters to drop below 4% ABV. Both Watney and Youngs called theirs Special Bitter, beers of a similar strength to London Pride. They sold for 2d a pint more than Ordinary Bitter. A premium I'd be willing to pay for the extra oomph.

It's a simple recipe. Which I've made even simpler by replacing the glucose and the proprietary sugar PEX with more No.2 invert. The sugar content is quite low. 10% to 15% was more usual. In case wondering, the current version of London Pride has quite a different grist. Fullers now brew all-malt. There's 5% crystal malt, 0.25% chocolate malt and the rest is pale malt.

The original mashing scheme was an underlet mash. It started at 144° F and stood for half an hour. There was then an underlet that raised the temperature to 152° F and it was stood for 2 hours. Feel free to replicate that if you want to go for full authenticity.

1958 Fullers SPA		
pale malt	7.75 lb	79.49%
flaked maize	1.50 lb	15.38%
no. 2 sugar	0.50 lb	5.13%
Fuggles 90 min	1.00 oz	
Fuggles 60 min	0.75 oz	
Goldings 30 min	0.75 oz	
OG	1043.2	
FG	1011.4	
ABV	4.21	
Apparent attenuation	73.61%	
IBU	34	
SRM	12	
Mash at	152° F	
Sparge at	165° F	
Boil time	90 minutes	
pitching temp	60° F	
Yeast	WLP002 English Ale	

Mini Book Series volume XXX: Let's Brew!

1955 Flowers PX

You may be starting to detect a slight 1950's theme going on in this series. There's a reason for that. Though I'm not going to tell you it. I don't want to ruin the mystery.

This beer comes from another brewery lucky enough to have been bought my Whitbread. Lucky for me, that is. Because they were very good at retaining all sorts of documents from those they took over. Including brewing records.

Let's begin with the name. I'd probably be scratching my head trying to work out what the hell PX stood for – and coming up with all sorts of wild guesses – if I hadn't seen adverts and labels for Flowers Palex. Which is obviously this beer. It had a darker sibling, which we'll be getting to later, called Brownex.

Should you ask what style this was, I'd say Light Ale. Though the label says "Extra Light Mild Ale". And they also had a beer called LA, which I'm guessing stood for Light Ale. The gravity of the two was just a few percentage points different and the recipes identical. Seems like a bit of a waste of time.

I'm not going to claim that the recipe is particularly exciting. Basically, it's just pale malt and No. 1 invert sugar. With a touch of wheat malt and malt extract. Not quite sure why the latter was so popular after WW II. Was it an attempt to make up for the lack of American malt with its higher diastatic power? I assume the wheat is there to improve head retention. At under 4% of the total grist it couldn't have impacted the flavour much.

Flowers used the dropping system of fermentation. At least there's a row called "dropped to" in the records. No more detail, than that, sadly. Not even the date and time of dropping. Though I guess no-one is likely to try to recreate that at home. It seems to have been a common method in the South. While in the Midlands and North Yorkshire squares were popular. Something even harder to recreate in your garage.

The FG is on the high side, leaving the finished beer under 3% ABV. This appears to have been deliberate as it's similar in both examples I have. And the LA parti-gyled with this one had a longer fermentation and significantly lower FG.

The colour calculated from the ingredients came out slightly lower than the one quoted in the log, meaning there was probably some sort of colour correction with caramel. But the difference is so small – 4 SRM rather than 5.5 – that there doesn't seem much point bothering with it on a homebrew level. It looks to me as if they deliberately aimed a little low so they could always hit the exact same shade. You can raise the colour easily enough but you try lowering it.

In such a light beer, those 27 IBUs will seem like more. Though the relatively high FG should leave it with a little body.

1955 Flowers PX		
pale malt	5.25 lb	82.35%
wheat malt	0.25 lb	3.92%
no. 1 invert sugar	0.75 lb	11.76%
malt extract	0.13 lb	1.96%
Fuggles 90 min	0.75 oz	
Fuggles 60 min	0.50 oz	
Goldings 30 min	0.50 oz	
Goldings dry hop	0.25 oz	
OG	1030.3	
FG	1011.5	
ABV	2.49	
Apparent attenuation	62.05%	
IBU	27	
SRM	5.5	
Mash at	153º F	
Sparge at	170º F	
Boil time	90 minutes	
pitching temp	60º F	
Yeast	WLP007 Dry English Ale	

Mini Book Series volume XXX: Let's Brew!

1955 Flowers GL

As you can see, the 1950's theme continues. I'm enjoying it, even if you aren't. It's another Flowers recipe. Doubtless you can see where this is leading. Yes, I'll be dragging you through the full Flowers range. So exciting.

No idea whatsoever. About what GL stands for, before you ask. It's some sort of Pale Ale, I know that.

Forget that. I now know exactly what it stands for. A quick search in the newspaper archive came up with an advert for Flowers Green Label:

Leamington Spa Courier - Friday 21 August 1953, page 9.

Looks like it was a posh bottled beer. Funny thing, that name. I always think of Websters when I hear Green Label. It was the name of the Light Mild back in the 1970's. Though in adverts they usually forgot to mention it was a Mild.

But there's another association between Flowers and Green. Because right at this time they merged with JW Green of Luton:

> **"Brewery merger approved**
> At an extraordinary general meeting of the shareholders in J. W Green, the brewers, held at Luton today, a large attendance unanimously approved the resolution dealing with the increase of capital, etc., in order to implement the amalgamation with Flower and Sons, of Stratford-on-Avon. Mr. Bernard Dixon, chairman J. W. Green, thanked the shareholders on behalf the board for the wholehearted support and approval which they had given to this matter.
>
> He further expressed the appreciation his board of the manner in which the shareholders in Flower and Sons had responded to the offer. The target of 91 per cent was reached the latter part of last week, the position being that acceptances had come in amounting to 99 per cent, of both Ordinary and Preference capital in Flower and Sons."
> Yorkshire Post and Leeds Intelligencer - Thursday 25 March 1954, page 7.

The combined company eventually fell prey to Whitbread. Who built a new keg brewery in Luton and close Flowers brewery in Stratford-upon-Avon.

I think it's time to get on with the beer itself. Continuing with the theme of their other beers, it has a very simple grist: pale malt, sugar with a touch of wheat malt and malt extract. Though there must be some colour adjustment going on as the colour is quite dark for a Bitter. If you want to go 100% authentic, you'll need to add some caramel.

The youngsters amongst you will doubtless be pleased to learn that Green Label was quite heavily hopped, coming in at over 40 IBUs, according to BeerSmith. With its relatively high FG and generous hopping, that must have been a very full, bitter beer. Looks quite interesting to me.

Funnily enough, this is the one Flowers beer that wasn't dropped. Though that could just be the particular example I have.

Mini Book Series volume XXX: Let's Brew!

1955 Flowers GL		
pale malt	8.25 lb	82.50%
wheat malt	0.50 lb	5.00%
no. 1 invert sugar	1.00 lb	10.00%
malt extract	0.25 lb	2.50%
Fuggles 90 min	1.00 oz	
Goldings 60 min	1.00 oz	
Goldings 30 min	1.00 oz	
OG	1047	
FG	1015	
ABV	4.23	
Apparent attenuation	68.09%	
IBU	42	
SRM	7.5	
Mash at	152° F	
Sparge at	160° F	
Boil time	90 minutes	
pitching temp	60° F	
Yeast	WLP007 Dry English Ale	

1955 Flowers BX

I'm continuing my slow walk through the fields of Flowers 1950's beer range. This time it's the turn of their Brown Ale, Brownex.

It's a slightly weird name. Sounds like some sort of stain remover for underpants. In reality, it forms a pair with their Light Ale, Palex. I'm glad to have found both. Because Light Ale and Brown Ale are surprisingly rare in brewing records. The explanation is quite simple: they were often just tweaked bottled versions of another beer. Many Brown Ales were bottled Dark Mild, perhaps with slightly different priming. While Light Ale was a bottled weak Bitter.

A quick scan of the newspaper archives reveal that Brownex first appeared in the 1930's:

> **"A WINTER'S (T)ALE**
>
> "Brownex," a new brown ale, specially brewed as a cold weather drink, is now at the disposal of the discriminating purchaser. It is, of course, the brunette of the twins "Palex" and "Brownex" —"Palex," you may remember, is the special light summer ale which made its appearance this year. While "Palex" is extra light in colour, in gravity and flavour, so is "Brownex" heavy and darker in colour tone, heavier in weight and fuller in flavour. It is a warming tasteful drink with plenty of body in it and agreeable to degree.
>
> Its sponsors, Messrs. Flower and Sons, of Stratford-on-Avon, consider that its success will equal that of "Palex."
>
> "Brownex " is obtainable all Flower's houses, or from licensed grocers, bottles only (not on draught) at 3s. 6d. per dozen small, or 6s. 6d. per dozen large. Ample local stocks are available at Flower and Sons, Ltd., 377 High-street, Cheltenham."
> Cheltenham Chronicle - Saturday 18 November 1933, page 10.

Some interesting details in there. It implies that Brownex is stronger than Palex. That definitely wasn't true in 1955 – the gravities were identical. 3s. 6d.for a dozen small bottles implies a gravity of around 1037°. So not particularly strong. Below average gravity, in fact. Also fascinating that they pushed Palex as a summer drink and Brownex as a winter drink.

What on earth does "agreeable to degree" mean? That it's a bit agreeable? Reads like nonsense to me.

On with the beer. The combination of pale malt, crystal malt and No.3 invert looks like a classic Dark Mild grist. Though including lactose, presumably to add residual sweetness, isn't usual in Mild. The hopping is pretty light, but that's what you'd expect.

Will any of you brew this? Probably not, I suspect. It's a bit weak, well, unexciting. Though I'm certain large quantities of it were consumed 60 years ago. Who drinks Brown Ale in Britain today? A few old blokes and bikers.

Mini Book Series volume XXX: Let's Brew!

1955 Flowers BX		
pale malt	5.25 lb	79.25%
crystal malt 60 L	0.25 lb	3.77%
No. 3 invert sugar	0.50 lb	7.55%
lactose	0.50 lb	7.55%
malt extract	0.13 lb	1.89%
Fuggles 90 min	0.50 oz	
Fuggles 60 min	0.50 oz	
Goldings 30 min	0.25 oz	
OG	1030.4	
FG	1009	
ABV	2.83	
Apparent attenuation	70.39%	
IBU	19	
SRM	23	
Mash at	152° F	
Sparge at	160° F	
Boil time	90 minutes	
pitching temp	60° F	
Yeast	WLP007 Dry English Ale	

1955 Flowers IPA

I'm sticking with my 1950's Flowers theme. There is sort of a point to it. No, not sort of. There is a point.

To show the full range of beers coming out of a brewery in the 1950's. In some cases, it's surprisingly few. Not at Flowers. They brewed at least nine beers 4 Pale Ales, and one each of IPA, Mild, Brown Ale, Strong Ale and Stout. Though, a bit like many modern English brewers, they had several Pale Ales of fairly similar gravities. One of which we're looking at now: IPA.

I don't know if this was a draught beer as well as bottled. But it looks very similar to a type I sometimes call "Southern IPA". A couple of London brewers, at least, made one. Like Whitbread. Theirs from 1955 has the same gravity as this, 1034°, but is more highly attenuated and more heavily hopped[6]. Barclay Perkins brewed this type of low-gravity IPA, too. Though I'm not sure if it survived as long as 1955.

Talking of hopping, this is the most heavily hopped of Flowers Pale Ales, in terms of pounds per quarter. Which is the best way, as it takes gravity out of the equation. 7.5 lbs in the case of IPA, 7.25 lbs for Green Label and OB, 6 lbs for PX and LA. It's not a huge difference, but it is there.

The recipe is uncomplicated: pale malt, sugar, malt extract and Goldings. Not a huge amount I can say about that, is there? No. 1 is a guess, as the log just says "invert". There's a touch of some sugar called DSI, too. No idea what that is.

---

[6] Whitbread brewing record held at the London Metropolitan Archives, document number LMA/4453/D/01/122

Mini Book Series volume XXX: Let's Brew!

1955 Flowers IPA		
pale malt	7.00 lb	93.32%
No. 1 invert	0.38 lb	5.01%
malt extract	0.13 lb	1.67%
Goldings 90 min	0.75 oz	
Goldings 60 min	0.75 oz	
Goldings 30 min	0.75 oz	
OG	1034.2	
FG	1009	
ABV	3.33	
Apparent attenuation	73.68%	
IBU	36	
SRM	6	
Mash at	153° F	
Sparge at	160° F	
Boil time	90 minutes	
pitching temp	60° F	
Yeast	WLP007 Dry English Ale	

Mini Book Series volume XXX: Let's Brew!

1955 Flowers OB

Yet another Flowers beer. Don't worry – only another three to go after this one. Though expect a sudden inexplicable switch to 19th-century Scottish beers soon. For which I have a very good reason. Two very good reasons, in fact.

This time I really don't have any idea what OB stands for. None of the labels I have matches. The best match I can come up with comparing the beer to analyses of Flowers beers in the Whitbread Gravity Book in Brewmaster, a bottled Pale Ale. Could the B in OB be for Brewmaster? Possibly. But I'm not going to get too carried away.

I could probably tell for sure by looking a little further back in Flowers brewing records. Because Brewmaster wasn't originally a Flowers brand. It came from J.W. Green of Luton, with whom Flowers merged in the spring of 1954. I say merged. Effectively J.W. Green took over Flowers, though oddly the name of the new company was Flowers Breweries, Ltd. I'll be telling you more about the merger later. But for the moment let's concentrate on this beer.

It's been pointed out to me that there was a beer called Flowers Original Bitter. I shouldn't have needed it pointing out as I almost certainly drank it back in the 1980's. That's why I couldn't find a label: it was a draught beer.

It's another minimalist classic, containing only a handful of ingredients. Though I suspect there was some caramel used for colour correction. You won't get a beer as dark as the colour specified on the brew sheet with the ingredients listed. Just a cosmetic things, really, so don't feel obliged to do it. I doubt it has any noticeable effect on the beer's flavour.

Goldings are a pure guess as the hop variety. Mostly based on the fact that it's a highish gravity Pale Ale. Good-quality Pale Ales were usually hopped with Goldings.

Nothing left but to hit you with the recipe.

1955 Flowers OB		
pale malt	8.75 lb	92.11%
No. 1 invert	0.50 lb	5.26%
malt extract	0.25 lb	2.63%
Goldings 90 min	1.00 oz	
Goldings 60 min	1.00 oz	
Goldings 30 min	0.75 oz	
OG	1043.4	
FG	1011	
ABV	4.29	
Apparent attenuation	74.65%	
IBU	41	
SRM	7	
Mash at	152° F	
Sparge at	160° F	
Boil time	90 minutes	
pitching temp	60° F	
Yeast	WLP007 Dry English Ale	

Mini Book Series volume XXX: Let's Brew!

1955 Flowers Stout

And finally we're there. With the last in the set of Flowers beers. You can recreate an authentic 1950's Warwickshire pub experience in the privacy of your own shed. Or your home, if you're single.

I've argued several times that the idea that all English Stouts became sweet after WW I is way wide of the mark. Drier, quite highly-attenuated versions continued to be produced right through until at least the 1970's. But I won't deny Sweet Stouts were very popular. Especially in the 1950's. This is a Stout of that type.

The lactose is a bit of a giveaway that this is a Sweet Stout. Other than that, the grist has a fairly standard combination of pale, crystal and black malts plus sugar. The wheat malt I assume is for head retention. And, as always, there's a touch of malt extract. The sugar in the original is something called Palatose, which I guess is some sort of proprietary dark sugar. Given the very dark colour of the finished beer, there must have been something pretty dark added. Perhaps just caramel.

Despite being a Sweet Stout, there's quite robust hopping. Looks like they were going for the bittersweet of the stronger version of Mackeson. Which makes it more interesting than some Stouts of this type. No doubt it was eventually replaced by Mackeson after Flowers fell into Whitbread's hands. No point in competing with yourself.

The hops are a guess. All I know is that they came from Kent. Fuggles seem a good bet. This sort of Stout wouldn't usually be a candidate for posher hops like Goldings.

1955 Flowers Stout		
pale malt	5.25 lb	59.39%
crystal malt 60 L	0.33 lb	3.73%
No. 3 invert	0.67 lb	7.58%
lactose	1.00 lb	11.31%
wheat malt	0.67 lb	7.58%
black malt	0.67 lb	7.58%
malt extract	0.25 lb	2.83%
Fuggles 90 min	1.00 oz	
Fuggles 60 min	1.00 oz	
Fuggles 30 min	0.50 oz	
OG	1039.8	
FG	1014.5	
ABV	3.35	
Apparent attenuation	63.57%	
IBU	35	
SRM	75	
Mash at	152° F	
Sparge at	160° F	
Boil time	90 minutes	

pitching temp	58° F
Yeast	WLP007 Dry English Ale

I'll have to think of another brewery now. What have I got? Fullers is a possibility. As is Ushers of Trowbridge. Or maybe I'll just go 19th century.

Mini Book Series volume XXX: Let's Brew!

1937 Greene King AK

I'm always delighted to add a new AK to my collection. And this is no exception.

It's thanks to Ed Wray, who took a few snaps of Greene King's brewing records, again. This is derived from a photograph he sent me rather than me just nicking it from his blog.

The OG of this beer is very revealing. Revealing about the reason so many AKs disappeared. With a gravity already in the low 1030's, the drop in beer strength as a result of WW II left beers like this unviably weak. Just like 4d Ale.

The grist doesn't have anything very unusual about. There is Fiona, a type of diastatic malt extract that was added in the mash tun. It's not even that odd, plenty of beers of this period contained malt extract. It's just the type, Fiona rather than DME, that is slightly out of the ordinary.

It's clear that the war must have knocked Greene King's Best Bitter, IPA, down into Ordinary Bitter country. Which is presumably when and why AK was discontinued.

I'd love to see more of Greene King's brewing records. They're easy to read and contain all the most important information.

1937 Greene King AK		
pale malt	5.75 lb	76.67%
crystal malt 60L	0.25 lb	3.33%
flaked maize	0.50 lb	6.67%
no. 2 sugar	0.75 lb	10.00%
diastatic malt extract	0.25 lb	3.33%
Fuggles 90 mins	1.00 oz	
Goldings 30 mins	0.50 oz	
Saaz 30 mins	0.50 oz	
Goldings dry hops	0.75 oz	
OG	1033.8	
FG	1011.1	
ABV	3.00	
Apparent attenuation	67.16%	
IBU	27	
SRM	7	
Mash at	150° F	
Sparge at	170° F	
Boil time	90 minutes	
pitching temp	61° F	
Yeast	WLP025 Southwold	

Mini Book Series volume XXX: Let's Brew!

1937 Greene King IPA

While I'm looking at Greene King I may as well do their IPA, too.

I'd love to know more about the history of this beer. If only to have more arguments against those who accuse of not being an "authentic" IPA because it doesn't fit their preconceptions. What I do know, is that it filled the Best Bitter spot in their pre-war line-up. We can blame the war for knocking the gravity down to its current level.

If I were Greene King, I'd be annoyed with the developments which have left their flagship beer under attack by geeks who, let's face it, mostly know eff all about the real history of IPA. Or any other beer history, for that matter.

You may have noticed that I'm waffling a bit. I need to fill out this post, but there's little to add to what I said about AK. The two were parti-gyled together, meaning this is just slightly stronger version of AK. Though there was one difference: caramel was added to AK to make it slightly darker.

1937 Greene King IPA		
pale malt	6.75 lb	77.14%
crystal malt 60L	0.25 lb	2.86%
flaked maize	0.50 lb	5.71%
no. 2 sugar	1.00 lb	11.43%
diastatic malt extract	0.25 lb	2.86%
Fuggles 90 mins	1.25 oz	
Goldings 30 mins	0.75 oz	
Saaz 30 mins	0.50 oz	
Goldings dry hops	1.00 oz	
OG	1040.7	
FG	1012.5	
ABV	3.73	
Apparent attenuation	69.29%	
IBU	33	
SRM	5	
Mash at	150° F	
Sparge at	170° F	
Boil time	90 minutes	
pitching temp	61° F	
Yeast	WLP025 Southwold	

1950 Lees Bitter

Time to head off up North for some honest. A lovely, straightforward Bitter.

Lees brewed two Milds in the 1950's, but only one Bitter. Called, er, Bitter. With an OG of 1041, it was a pretty decent strength for an Ordinary Bitter. I'm not sure of the ABV, because Lees couldn't be arsed to fill in racking gravities in this period. I've guessed that attenuation was around 75%, which seems reasonable enough.

Older Bitter recipes are mostly very simple. As is this one – just pale malt, the tiniest touch of black malt and sugar. Oh, and a dash of enzymatic malt. Not sure if you can still get that. It was a big deal in the 1950's, when brewers saw it as a wonder ingredient. Feel free to just use more pale malt.

The sugar is the problem. In the original, it's a combination of an unspecified invert, CWA and something called proteinex. I've simplified it to all No. 2, though you could use a combination of No. 1 and No. 2.

Nothing is revealed about the hops in the brewing record, other than that they're English. Fuggles and Goldings seem a reasonable assumption. As this is a Bitter, you could also go with all Goldings. I'd be amazed if the dry hops were anything other than Goldings.

As for the mash, I've simplified that a little. There was an initial mash at 148° F for 20 minutes, then an underlet to raise the temperature to 150° F, at which it was held for 100 minutes. Given how common this form of mashing was in the 20th century, I'm surprised how little I've seen it mentioned. It was bog standard in London, but was used elsewhere, too.

As it's so simple, there's not a great deal to say. Except give the recipe a try and imagine the glamour of Manchester in 1950 as you drink it.

Mini Book Series volume XXX: Let's Brew!

1950 Lees Bitter			
pale malt		7.75 lb	87.25%
black malt		0.008 lb	0.09%
enzymic malt		0.125 lb	1.41%
No. 2 invert		1.00 lb	11.26%
Fuggles 90 min		1.00 oz	
Goldings 30 min		1.00 oz	
Goldings dry hops		0.25 oz	
OG		1041	
FG		1010	
ABV		4.10	
Apparent attenuation		75.61%	
IBU		27	
SRM		7	
Mash at		150° F	
Sparge at		170° F	
Boil time	90 minutes		
pitching temp		60° F	
Yeast	Wyeast 1318 London ale III (Boddingtons)		

Mini Book Series volume XXX: Let's Brew!

1984 Maclay PA 6d

I forgot to post a recipe yesterday as usual. I've just been so busy with that book thingy.

No, this recipe isn't in the book. That only goes as far as 1970. I'm trying not to post stuff from the book. Then you bastards have more incentive to buy it.

PA 6d, or 60/- as it was known in the pub, was a long-running beer of Maclay's, being brewed from at least 1938 right up until they closed. In the 1930's, it was their mid-strength Pale Ale at 1038°, slotting in between PA 5d and PA 7d, at 1032° and 1042°, respectively. After WW II, it was their bottom=level beer.

It's a beer I was very fond of, when I could find it. A very pleasant Dark Mild. Oh yes, you'll need to ass a shit load of caramel to get the right colour. It's way, way paler as brewed, more like 4-5 SRM.

The malt percentage increased in the early 1980's when Maclay dropped flaked maize. The recipe otherwise – No. 1 invert, a sugar called DCS and a bit of malt extract – remained exactly the same. I've substituted No. 3 invert for DCS.

The hops were a mix of British Columbian and English. As usual, varieties are my guess. You can swap them around, should you so be inclined.

The two mashing temperatures are for the initial infusion and after adding more hot water via the underlet after about 30 minutes. A sort of step mash, in effect.

1984 Maclay PA 6d		
pale malt	6.00 lb	90.57%
malt extract	0.17 lb	2.57%
No. 1 invert	0.33 lb	4.98%
No. 3 invert	0.125 lb	1.89%
Cluster 90 min	0.50 oz	
Fuggles 60 min	0.50 oz	
Goldings 30 min	0.25 oz	
Goldings dry hops	0.25 oz	
OG	1030	
FG	1007	
ABV	3.04	
Apparent attenuation	76.67%	
IBU	22	
SRM	25	
Mash at	148/157° F	
Sparge at	165° F	
Boil time	90 minutes	
pitching temp	61° F	
Yeast	WLP028 Edinburgh Ale	

Mini Book Series volume XXX: Let's Brew!

Mini Book Series volume XXX: Let's Brew!

1984 Maclay Export

Seeing as we've had Maclay's 60/- from the 1980's, we may as well have the 80/-, as well.

The recipe is exactly the same, obviously. Maclay only had one recipe at this point. So exactly the same percentages of pale malt, malt extract, No. 1 Invert sugar and DCS. For the latter I've substituted No. 3 Invert. It seems a reasonable enough guess. Too match the colour of the original you'll need to add some caramel. I'd guess it was around 8-10 SRM.

It's a beer that I know I drank occasionally. Though, if it was available, my preference was the 60/-. A perfectly decent drinking beer. Which is exactly how it looks on paper. Not really sure what else I can tell you. Er, buy my new book. That's a good one. This recipe isn't in the books by the way.

1984 Maclay Export		
pale malt	7.75 lb	90.70%
malt extract	0.17 lb	1.99%
No. 1 invert	0.50 lb	5.85%
No. 3 invert	0.13 lb	1.46%
Cluster 90 min	0.50 oz	
Fuggles 60 min	0.50 oz	
Goldings 30 min	0.50 oz	
Goldings dry hops	0.25 oz	
OG	1039	
FG	1011	
ABV	3.70	
Apparent attenuation	71.79%	
IBU	24	
SRM	5	
Mash at	148/157° F	
Sparge at	165° F	
Boil time	90 minutes	
pitching temp	60.5° F	
Yeast	WLP028 Edinburgh Ale	

Mini Book Series volume XXX: Let's Brew!

1984 Maclay SPA

I may as well give you the full set of shillings, now we've had 60 and 80 Bob.

SPA, or 70/- or Heavy, wasn't that old a beer. It only seems to date from after WW II. The first spotting I have of it is 1951. In the later war years, Maclay brewed just two Pale Ales, PA 6d and Export. PA5d, their weakest Pale Ale, was dropped, presumably because the strength of PA 6d had dropped to its level.

There was some rearrangement after the war and SPA was introduced as a new mid-strength Pale Ale. It had about the same OG as PA 6d had had before the war. The stronger Export was emerged from WW II surprisingly unscathed, with an OG just a couple of points lower than in 1939.

Once they'd moved to this new three Pale Ale set up, Maclay brewed it relentlessly for the next forty years, with only small changes to the recipes and gravities. Incredibly boring, really. Which isn't to say that the beers were bad, they weren't. Just that for the historian there's not a huge amount of material.

And there you have it: the full set of Maclay's beers from 1984.

1984 Maclay SPA		
pale malt	6.75 lb	89.82%
malt extract	0.14 lb	1.86%
No. 1 invert	0.50 lb	6.65%
No. 3 invert	0.13 lb	1.66%
Cluster 90 min	0.50 oz	
Fuggles 60 min	0.50 oz	
Goldings 30 min	0.25 oz	
Goldings dry hops	0.25 oz	
OG	1034	
FG	1009	
ABV	3.31	
Apparent attenuation	73.53%	
IBU	21	
SRM	5	
Mash at	148/157° F	
Sparge at	165° F	
Boil time	90 minutes	
pitching temp	61° F	
Yeast	WLP028 Edinburgh Ale	

Mini Book Series volume XXX: Let's Brew!

1933 Perry IPA

Just for a little variety, an Irish IPA. Ireland isn't a country particularly associated with the style, but in the past most British styles were brewed there as well as Stout.

Perry's brewery was located in Rathdowney, county Laois. It was founded around 1800 by the Perry family, becoming a limited company in 1877. It struggled it the 1950's and was bought by Cherry's Breweries in 1959 and closed in 1966.

I must say for a 1930's beer, it was a pretty high gravity. In fact, it's not much weaker than the classic 19th-century Pale Ale gravity of 1060-1065°. A decent degree of attenuation leaves a pretty strong beer of almost 6% ABV.

Not much to say about the recipe, which is just pale malt and English and US hops. The quite large quantities leaving a beer with quite a lot of bitterness. Style Nazis might even believe it has the right to call itself an IPA.

1933 Perry IPA		
pale malt	13.75 lb	100.00%
Cluster 165 min	1.75 oz	
Fuggles 60 min	1.75 oz	
Goldings 30 min	1.75 oz	
Goldings dry hop	0.50 oz	
OG	1058.2	
FG	1013.9	
ABV	5.86	
Apparent attenuation	76.12%	
IBU	76	
SRM	5	
Mash at	150° F	
Sparge at	170° F	
Boil time	165 minutes	
pitching temp	60° F	
Yeast	Wyeast 1084 Irish ale	

Mini Book Series volume XXX: Let's Brew!

1966 Perry Phoenix Ale

A beer from right at the end of Perry's existence, the ironically-named Phoenix Ale.

If you'd just shown me the recipe and not told me where it was from, I'd have guessed this was an English Ordinary Bitter. Pale malt, invert sugar and a bit of caramel for colour and that's it. Along with a reasonable amount of English hops.

The colour is pretty dark for a Bitter. Do you know what I think this is? An early example of an Irish Red Ale. I'd be interested to know why Irish brewers started colouring their Pale Ales darker. Did one brewery do it and then others copy them?

1966 Perry Phoenix Ale		
pale malt	6.75 lb	89.80%
caramel	0.017 lb	0.23%
No. 2 invert sugar	0.75 lb	9.98%
Fuggles 105 min	1.00 oz	
Fuggles 60 min	1.00 oz	
Fuggles 30 min	1.00 oz	
OG	1037.5	
FG	1010	
ABV	3.64	
Apparent attenuation	73.33%	
IBU	41	
SRM	11	
Mash at	149° F	
Sparge at	176° F	
Boil time	105 minutes	
pitching temp	61° F	
Yeast	Wyeast 1084 Irish ale	

1838 Reid IPA

Odd that I've never used this recipe before. Given that I've had it for years and it's the earliest IPA recipe I have.

It's strange that it should be from Reid as they were essentially a Porter brewery. A couple of decades later they dropped Ales completely and concentrated on just Porter and Stout. Which was a weird thing to do as that was just when Ales were starting to outshine Porter.

You can't get much simpler than this recipe: while malt and East Kent hops. Lots and lots of East Kent hops. Would you believe that I've actually reduced the quantity? It came to 14.5 ozs. based on the amount in the original brewing record. But it was brewed in May and the hops were from 1837.

There's not really much I can say about this beer, it's so simple. Apart from the original mashing scheme.

action	water (barrels)	temp.	tap temp.
mash	251	168° F	150° F
mash	181	190° F	175° F
sparge	85	180° F	169° F
sparge	70	160° F	166° F
sparge	70	160° F	open taps

I'm surprised at how hot the second mash was. That must have killed off all the enzymes stone dead. Though, as they were only sparging afterwards, I guess that didn't really matter.

One last thing: this beer was vatted. Not what you'd normally expect of an IPA. Usually it as aged in trade cask. But I suppose that Reid, as a Porter brewer, had plenty of vats.

1838 Reid IPA		
pale malt	13.00 lb	100.00%
Goldings 90 mins	4.00 oz	
Goldings 60 mins	4.00 oz	
Goldings 30 mins	4.00 oz	
Goldings dry hops	1.00 oz	
OG	1056	
FG	1007	
ABV	6.48	
Apparent attenuation	87.50%	
IBU	148	
SRM	5	
Mash at	152° F	
Sparge at	160° F	
Boil time	90 minutes	
pitching temp	61° F	
Yeast	Wyeast 1099 Whitbread Ale	

Mini Book Series volume XXX: Let's Brew!

1947 Shepherd Neame LDA

Now I've started I may as well finish the full set of low-gravity Shepherd Neame Pale Ales. And this is the weakest of the set.

In fact, it has the lowest gravity you'll ever see in post-WW I beers. No-one brewed a beer below 1027° because however low the gravity was, the minimum beer duty was set at 1027°. It made no sense to make a weaker beer as you'd be paying the tax for a 1027° beer anyway. It the late 1940's you see quite a few beers at this minimum level. Shepherd Neame had three: this, Mild and Stout.

LDA was always parti-gyled with something else. In this case BB, the one step up Pale Ale. Interestingly, this recipe is different from the single-gyle brew of BB in that it contains No. 3 invert sugar. And quite a bit of it: 20% of the grist. Which means the BB from this brew must have been darker in colour.

Or did it? Just had a closer look at the brewing record. It clearly shows that all the No. 3 was in the second copper with the weaker wort. And the BB only had 6 barrels (of 121 in total) from the second wort. Meaning the No. 3 was really only in the LDA. Ah, the joys of parti-gyling.

For some reason LDA is always written in red in the brewing books. Why is that? At first I thought it may have been because it was a bottled beer. But surely the Stout was only bottled, too. And that isn't written in red ink. Bit of a mystery, that one. Red ink usually indicates something unusual, something that changed in that brew or something that went wrong.

There can't have been a huge amount of drunkenness in the late 1940's, judging by the strength of most beers. I doubt anyone over the age of 8 could get pissed on this one.

Almost forgot to tell you what style this is. It's a Light Ale. LDA usually stands for "Light Dinner Ale" which around this time was shortened to just Light Ale.

Mini Book Series volume XXX: Let's Brew!

1947 Shepherd Neame LDA		
pale malt	3.75 lb	67.57%
flaked barley	1.00 lb	18.02%
no. 3 sugar	0.75 lb	13.51%
malt extract	0.05 lb	0.90%
Fuggles 120 mins	0.50 oz	
Goldings 30 mins	0.50 oz	
OG	1027.1	
FG	1007.2	
ABV	2.63	
Apparent attenuation	73.43%	
IBU	15	
SRM	8	
Mash at	151° F	
Sparge at	170° F	
Boil time	120 minutes	
pitching temp	62.75° F	
Yeast	a Southern English Ale yeast	

Mini Book Series volume XXX: Let's Brew!

1947 Shepherd Neame BB

Since we've had Shepherd Neame's watery Mild from 1947, we may as well have their watery Ordinary Bitter, too.

Don't get the idea that I'm blaming them or anything. Brewers had no option but to brew very low-gravity beers in the immediate aftermath of WW II. It was called Austerity Britain for a good reason.

This beer is a real, real rarity. Especially in the difficult years after the war. Because it contains no sugar. The tiny percentage of diastatic malt extract I'm sure is just there for mash efficiency purposes. The amount is so small it couldn't have contributed anything to the flavour or character of the beer. They were compelled by the government to use the flaked barley.

After the Free Mash Tun Act of 1880 almost no-one brewed all-malt. I'm straining my mind to think of any that I've seen. The occasional one-off, but that's about it. Whereas Shepherd Neame used only malt in their Pale Ales from 1920 right through to the 1960's. With the exception of WW II and its immediate aftermath, when they were compelled to use flaked barley by the government.

The relatively high attenuation of this beer might have left it tasting a little thin.

Around half the hops are designated "SN" in the record. I assume this means that they were from Shepherd Neame's own hop gardens. The dry hops are a guess as the records don't list them. It would have been strange indeed if a Bitter weren't dry hopped.

1947 Shepherd Neame BB		
pale malt	5.75 lb	78.55%
flaked barley	1.50 lb	20.49%
malt extract	0.07 lb	0.96%
Fuggles 120 mins	0.75 oz	
Goldings 30 mins	0.50 oz	
Goldings dry hops	0.25 oz	
OG	1031.3	
FG	1006.6	
ABV	3.27	
Apparent attenuation	78.91%	
IBU	19	
SRM	3	
Mash at	152° F	
Sparge at	170° F	
Boil time	120 minutes	
pitching temp	62.75° F	
Yeast	a Southern English Ale yeast	

Mini Book Series volume XXX: Let's Brew!

1947 Shepherd Neame BA

I hope you're enjoying gambolling through pasture of 1940's brewing. Doesn't it make you glad to be alive? In a different decade, obviously. The 1940's sound pretty grim. Especially the post-war years.

You'll be pleased to hear that we're leaving watery beers aside for a . . . slightly less watery beer. One with all the punch of an Ordinary Bitter. Let's face, this is pretty much the same beer as BB. Just a little bit stronger. It's a weird world, the late 1940's. Where a brewery might have four or five beers under 1033°.

I'm going to struggle to draw this out over 100 words. Er, pretty boring grist: pale malt, the obligatory flaked barley and a touch of malt extract. Again, around half of the hops look as if they've come from Shepherd Neame's own hop garden.

Just a slightly stronger version of the BB. That's it really. Just about done with Shep's 1947 beer range. Just one to go: LDA. Guess what that is. Go on. Not got it? A waterier version of BA. Hard to believe that a beer of 1034° could be a brewery's strongest. But it's true. BA was the strongest beer Shep's brewed in 1947. Happy days? I don't think so.

1947 Shepherd Neame BA			
pale malt		6.50 lb	80.55%
flaked barley		1.50 lb	18.59%
malt extract		0.07 lb	0.87%
Fuggles 120 mins		0.75 oz	
Goldings 30 mins		0.75 oz	
Goldings dry hops		0.25 oz	
OG		1034.3	
FG		1006.1	
ABV		3.73	
Apparent attenuation		82.22%	
IBU		22	
SRM		3	
Mash at		151° F	
Sparge at		170° F	
Boil time		120 minutes	
pitching temp		63° F	
Yeast	a Southern English Ale yeast		

Mini Book Series volume XXX: Let's Brew!

1956 Shepherd Neame SXX

We'll be looking at a typical a new beer of the 1950's: a stronger Bitter.

Around 1950 Shepherd Neame added two new Bitters, SXX and PA, with higher gravities than their existing Pale Ales BA and BB, at the same time dropping the weakest of their old range, AK. BA, the strongest of the old set, had an OG of just 1034°.

It was a pattern followed by many breweries. With the gravities of their pre-war flagship Pale Ales seriously eroded, they took the opportunity provided by a loosening of restrictions to launch something stronger. It must have been a joy for drinkers who had spent a decade having to put up with ever weaker beer sold at an ever higher price.

SXX was the stronger of the two new Bitters and, at 4% ABV, had a decent amount of oomph. Of course, all of the Bitters were parti-gyled together in various combinations. That's just the way everyone brewed back then. The technique really was a key feature of British brewing in the 19th and 20th centuries. And it's still practised by many older breweries. Including Shepherd Neame, I believe.

It's another very simple recipe. All pale malt, except for a touch of malt extract. The latter was quite popular in the 1950's. Not sure what its function was. In this case it was diastatic malt extract, which leads me to believe that its function is to aid the mashing process. Perhaps it was to compensate for the loss of malt made from Californian barley.

The hops were all their own. No idea what varieties, but Fuggles and Goldings seem a good bet. Note that at two hours the boil is quite long. 90 minutes was more typical by this period.

1956 Shepherd Neame SXX		
pale malt	9.00 lb	97.93%
malt extract	0.19 lb	2.07%
Fuggles 120 mins	0.75 oz	
Goldings 60 mins	0.75 oz	
Goldings 30 mins	0.75 oz	
Goldings dry hops	0.25 oz	
OG	1039.3	
FG	1009.4	
ABV	3.96	
Apparent attenuation	76.08%	
IBU	30	
SRM	4	
Mash at	152° F	
Sparge at	170° F	
Boil time	120 minutes	
pitching temp	61.5° F	
Yeast	a Southern English Ale yeast	

Mini Book Series volume XXX: Let's Brew!

1956 Shepherd Neame Abbey Ale

AA – what the hell does that mean? That's what I thought when I first stumbled across this beer in Shepherd Neame's records. Luckily, I've analyses for a beer of theirs called Abbey Ale. And label images.

It must have been introduced around 1953, a typical time for stronger beers to be introduced. I say that because it isn't in their 1952 brewing book, but is in the 1956 one.

This is a difficult beer to categorise. In my gravity spreadsheet, I've classified it as a Pale Ale. Based mostly on its colour, which is pretty pale at around 10 EBC / 5 SRM. Which you'll note is much paler than the calculated colour in the recipe below. That will be on account of the gyling. In reality, the proportion of No. 3 invert sugar would have been lower.

OK back to the drawing board. That's clearly come out wrong. Abbey Ale contained very little of the second wort – only 4 of the 98 barrels. Assuming all the No. 3 went in the second copper, that drastically reduces the percentage of the sugar in Abbey Ale. From 25% to 9%.

As I was saying, a difficult one to categorise, this one. I've got it down as a Strong Ale in my brewing log spreadsheet. That was mainly because it was parti-gyled with a couple of Brown Ales. I'd assumed that it was darker than it was. I think I'll standardise on Pale Ale. Though it is weird that it wasn't parti-gyled with the Pale Ales.

Ah. I think I know why it wasn't parti-gyled with the Bitters. Abbey Ale was a bottled beer, as were all the beers it was parti-gyled with. That probably explains it. And also the presence of wheat malt. For head retention, is my guess. Something more important in a bottled beer.

Not much else to say, other than that the attenuation isn't great. I was going to say tank conditioning before bottling would have lowered that a bit. But having looked at the two analyses of Abbey Ale I have, I'm not so sure. The one from 1954 is, indeed, more highly attenuated at 76%. That from 1961, however, is only 67% attenuated.

1956 Shepherd Neame Abbey Ale		
pale malt	7.75 lb	85.45%
wheat malt	0.50 lb	5.51%
no. 3 sugar	0.75 lb	8.27%
malt extract	0.07 lb	0.77%
Fuggles 105 mins	1.00 oz	
Goldings 60 mins	0.50 oz	
Goldings 30 mins	0.50 oz	
OG	1044.3	
FG	1016.9	
ABV	3.62	
Apparent attenuation	61.85%	
IBU	27	
SRM	8	
Mash at	153º F	
Sparge at	170º F	
Boil time	105 minutes	
pitching temp	60.25º F	
Yeast	a Southern English Ale yeast	

Mini Book Series volume XXX: Let's Brew!

1956 Shepherd Neame PA

I sometimes wonder what my least popular recipes have been, Ones that no-one could be arsed to brew.

I suspect that a few of the post-WW II austerity beers fall into that category. Including this one. Because it's one of those perennially dull styles, Ordinary Bitter.

Though, in PA's defence, it is basically all-malt. I'm not going to count the tiny amount of malt extract as adjuncting it up. Which makes it more unusual than you might suspect. British brewers didn't really do all-malt in the 20th century. Almost everything, with the exception of Guinness, contained sugar.

It's such a simple recipe that it's scarcely worth writing down. Pale malt and classic English hops. The hop varieties are I guess. All I know is that they came from Shepherd Neame's own hop farms in Kent.

Looking at analyses from the Whitbread Gravity Book, it looks as if the colour was corrected to a slightly darker shade of around 6 SRM. Probably not worth bothering with on a homebrew level.

Er, and that's. The recipe is so simple, it's left me lost for words.

1956 Shepherd Neame PA		
pale malt	9.00 lb	99.01%
malt extract	0.09 lb	0.99%
Fuggles 120 mins	0.75 oz	
Goldings 60 mins	0.50 oz	
Goldings 30 mins	0.50 oz	
Goldings dry hops	0.25 oz	
OG	1035.5	
FG	1011.6	
ABV	3.16	
Apparent attenuation	67.32%	
IBU	24	
SRM	4	
Mash at	152° F	
Sparge at	170° F	
Boil time	120 minutes	
pitching temp	62° F	
Yeast	a Southern English Ale yeast	

1869 Simonds XXX Pale

Simonds, of Reading in the South of England, were noted for their Pale Ales. Managing to build a considerable business on the back of their popularity.

In 1960 they were bought by Courage and Barclay, the combined company being renamed Courage, Barclay, Simonds. Their brewery in the centre of reading was closed in 1979 and replaced by a massive new brewery just outside town called Worton Grange. The new plant had a capacity of 6 million barrels, or around 10% of all the beer consumed in the UK. It didn't last that long, closing in 2010.

I can remember the fuss when the closure of the original brewery was announced. CAMRA waged a fruitless campaign to keep it open. Thinking back, their attempts to save breweries always ended in failure. But perhaps actually keeping a specific brewery running wasn't necessarily the point of their campaigns.

XXX looks like a typical top-of-the-range 19th-century Pale Ale: an OG of 1065° and a shitload of English and American hops.

1869 Simonds XXX Pale		
pale malt	15.25 lb	100.00%
Cluster 90 min	1.75 oz	
Fuggles 90 min	6.00 oz	
Goldings 30 min	3.00 oz	
Goldings dry hops	3.00 oz	
OG	1065.4	
FG	1021	
ABV	5.87	
Apparent attenuation	67.89%	
IBU	130	
SRM	6	
Mash at	154° F	
Sparge at	172° F	
Boil time	90 minutes	
pitching temp	58° F	
Yeast	White Labs WLP023 Burton Ale	

Mini Book Series volume XXX: Let's Brew!

1952 Strong SAK

You might be starting to notice a theme here. Or two themes. Or three. I'm not quite sure how many of them there are myself.

It's good to stray outside London every now and again. I'm gradually building up a better set of provincial brewing records. Because the capital wasn't always typical of the country as a whole. Porter is a good example. Draught Porter was gone from most of England, Scotland and Wales by 1900. Yet in London it limped on until WW II.

Pre-WW I there seems to have been more regional variation in strength. Some country brewers had products considerable weaker than their London equivalents. But two world wars and pretty standardised prices (in some periods regulated prices) flatten those variations out. By the 1950's there was little difference between the gravity of a beer in London and elsewhere.

But everything still wasn't completely standard around the country. In the 1950's you'd expect Mild to be the weakest and cheapest draught beer on offer in a pub. That wasn't the case at strong. Their weakest draught was an AK, or Ordinary Bitter.

Take a look:

Strong draught beer prices 1955			
beer	style	OG	price per pint
SAK	Bitter	1030.5	13d
XXX	Mild	1033.5	14d
PA	Best Bitter	1036.6	15d
SSB	Strong Ale	1045.4	20d
Sources:			
Strong brewing record, document number 79A01-A3-3-27			
A Strong & Co, price list dated 4th July 1955.			

Which makes Strong SAK an unusually weak Bitter. Looks rather like Boy's Bitter, the West Country style of weak Bitter that seemed to fill the slot taken by Mild in the rest of the country. A Bitter of barely 3% ABV intended to be drunk by the gallon.

It's a pretty simple recipe, just base malt and sugar. Now if Kristen were here he'd be telling you about how light and crisp the beer is. Or somesuch. I'm not him. So I'll tell this beer is particularly crisp and light. It's bound to be with the high level of attenuation and all that sugar. Should make a very pleasant summer supping beer.

1952 Strong SAK		
mild malt	4.00 lb	55.17%
PA malt	2.25 lb	31.03%
no. 3 invert sugar	0.125 lb	1.72%
table sugar	0.50 lb	6.90%
candy sugar	0.25 lb	3.45%
malt extract	0.125 lb	1.72%
Fuggles 90 min	0.50 oz	
Fuggles 60 min	0.50 oz	
Goldings 30 min	0.50 oz	
OG	1030.5	
FG	1006	
ABV	3.24	
Apparent attenuation	80.33%	
IBU	22.5	
SRM	7.5	
Mash at	153° F	
Sparge at	160° F	
Boil time	90 minutes	
pitching temp	60° F	
Yeast	WLP007 Dry English Ale	

Mini Book Series volume XXX: Let's Brew!

1952 Strong Golden Ale

I long ago learned that there's nothing new under the sun when it comes to brewing. No matter what today's "innovators" might claim, pretty much everything has already been done.

So you shouldn't be surprised to discover that Golden Ale dates back much further than the 1980's. And not just as far back as the 1950's. A quick search in the newspaper archive popped up a beer called Golden Ale from almost a century earlier than that.

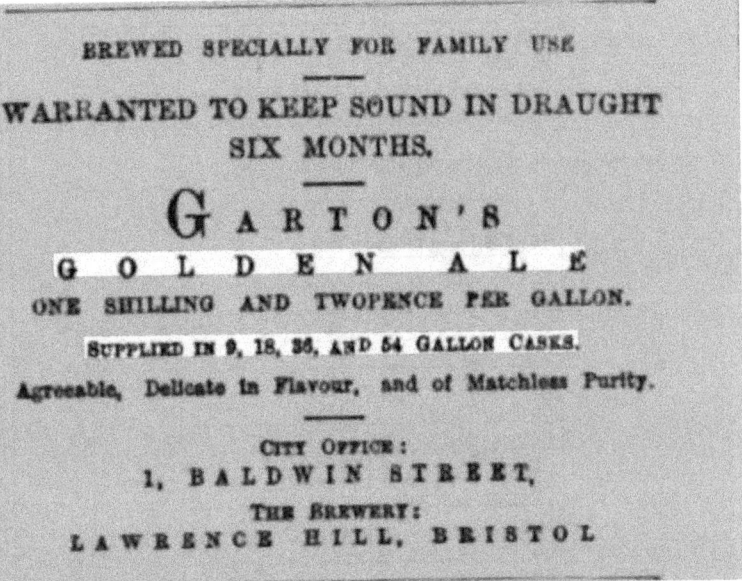

Bristol Times and Mirror - Thursday 07 May 1868, page 4.

A quick look at the colour confirms that it wasn't just a fancy name for a bottled Pale Ale, but a significantly paler beer. It's about the same colour as Pilsner Urquell. Though my guess is that if you'd asked for a Light Ale in a Strong's pub, this is what you would have been served.

It's another very simple recipe: pale malt and sugar. That's it. Oh, and a tiny dash of malt extract. I've picked Goldings as the hops because it contained Kent and Farnham hops, according to the brewing record. And it's pretty hop-accented, so you'd expect good quality hops to have been used. For its gravity, it has the heaviest hopping of any of Strong's beers.

What else can I tell you? How much it cost down the pub. That's always handy to know.

This was Strong's range of bottled beers:

Strong bottled beer prices 1955				
beer	style	OG	price per half pint	price per pint
Golden Ale	Light Ale	1033.5	10d	19d
Brown Ale	Brown Ale	1033.5	10d	19d
Black Bess Stout	Stout	1036.6	10d	19d
SPA	Pale Ale	1045.4	12d	
SSB	Strong Ale	1045.4	12d	
Sources: Strong brewing record, document number 79A01-A3-3-27. A Strong & Co, price list dated 4th July 1955.				

As you can see, they kept the pricing structure simple.

1952 Strong Golden Ale		
PA malt	5.50 lb	78.57%
no. 1 sugar	0.75 lb	10.71%
glucose	0.375 lb	5.36%
candy sugar	0.125 lb	1.79%
malt extract	0.25 lb	3.57%
Goldings 90 min	0.75 oz	
Goldings 60 min	0.75 oz	
Goldings 30 min	0.75 oz	
Goldings dry hops	1.00 oz	
OG	1033.5	
FG	1007.5	
ABV	3.44	
Apparent attenuation	77.61%	
IBU	37	
SRM	4	
Mash at	153° F	
Sparge at	160° F	
Boil time	90 minutes	
pitching temp	60° F	
Yeast	WLP007 Dry English Ale	

Mini Book Series volume XXX: Let's Brew!

1952 Strong SPA

We've just about finished off the set of Strong's beers from the 1950's. Quite an interesting set.

This time it's their, er, strong Pale ale. A beer that was sold in bottled format only. Bottled beer was on the rise again in the 1950's after being beaten down by wartime restrictions. Less popular styles like Stout retreated from draught, but other beers were designed to be bottled only. Things like Brown Ale and Light Ale.

This gives a flavour of the shift in consumer preference from cask to bottled beer:

> "A CONTINUOUS and growing demand for bottled was reported by H.W. Lake, MC. the chairman of directors at the Annual General Meeting of Cheltenham and Hereford Breweries, Ltd which was held the Fleece Hotel, Cheltenham. yesterday.
>
> In his remarks amplifying his statement circulated to shareholders, he said "In this part of the world people are changing. They like beer out of a bottle and not out of a cask.
>
> "While this is proceeding here to such an extent, I want to tell you that this Company is prepared for this change.
>
> "Under the direction of the brewers helped by Mr Hopcraft, we have a bottling plant which can cope with all the present demands and it is up to us to thank the management and the brewers that they have able to design improvements in our bottle store, by which we ran cope with this extraordinary demand for bottled beer which increases every year, and looks like increasing."
>
> . . . .
>
> "The outstanding feature this year is that although the output of beer in cask declines, the demand for bottled beer continually increases. We are, however, now able to meet all demands for bottled goods, having concentrated our bottling at Cheltenham with a complete range of modern plant running smoothly and economically.""
> Gloucester Citizen - Saturday 16 December 1950, page 2.

Getting back to the beer in question, it has one notable feature: it's very pale. At 13.5 on the old Lovibond scale, it's only a tad darker than the 12.5 of their Golden Ale. It'd got me thinking about the colour of Pale Ale. I've often wondered just how pale 19th-century versions were. What was a typical colour in the early 1950's?

So I had a look at other Pale Ales of the same era. I've plenty of analyses. And I've arranged them nicely in a table:

Pale Ale colour in 1952

Year	Brewer	Spotlight	Price	size	package	OG	colour
1952	Ansell	Pale Ale	10d	half pint	bottled	1038.3	19
1952	Cobbs Brewery	Pale Ale	10d	half pint	bottled	1031.5	26
1952	Barclay Perkins	Pale Ale	15d	pint	draught	1034.6	19
1952	Barclay Perkins	Pale Ale	16d	pint	draught	1033.22	24
1952	Barclay Perkins	H & O Pale Ale	16d	pint	draught	1032.78	23
1952	Bass	Pale Ale		half pint	bottled	1036.7	20
1952	Bass	Pale Ale	19d	pint	draught	1044.81	22
1952	Bass	Pale Ale	19d	pint	draught	1046.44	24
1952	Beasley	Pale Ale	17d	pint	draught	1037.18	30
1952	Benskins	Pale Ale	18d	pint	draught	1038.98	23
1952	Charrington	Pale Ale	15d	pint	draught	1034.06	18
1952	Courage	Pale Ale	16d	pint	draught	1037.47	24
1952	Courage	Pale Ale	19d	pint	draught	1039.99	26
1952	Courage	Pale Ale	18d	pint	draught	1039.04	32
1952	Ind Coope	Pale Ale	19d	pint	draught	1044.08	26
1952	Ind Coope	Pale Ale	19d	pint	draught	1043.7	23
1952	Ind Coope	Coronet Pale Ale	19d	pint	draught	1044.86	23
1952	Ind Coope	Pale Ale	11d	half pint	bottled	1035.6	22
1952	Lacons	Pale Ale	17d	pint	draught	1037.98	30
1952	Lacons	Pale Ale	18d	pint	draught	1037.93	25
1952	Lacons	Bitter	17d	pint	draught	1037.36	28
1952	Lees	Bitter				1040.0	20
1952	Lees	Pale Ale				1040.0	20
1952	Mann Crossman	Macs No.1 Pale Ale	20d	pint	draught	1044.91	20
1952	McMullen	Pale Ale	10.5d	half pint	bottled	1038.2	30
1952	Meux	Pale Ale	17d	pint	draught	1036.04	20
1952	Taylor Walker	Pale Ale	17d	pint	draught	1037.65	24
1952	Tetley	Pale Ale	16d	pint	draught	1036.27	20
1952	Tollemache	Resch's Bitter Ale	18d	pint	draught	1035.96	23
1952	Tooth & Co	Pale Ale		half pint	bottled	1043.1	13
1952	Truman	Pale Ale	17d	pint	draught	1037.15	20
1952	Truman	Pale Ale	17d	pint	draught	1037.14	24
1952	Truman	Pale Ale	17d	pint	draught	1036.72	20
1952	Truman	Pale Ale	17d	pint	draught	1036.52	24
1952	Watney	Pale Ale	17d	pint	draught	1037.42	24
1952	Watney	Pale Ale	17d	pint	draught	1035.72	26
1952	Wenlock	Pale Ale	17d	pint	draught	1036.09	32
1952	Wenlock	Pale Ale	16d	pint	draught	1036.69	27
1952	Whitbread	Pale Ale	17d	pint	draught	1038.12	28
1952	Younger	"Monk" Export	17d	pint	draught	1035.92	26
1952	Wm.Younger		1/1d	half pint	bottled	1046.9	24
	Average					1038.4	23.7

Sources:

Mini Book Series volume XXX: Let's Brew!

Truman Gravity Book held at the London Metropolitan Archives, document number B/THB/C/252.
Whitbread Gravity book held at the London Metropolitan Archives, document number LMA/4453/D/02/001.
Lees brewing records

The only one that's paler is from Australia. Only a handful have a colour of less than 20. It's clear that SPA was unusually pale.

The table also tells us that SPA was up at the top end of the strength scale for Pale Ales. Only two are stronger and one of those is Bass.

The recipe is extremely simple: pale malt, sugar and English hops. Attenuation is relatively low, meaning the finished beer should have plenty of body, probably drinking stronger than it really is. A beer I'd really like to taste.

1952 Strong SPA		
pale malt	6.75 lb	74.34%
no. 1 sugar	1.00 lb	11.01%
glucose	0.75 lb	8.26%
candy sugar	0.25 lb	2.75%
malt extract	0.33 lb	3.63%
Fuggles 90 min	0.75 oz	
Goldings 60 min	0.75 oz	
Goldings 30 min	0.75 oz	
Goldings dry hops	0.25 oz	
OG	1045.4	
FG	1015.2	
ABV	4.00	
Apparent attenuation	66.52%	
IBU	31	
SRM	4.5	
Mash at	152° F	
Sparge at	160° F	
Boil time	90 minutes	
pitching temp	62° F	
Yeast	WLP007 Dry English Ale	

Mini Book Series volume XXX: Let's Brew!

1885 Thomas Usher 80/-

Another 80 Shilling recipe. And another beer you can hear me talk about on Sunday at Beer Nouveau in Manchester.

The same comments apply as to the William Younger 80/-. This beer has nothing to do with modern 80/-. Though I can see why people get confused.

Being a little later, it should be no surprise that the recipe isn't all-malt. Though it was allowed to brew using sugar after 1847, most breweries didn't. There was a flurry of experiments in London breweries in the late 1840's, then back to all-malt grists. I'm not sure why. Perhaps the duty paid on sugar used in brewing made it economically unattractive.

Unusually, all the malt in this brew was made from local Scottish barley. You might be surprised how rare that was. The brewing record is very vague about the sugar. It's listed just as "sacharine" which basically just means sugar. I've guessed at pure cane sugar. I could be wrong.

Moving on to the hops, they're listed as California and Alsace, hence the Cluster and Strisselspalt combination. Note that, although all the malt was local, the hops were all imported. It's not that unusual to find brews where the only ingredients not imported were the water and yeast.

Don't miss your chance to drink this beer on Sunday. It might be your only chance.

1885 Thomas Usher 80/-		
pale malt	10.75 lb	87.76%
cane sugar	1.50 lb	12.24%
Cluster 90 min	1.00 oz	
Cluster 60 min	1.00 oz	
Strisselspalt 30 min	0.50 oz	
OG	1058	
FG	1023	
ABV	4.63	
Apparent attenuation	60.34%	
IBU	45	
SRM	4	
Mash at	155° F	
Sparge at	175° F	
Boil time	120 minutes	
pitching temp	59° F	
Yeast	WLP028 Edinburgh Ale	

Mini Book Series volume XXX: Let's Brew!

1855 Truman EI Contract IPA

Truman dabbled with brewing Pale Ale even before they acquired a brewery in Burton.

Their Contract Pale Ale is particularly interesting, being a beer specifically brewed for the East India Company. The company regularly placed advertisements asking breweries to submit tenders for Pale Ale and Porter to be shipped to India.

To all those who insist that IPA is and always has been a strong beer, I'll point out that this was the lowest OG beer Truman brewed. Their weakest Mild had a gravity of 1066° and even their Porter was 1057°.

At a time when breweries regularly used hops that were two, three or even five years old, it's worth noting that this beer, which was brewed in November, used all 1855 season hops. So about as fresh as hops get. So for once I've not reduced the hopping rate to account for hop deterioration over time. The hops are described as MK, i.e. Mid Kent, in the brewing record.

Unsurprisingly, the grist is 100% pale malt. As were most beers other than Porter and Stout at the time. Not really much else I can say, is there?

1855 Truman EI Contract IPA		
pale malt	12.75 lb	100.00%
Goldings 90 mins	3.25 oz	
Goldings 60 mins	3.25 oz	
Goldings 30 mins	3.25 oz	
Goldings dry hops	0.50 oz	
OG	1055	
FG	1014	
ABV	5.42	
Apparent attenuation	74.55%	
IBU	121	
SRM	5	
Mash at	154° F	
Sparge at	170° F	
Boil time	90 minutes	
pitching temp	69° F	
Yeast	Wyeast 1099 Whitbread Ale	

Mini Book Series volume XXX: Let's Brew!

1877 Truman P1

In the 19th century several brewers from other parts of the country set up brewing operations in Burton. The idea was simple: take advantage of the Burton water to brew Pale Ale.

Truman took the plunge in 1873, when they bought the Phillips Brothers' brewery which had been established a few years earlier. After rebuilding the brewery, they proceeded to brew Pale Ales and Burton Ales there to supplement the Porter and Mild Ale they brewed on Brick Lane. It wasn't a huge success and never really ran at full capacity. It closed in 1971.

P1 was their flagship Pale Ale. Or IPA. Not sure what they billed it as. But with a gravity of 1067° and over 150 calculated IBUs, that's what it looks like to me.

The grist is typical of the pre 1880 Free Mash Tun Act, being just pale malt. Sometimes brewers used some sugar, which was allowed, in this period, but mostly brewers stuck to just malt. It's only after 1880 that sugar usage really took off. Along with the use of unmalted grain, usually maize.

I'm pretty certain this was brewed as a Stock Pale Ale, which means that it would have been aged for at least six months before sale, possibly longer.

1877 Truman P1		
pale malt	15.50 lb	100.00%
Cluster 210 mins	3.50 oz	
Goldings 60 mins	3.50 oz	
Goldings 30 mins	3.50 oz	
Goldings dry hops	1.00 oz	
OG	1067	
FG	1022	
ABV	5.95	
Apparent attenuation	67.16%	
IBU	154	
SRM	6	
Mash at	150° F	
Sparge at	170° F	
Boil time	210 minutes	
pitching temp	57° F	
Yeast	Wyeast 1099 Whitbread Ale	

1883 Truman P2

Stablemate to P1 was the equally inspiringly-named P2.

A little weaker and rather less hoppy than P1, P2 is still a powerful beer. Note that even though it was brewed after 1880, it's still all malt. A sign that it was a classy beer. Though quite often expensive Pale Ales did contain sugar, which was used to keep both the colour and body as light as possible.

P2 was probably also brewed as a Stock Ale, but my guess would be that it wasn't aged for as long as P1, probably more like three months is trade casks.

1883 Truman P2		
pale malt	14.50 lb	100.00%
Cluster 180 mins	1.75 oz	
Goldings 60 mins	1.75 oz	
Goldings 30 mins	1.75 oz	
Goldings dry hops	1.00 oz	
OG	1062	
FG	1021	
ABV	5.42	
Apparent attenuation	66.13%	
IBU	77	
SRM	5	
Mash at	151° F	
Sparge at	170° F	
Boil time	180 minutes	
pitching temp	58° F	
Yeast	Wyeast 1099 Whitbread Ale	

1883 Truman P1 S

The S in the name of this version of P1 confirms that this is definitely a Stock Ale.

It's pretty much like the 1877 version, with one exception: the type of hops used. Whereas the earlier P1 only had English and American hops, this has two continental varieties as well: Saaz and Spalt. Though the latter is just called "Bavarian" in the log. That usually means Spalt, but I guess it could also be Hallertau.

I'd give this one at least six months ageing, but preferably more like a year. If authenticity is your thing.

1883 Truman P1 S		
pale malt	15.50 lb	100.00%
Cluster 180 mins	2.50 oz	
Fuggles 90 mins	2.50 oz	
Spalter 60 mins	2.50 oz	
Saaz 30 mins	2.50 oz	
Goldings dry hops	1.50 oz	
OG	1067	
FG	1018	
ABV	6.48	
Apparent attenuation	73.13%	
IBU	136	
SRM	5	
Mash at	150° F	
Sparge at	160° F	
Boil time	180 minutes	
pitching temp	56° F	
Yeast	Wyeast 1099 Whitbread Ale	

Mini Book Series volume XXX: Let's Brew!

1887 Truman LB

In the 1887 Truman (Burton) brewing record a new beer appears. A type of Pale Ale called LB.

My guess would be that that stands for "Light Bitter". Though with a gravity north of 1060°, it's not exactly my idea of light. Given the name, I suspect that this is a Running rather than a Stock Pale Ale.

What's odd, is that despite having some invert sugar in the grist, the attenuation is worse than the Stock Pale Ales we've seen. No idea why that should be, though the quantity of sugar isn't enormous.

One thing I should remind you of. As Truman's Pale Ales were brewed in a proper Burton brewery, they would have been cleansed in union sets. Note that I didn't say fermented in union sets. Because that wasn't the primary function of the unions. And the beer would have already been fermenting for days before it ever went into the unions.

No need to age this one, then. That's a relief, isn't it?

1887 Truman LB		
pale malt	13.00 lb	92.86%
No. 1 invert sugar	1.00 lb	7.14%
Cluster 180 mins	1.25 oz	
Goldings 60 mins	1.25 oz	
Goldings 30 mins	1.25 oz	
Goldings dry hops	0.50 oz	
OG	1064	
FG	1022	
ABV	5.56	
Apparent attenuation	65.63%	
IBU	55	
SRM	6	
Mash at	152° F	
Sparge at	170° F	
Boil time	180 minutes	
pitching temp	57° F	
Yeast	Wyeast 1099 Whitbread Ale	

Mini Book Series volume XXX: Let's Brew!

1963 Watneys Keg Red Barrel

Now here's a beer I never imagined I'd be writing a recipe for, the infamous Watneys Red Barrel.

This isn't taken from a brewing record, but an even more detailed source: the Watney Mann Quality Control manual. I know. Given their reputation, that's a bit of a joke. Though they do seem to have tried to brew Red Barrel to a reasonable quality. It's one of their few beers without any ullage or other crap blended in.

There's nothing at all wrong with the recipe. It's just malt and sugar. Remember this is a time when the vast majority of beer brewed in the UK contained adjuncts, usually in the form of flaked maize. Here there's nothing dodgier than No.3 invert sugar.

Of course, to truly recreate the original you'll need to pasteurise it to death and then fizz it up with force carbonation. Or you could serve it as God intended, unfizzzed from a cask. And see how nice a beer it could have been, had Watneys not been obsessed with kegging everything.

I can remember when they brought back cask in the early 1980's. They didn't have any casks so Fined Stag Bitter was filled into specially adapted kegs. It wasn't the world's greatest beer. Probably because (I'm guessing here) they blended in 10% ullage like with their other beers.

1963 Watneys Keg Red Barrel		
pale malt	7.50 lb	87.41%
crystal malt 60 L	0.33 lb	3.85%
No. 3 invert sugar	0.50 lb	5.83%
malt extract	0.25 lb	2.91%
Fuggles 105 min	1.50 oz	
Goldings 15 min	0.75 oz	
Goldings dry hops	0.125 oz	
OG	1039.2	
FG	1006	
ABV	4.39	
Apparent attenuation	84.69%	
IBU	30	
SRM	8	
Mash at	158° F	
Sparge at	175° F	
Boil time	105 minutes	
pitching temp	60° F	
Yeast	WLP023 Burton Ale	

Mini Book Series volume XXX: Let's Brew!

1972 Watneys Red

For the sake of completeness, here's the successor to Red Barrel, Watneys Red.

I can remember the advertising campaign when it launched. All this faux-communist stuff. It was launched in 1971. Not the best timing, as it was just before the cask revival. Wikipedia sys it was just a rebranding of Red Barrel. I don't buy that. The recipe and the OG are pretty different. It looks like a new beer to me.

I'll be honest with you. I'm a bit light on details for this beer. The Watney Mann Quality Control manual lists the ingredients and the OG and FG I got from an analysis in the Whitbread Gravity Book.

The sugar Is listed as something called Fermax. No idea what that is, so I've substituted No.2 invert. I've no idea how close that is. But, the colour of the finished beer came out right so it can't be that far wide of the mark.

As with Red Barrel, you'll need to process the buggery out of it if you want to go for full authenticity. And preferably drink it in a room with a shitty brick bar and a garish red and purple carpet, packed with tattooed blokes who are all chain smoking while watching racing on a black and while telly.

1972 Watneys Red		
pale malt	5.75 lb	76.67%
lightly roasted barley 400 L	0.25 lb	3.33%
No. 2 invert sugar	1.50 lb	20.00%
Fuggles 105 min	0.75 oz	
Fuggles 60 min	0.75 oz	
Goldings 15 min	0.75 oz	
OG	1037.1	
FG	1009.5	
ABV	3.65	
Apparent attenuation	74.39%	
IBU	30	
SRM	9	
Mash at	158° F	
Sparge at	175° F	
Boil time	105 minutes	
pitching temp	60° F	
Yeast	WLP023 Burton Ale	

1909 Whitbread IPA

Whitbread first brewed their IPA in 1900. Making this a fairly early iteration of the beer.

Just to confuse modern style Nazis, it was lower in gravity that the Pale Ale that they had been brewing since 1865. That beer had an OG of around 1060°. One thing that does fit in with modern ideas is the hopping rate, which was slightly higher for the IPA.

There's not much to the recipe. Just pale malt, invert sugar and a load of Goldings. Not as crazy as in some 19th-century beers, but enough to give calculated IBUs in the 60s.

It's possible at this date that the colour was adjusted with caramel at racking time.

1909 Whitbread IPA		
pale malt	8.00 lb	80.00%
no. 1 sugar	2.00 lb	20.00%
Goldings 90 mins	1.75 oz	
Goldings 60 mins	1.75 oz	
Goldings 30 mins	1.75 oz	
Goldings dry hops	0.50 oz	
OG	1049.6	
FG	1015	
ABV	4.58	
Apparent attenuation	69.76%	
IBU	68	
SRM	6	
Mash at	151° F	
Sparge at	165° F	
Boil time	105 minutes	
pitching temp	59° F	
Yeast	Wyeast 1099 Whitbread ale	

Mini Book Series volume XXX: Let's Brew!

1909 Whitbread PA

So you can do the comparing thing with the IPA, here's Whitbread's Pale Ale, too.

The recipes are, unsurprisingly, very similar. Pale malt, invert sugar and Goldings. In fact, exactly the same quantity of Goldings, though as this is a stronger beer, the IBUs come out a bit lower. My guess would be that because IPA was a lighter beer, the perceived difference in bitterness would be greater than the numbers suggest.

1909 Whitbread PA		
pale malt	10.25 lb	80.39%
no. 1 sugar	2.50 lb	19.61%
Goldings 90 mins	1.75 oz	
Goldings 60 mins	1.75 oz	
Goldings 30 mins	1.75 oz	
Goldings dry hops	0.50 oz	
OG	1062.7	
FG	1019	
ABV	5.78	
Apparent attenuation	69.70%	
IBU	61.5	
SRM	8	
Mash at	151° F	
Sparge at	165° F	
Boil time	105 minutes	
pitching temp	59° F	
Yeast	Wyeast 1099 Whitbread ale	

Mini Book Series volume XXX: Let's Brew!

1957 Whitbread IPA

English IPA. There has been so much total and utter bollocks spoken about the style. Most definitions seem to be what Americans think English IPA should be like. Not based on something as dull as beers actually brewed in the UK.

It's always good fun picking a style in BeerSmith. As this is an IPA brewed in England, I plumped for English IPA. 1050° to 1075° it tells me is the gravity range. Where the fuck did they get that from? I'm pretty certain that between 1820 and 1990 there wasn't a single IPA breed in the UK with an OG over 1070°. The classic IPA gravity in the 19th century was 1065°. After WW I, Bass and Worthington excepted, there wasn't an IPA with a gravity over 1055°. Just thought I'd make that clear.

In the 20th century, one of the commonest types of IPA was like Whitbread's. A low-gravity, very pale, quite hoppy, bottled beer. Other London brewers had similar beers. Barclay Perkins, for example. It's pretty much died out, though Harveys still make one.

It's another painfully simple Whitbread recipe. Pale malt, crystal malt and invert sugar. Where could you go wrong with that? This is one of the very few beers where the colour calculated in BeerSmith pretty much matches the one in the brewing record. Meaning the colour wasn't adjusted with caramel. Or with only a very little.

The hops were a mix of Mid Kent and East Kent, which I've interpreted as Fuggles and Goldings. It's another beer with a relatively short boil. Which was pretty standard at Whitbread after WW II.

1957 Whitbread IPA		
PA malt	6.50 lb	83.87%
crystal malt 40L	0.50 lb	6.45%
no. 1 sugar	0.75 lb	9.68%
Fuggles 75 min	0.75 oz	
Goldings 40 min	1.00 oz	
Goldings 20 min	1.00 oz	
OG	1035.8	
FG	1006.5	
ABV	3.88	
Apparent attenuation	81.84%	
IBU	36	
SRM	6	
Mash at	147° F	
Sparge at	168° F	
Boil time	75 minutes	
pitching temp	64° F	
Yeast	Wyeast 1099 Whitbread ale	

Mini Book Series volume XXX: Let's Brew!

1959 Whitbread PA

It seems like an age since I last did a Whitbread recipe. Probably because it was ages ago.

Whitbread PA, the brewery's main Bitter, had been around for a long time. It first appeared in 1865 and was brewed continuously until Chiswell Street closed in the mid 1970's. Though it changed quite a bit over the years. Initially it was 6.5% ABV, though obviously a couple of world wars whittled that down. And there was a name change after WW II, at least at the point of sale, where it became known as Tankard. Or perhaps that was just the keg version.

In the 1950's, Whitbread brewed two Bitters: PA at 1039° and IPA/WPA at 1035°. So I suppose Best Bitter and Bitter. IPA eventually transformed itself into Trophy. I would tell you more about that, but I'm saving it for when I publish a recipe.

There is a beautiful simplicity to this recipe. It's just pale malt, crystal malt and No. 1 invert sugar. So simple I'm struggling for something to say. Er, note how Whitbread didn't use any adjuncts (sugar is a malt substitute, not an adjunct). Which was good of them. Except during WW II, when they were obliged to use flaked barley, flaked rye and flaked oats.

One fact worth noting is that this beer was brewed from 100% British ingredients. British malt and Kent hops. This would have been unusual, other than in wartime, at any point in the previous century. But a huge increase in barley production during the war and a fall in the quantity of hops needed left the UK self-sufficient in brewing materials. Other than the occasional continental hop, it's rare to see any imported raw materials in the 1950's.

You're going to have to make do with that as I'm ausgebollocksed. Just the recipe left.

1959 Whitbread PA		
PA malt	6.25 lb	75.76%
crystal malt 60L	0.50 lb	6.06%
no. 1 sugar	1.50 lb	18.18%
Whitbread Golding Varieties 75 min	1.00 oz	
Fuggles 60 min	0.50 oz	
Goldings 15 min	0.50 oz	
OG	1039.3	
FG	1011	
ABV	3.74	
Apparent attenuation	72.01%	
IBU	28	
SRM	12	
Mash at	148° F	
Sparge at	165° F	
Boil time	75 minutes	
pitching temp	62° F	
Yeast	Wyeast 1099 Whitbread ale	

Mini Book Series volume XXX: Let's Brew!

Whitbread Session IPA

There's a reason for this. Which will become apparent later, but which I'm too sick to be arsed with telling you.

1909 Whitbread IPA

pale malt	8.00 lb	80.00%
no. 1 sugar	2.00 lb	20.00%
Goldings 90 mins	1.75 oz	
Goldings 60 mins	1.75 oz	
Goldings 30 mins	1.75 oz	
Goldings dry hops	0.50 oz	
OG	1049.6	
FG	1015	
ABV	4.58	
Apparent attenuation	69.76%	
IBU	68	
SRM	6	
Mash at	151º F	
Sparge at	165º F	
Boil time	105 minutes	
pitching temp	59º F	
Yeast	Wyeast 1099 Whitbread ale	

1909 Whitbread PA

pale malt	10.25 lb	80.39%
no. 1 sugar	2.50 lb	19.61%
Goldings 90 mins	1.75 oz	
Goldings 60 mins	1.75 oz	
Goldings 30 mins	1.75 oz	
Goldings dry hops	0.50 oz	
OG	1062.7	
FG	1019	
ABV	5.78	
Apparent attenuation	69.70%	
IBU	61.5	
SRM	8	
Mash at	151º F	
Sparge at	165º F	
Boil time	105 minutes	
pitching temp	59º F	
Yeast	Wyeast 1099 Whitbread ale	

Mini Book Series volume XXX: Let's Brew!

1924 Whitbread IPA		
pale malt	6.00 lb	82.76%
no. 1 sugar	1.25 lb	17.24%
Fuggles 90 mins	1.00 oz	
Fuggles 60 mins	1.25 oz	
Goldings 30 mins	1.25 oz	
Goldings dry hops	0.25 oz	
OG	1035	
FG	1007	
ABV	3.70	
Apparent attenuation	80.00%	
IBU	51	
SRM	5	
Mash at	153° F	
Sparge at	165° F	
Boil time	90 minutes	
pitching temp	60° F	
Yeast	Wyeast 1099 Whitbread ale	

1944 Whitbread IPA		
pale malt	5.75 lb	82.14%
crystal malt 60L	0.75 lb	10.71%
no. 1 sugar	0.50 lb	7.14%
Fuggles 75 mins	0.75 oz	
Fuggles 60 mins	0.75 oz	
Goldings 20 mins	0.75 oz	
Goldings dry hops	0.25 oz	
OG	1031	
FG	1005.5	
ABV	3.37	
Apparent attenuation	82.26%	
IBU	31	
SRM	7	
Mash at	150° F	
Sparge at	165° F	
Boil time	75 minutes	
pitching temp	64° F	
Yeast	Wyeast 1099 Whitbread ale	

Mini Book Series volume XXX: Let's Brew!

1962 Whitbread Ex PA

For once, this is a Whitbread recipe that I didn't harvest myself. As I mentioned before, this is courtesy of Peter Symons.

Rushing through the Whitbread brewing logs, I managed to miss the export Pale Ale. They probably didn't brew it that often, which is my excuse for failing to spot it. I believe this is the beer that was intended for the Belgian market, along with Extra Stout.

It's not a complicated recipe, just pale malt, a touch of crystal and No. 1 invert sugar. It isn't, as you might expect, a scaled-up version of their domestic PA, containing a much less crystal malt. I guess, with the increased gravity, they didn't need as much crystal malt for colour or body.

The original contains a small amount of hops from Alsace. But it was such a small amount – 60 lbs in a total of 1,200 lbs – that I've just left it out. If you feel inclined to go the full authenticity hog, use 0.25 oz. Strisselspalt and knock down the Fuggles addition by the same amount.

It's considerably more heavily hopped than the domestic PA – 49 calculated IBU as opposed to 28. That's fairly bitter. The dry hops are a guess as Whitbread didn't record dry hops in their brewing logs.

This beer, unlike most of Whitbread's range, is still brewed. Somewhere in Belgium, by AB-Inbev. How much the current version resembles that of 1962 is difficult to say. Though I doubt the Belgians are using No. 1 invert sugar. It's probably been replaced by some sort of Belgian brewing sugar. And perhaps contains adjuncts.

1962 Whitbread Ex PA		
PA malt	8.75 lb	77.23%
crystal malt 60L	0.33 lb	2.91%
no. 1 sugar	2.25 lb	19.86%
Fuggles 90 min	1.50 oz	
Goldings 60 min	1.50 oz	
Goldings 30 min	1.50 oz	
Goldings dry hop	0.50 oz	
OG	1056.8	
FG	1018.4	
ABV	5.08	
Apparent attenuation	67.61%	
IBU	49	
SRM	5	
Mash at	150° F	
Sparge at	170° F	
Boil time	90 minutes	
pitching temp	62° F	
Yeast	Wyeast 1099 Whitbread ale	

Mini Book Series volume XXX: Let's Brew!

1957 Robert Younger Export

I'm maintaining my run of Let's Brews for at least one more week. I'm starting to get the hang of this lark again.

We're returning to Scotland after what seems like a very long absence. With a beer from one of the other Youngers, Robert of Edinburgh. The smaller and less fashionable Edinburgh Younger.

This is taken from their final brewing log. They were bought by Scottish & Newcastle in 1960 and closed in 1961. These were years of carnage for Scottish brewing. Between 1955 and 1965 pretty much all the independent brewers were bought up and mostly closed. The industry was left almost totally in the hands of large British brewing groups: Scottish & Newcastle, Bass Charrington, Allied Breweries, Watney and Whitbread. Which is the full set, except for Courage.

Robert Younger belong to the tradition of totally dull Scottish brewing records. They had a recipe. Just the one. From which they parti-gyled all of their beers, including their Stout. There's the classic 60/-, 70/-, 80/- combo. Though there's also a really watery 54/- at just 1028°.

The 1950's are when Scottish styles of 60/-, 70/- and 80/- really became fixed in their modern forms. Just to be totally clear about this, they're all types of Scottish Pale Ale. No matter how well 60/- was in passing itself off as Mild.

Now I've got started about Scottish styles, I may as well say something about hopping rates. As I already mentioned, 60/-, 70/- and 80/- are all types of Pale Ale. With the minimal hopping Scottish brewers employed, how could that be true? Other than that story being total bollocks, of course. It is true, however, that hopping rates fell more in Scotland than in England during the 20th century.

Shall we look at some examples? Yeah, 'course.

First archetypal English brewery Whitbread:

Whitbread hopping rates in 1957			
Beer	Style	OG	lbs hops / barrel
Best Ale	Mild	1030.4	0.71
IPA	IPA	1035.8	1.26
PA	Pale Ale	1039.6	0.93
Source: Whitbread brewing record held at the London Metropolitan Archives, document number LMA/4453/D/01/124.			

Now Robert Younger:

Mini Book Series volume XXX: Let's Brew!

Robert Younger hopping rates in 1957			
Beer	Style	OG	lbs hops / barrel
60/-	Pale Ale	1030	0.58
70/-	Pale Ale	1035	0.67
80/-	Pale Ale	1043	0.83
Source: Robert Younger brewing record held at the Scottish Brewing Archive, document number RY/6/1/2.			

Whitbread's Best Ale has 22% more hops than Robert Younger's 60/-, PA 20% more than 80/- (after adjustment for the difference in gravity). I'd call that a significant, though not enormous, difference. Though you can see why Scottish 60/-, coloured dark with caramel, could pass for Mild in England.

Export seems to have established itself as a style between the wars, representing a brewery's strongest draught Pale Ale. The 80/- designation seems to come later, possibly only after WW II. In this brewing log it appears as both Ex and 80/-.

As I've doubtless told you 1,000 times, Scottish brewers rarely used any malt other than pale, with the exception of in Stouts. This recipe is no exception. It's just pale malt, flaked maize, sugar and caramel. The latter purely for colour. Feel free to colour this beer any way you like. Because I'm sure Robert Younger sold it in many different shades. That's just what Scottish brewers did.

1957 Robert Younger Export		
pale malt	6.50 lb	70.27%
flaked maize	1.50 lb	16.22%
No. 2 invert	1.25 lb	13.51%
caramel	1.00 oz	10.81%
Bramling Cross 90 min	0.75 oz	
Bramling Cross 60 min	0.75 oz	
Goldings 30 min	0.375 oz	
OG	1045	
FG	1012	
ABV	4.37	
Apparent attenuation	73.33%	
IBU	33	
SRM	20	
Mash at	152° F	
Sparge at	170° F	
Boil time	90 minutes	
pitching temp	61° F	
Yeast	White Labs WLP028 Edinburgh Ale (McEwan's)	
	Wyeast 1728 Scottish ale (McEwans)	

Mini Book Series volume XXX: Let's Brew!

1879 William Younger 80/-

Now here's a special treat. No, not because it's a Scottish recipe. Nor because it's in my new book. Much better than that.

It's a beer you'll be able to taste this weekend. If you're in Manchester, that is. Because it's one of the beers that's been brewed up for my talk at Beer Nouveau in Manchester this Sunday. I'm certainly anticipating drinking it keenly. That is, after all, the main reason I do all of this. To get to drink old recipes.

For those of you not paying attention at the back, this type of 80/- has absolutely nothing at all to do with post-WW II 80/-. This version is a Scotch Ale, in this particular case, a type of Mild Ale. While modern 80/- is a sort of Pale Ale. I hope that's clear.

It's a simple beer. But they all were before 1880. This is right at the end of the period when only malt, hops and sugar were allowed. Hence the lack of any adjuncts in the grist. There are, however, two sorts of pale malt. About a third is described as "Chev.", which I'm pretty sure stands for "Cheviot", i.e. Scottish barley. The other is "CM oder". No idea what that means but, given the date, it's probably some sort of foreign barley.

The hops are listed as Californian, American, Kent and Spalt. I've left the latter out of the recipe because the quantity is so small, just 20 of the 220 lbs. Feel free to throw in half an ounce of them if you want to be really authentic.

1879 William Younger 80/-		
pale malt	13.75 lb	100.00%
Cluster 90 min	2.50 oz	
Goldings 30 min	2.50 oz	
Goldings dry hops	0.125 oz	
OG	1059	
FG	1020	
ABV	5.16	
Apparent attenuation	66.10%	
IBU	75	
SRM	5	
Mash at	150° F	
Sparge at	170° F	
Boil time	90 minutes	
pitching temp	61° F	
Yeast	WLP028 Edinburgh Ale	

Mini Book Series volume XXX: Let's Brew!

III Porter and Stout

Mini Book Series volume XXX: Let's Brew!

1950 Adnams DS Stout

I know. It isn't Wednesday. But I've a good reason for posting early, as you'll discover on Wednesday.

To tie in with my look at Adnams beers after WW II, I've decided to publish recipes, too. Starting at the same place, DS Stout.

It's typical of a certain type of post-war English Stout. A kind of beer everyone seems to have forgotten about. A gravity of 1040-45, 65-70% attenuation, a bit under 4% ABV. Too strong and too highly-attenuated to be a Sweet Stout, but less attenuated than Guinness. I've dozens of examples. Though as the 1950's progressed, some did turn sweeter. Presumably to put a clear distance between them and Guinness. Or simply because there was a demand for Sweet Stout.

I was intrigued to see that in the 1920's the attenuation of Stouts had been greater – mostly over 70%. I think I know the reason why it had fallen by 1950. They were deliberately leaving the FG high to give the beer some body, albeit at the expense of ABV.

Moving on to the beer itself, the grist is a combination of four malts: mild, chocolate, amber and crystal. I can't recall seeing that mix before. Most breweries had ditched amber malt before chocolate malt became very common. Looking through some older Adnams records I noticed that they switched from black to chocolate malt quite early, back in 1914. For the simple reason of that juxtaposition of malts, I'd love to try this beer.

The hopping is total guesswork. All I know for certain is that the hops were English. But as Fuggles accounted for around 75% of the British crop at this date, choosing Fuggles seems pretty safe. Especially as most of the other 25% were Goldings and you wouldn't usually use those in a Stout. They were meant for Pale Ales and other posh beers.

It looks as if a fair bit of the colour comes from caramel so it may come out a little pale if you don't use any.

Mini Book Series volume XXX: Let's Brew!

1950 Adnams DS		
mild malt	6.50 lb	73.24%
chocolate malt	0.625 lb	7.04%
amber malt	0.625 lb	7.04%
crystal malt 60 L	0.625 lb	7.04%
no. 3 sugar	0.375 lb	4.23%
caramel	0.125 lb	1.41%
Fuggles 90 min	1.00 oz	
Fuggles 30 min	1.00 oz	
OG	1040	
FG	1012.2	
ABV	3.68	
Apparent attenuation	69.50%	
IBU	30	
SRM	40	
Mash at	148° F	
Sparge at	170° F	
Boil time	120 minutes	
pitching temp	60° F	
Yeast	WLP025 Southwold	

Mini Book Series volume XXX: Let's Brew!

1933 Barclay Perkins Milk Stout

Can you believe that there are still Barclay Perkins brewing records that I haven't processed yet? But it's true. Somehow I got stuck in the late 1920's and never even got to the early 1930's records.

This beer is in one of the unprocessed sets. It's not made any simpler by the fact that Barclay Perkins had several brewing books at this point: one for their main brewery, one for the Lager plant and one for their small-batch brewery. Milk Stout was made in the latter.

Which tells me straight off that they weren't selling a huge amount of Milk Stout. This batch was just 18.75 barrels. At a time when they were brewing their standard Mild in batches of 500 barrels or more. So clearly not a huge seller at this point.

I'm not sure what happened later, as it doesn't turn up it the next small batch brewing book. Looking at analyses, the OG was lower in the later 1930's, around 1048. Which is suspiciously similar to the OG of London Stout. My guess is that they simply added lactose at racking time to some of that.

The grist is pretty complicated, with four malts plus roasted barley. Barclay Perkins were unusual in that sense. Most London brewers went for black or chocolate malt. Given the percentages, you have to wonder if the amber malt was diastatic. Unusually for a Barclay Perkins beer there's no flaked maize. Perhaps just as well, given the small percentage of base malt.

For once the hop additions aren't a guess. There are three types of hop, Fuggles, Worcester and Goldings, with two added "at inch" and the rest after an hour. I take "inch" to mean when the copper was filled with wort.

I've upped the FG and OG by 3 points to account for the "Milk Stout sugar" primings added at racking time. These had at OG of 1150° and were added at the rate of two gallons per barrel. I'm taking this to be some sort of proprietary sugar that was mainly lactose. I've upped the lactose amount accordingly[7].

---

[7] It handily says at the start of the brewing record that MSS (Milk Stout sugar) was 250° L. So about 65 SRM.

Mini Book Series volume XXX: Let's Brew!

1933 Barclay Perkins Milk Stout		
mild malt	4.75 lb	41.76%
brown malt	0.75 lb	6.59%
amber malt	1.25 lb	10.99%
crystal malt 80 L	0.75 lb	6.59%
roast barley	1.00 lb	8.79%
no. 3 sugar	1.00 lb	8.79%
lactose	1.75 lb	15.38%
caramel 2000 SRM	0.125 lb	1.10%
Fuggles 150 min	2.00 oz	
Goldings 90 min	1.00 oz	
OG	1055	
FG	1027.5	
ABV	3.64	
Apparent attenuation	50.00%	
IBU	41	
SRM	38	
Mash at	150° F	
Sparge at	172° F	
Boil time	150 minutes	
pitching temp	59° F	
Yeast	Wyeast 1099 Whitbread Ale	

Mini Book Series volume XXX: Let's Brew!

1901 Boddington Stout

Quiet my life isn't. I try to focus my efforts, but once again I'm fiddling in the knickers of several projects simultaneously. I won't bore you by repeating what they. Mostly because it's pretty damn effing obvious.

I've been a stupid twat. Only just twigging that I can easily combine my beery UK trips with archive visits. Which is where today's recipe originates. At the Manchester Central Library.

I almost left it too late. Officially you need to book offsite records – which the Boddies brewing records are – two weeks in advance. I was so dozy that I only asked 10 days in advance. Luckily, that was OK.

Right. You'll need to bear with me. I have to quickly finish off my Abt. Got a blood test at the quack tomorrow for which I need to be "nuchter", as they say in Dutch. Literally it means sober. In this case, it means without food or drink for 12 hours.

Finally, we've arrived at the beer in question. Boddington's entry-level Stout from 1901.

The recipe mixed my head up a treat, I can tell you. No dark malt at all in the log. Until I got two pages further. Where a note in the margin it details the quantities of black malt added to several beers. Not mentioned in the main part of the log, because it was added in the kettle, not the mash tun.

The sugars are a total guess. I just know there were two types. The recipe just barely gets to a Stout colour with my random jabs of No. 3 and No. 4 invert. Later logs show caramel. So that may well have been added to this beer as well.

In London this would never have counted as a Stout. Standard Porter had a higher OG. But I think this is just a case of a Porter being rebranded as Stout for commercial reasons. Boddington has a stronger version called Double Stout that was closer to the real Stout deal.

Maybe I'll pester you with that Double Stout soon. Unless some shiny thing distracts me.

1901 Boddington S		
pale malt	9.25 lb	85.33%
black malt	0.25 lb	2.31%
No. 3 Invert	0.67 lb	6.18%
No. 4 Invert	0.67 lb	6.18%
Cluster 135 mins	0.50 oz	
Fuggles 90 mins	1.00 oz	
Fuggles 60 mins	0.50 oz	
Fuggles 30 mins	0.50 oz	
OG	1051	
FG	1015	
ABV	4.76	
Apparent attenuation	70.59%	
IBU	36	
SRM	24	
Mash at	156° F	
Sparge at	165° F	
Boil time	135 minutes	
pitching temp	60° F	
Yeast	Wyeast 1318 London ale III (Boddingtons)	

Mini Book Series volume XXX: Let's Brew!

1915 Courage Porter

Like all London Porter breweries, Courage brewed a range of Porter and Stout. We're going to step through the set from 1915.

Don't expect hugely differing recipes. That's not the way breweries worked. They operated in a much simpler way. Through parti-gyling they'd spin several different-strength beers from a single recipe.

In addition to the classic pale, brown, black malt bend, there's also some sugar. I've guessed No. 4 invert, as that was the type usually intended for Stout. In the brewing record what it says is Sacc. SM. My money is on that standing for "Stout Mix". Which would definitely imply something along the lines of No. 4.

The gravity of 1050° is about typical for a pre-WW I London Porter. Early in the war, not much changed. And this was brewed in March 1915, less than one year in.

1915 Courage Porter		
pale malt	6.75 lb	60.00%
brown malt	2.25 lb	20.00%
black malt	1.00 lb	8.89%
No. 4 invert	1.25 lb	11.11%
Fuggles 90 mins	1.00 oz	
Fuggles 60 mins	1.00 oz	
Hallertau 30 mins	1.00 oz	
OG	1050	
FG	1018	
ABV	4.23	
Apparent attenuation	64.00%	
IBU	36	
SRM	46	
Mash at	148° F	
Sparge at	181° F	
Boil time	90 minutes	
pitching temp	64° F	
Yeast	Wyeast 1099 Whitbread Ale	

Mini Book Series volume XXX: Let's Brew!

1915 Courage Double Stout

Next up the strength ladder is Double Stout. A beer which would have been available both on draught and in bottle.

You could perhaps try doing a parti-gyle of this with either the porter or Imperial Stout. Though you might need extra equipment to do it the proper way. You'd need to hop and boil the mash wort and sparge wort separately, then blend them to hit the target gravities. It's not rocket science.

It amuses me to see Hallertau hops being used when the UK and Germany were at war. But it's not as uncommon as you might think. I've seen various German and Czech hops pop up in brewing records from both world wars. They weren't going to throw good hops away just because there was a war on. I wonder if drinkers ever knew their beeer contained German hops?

1915 Courage Double Stout		
pale malt	10.50 lb	59.15%
brown malt	3.50 lb	19.72%
black malt	1.75 lb	9.86%
No. 4 invert	2.00 lb	11.27%
Fuggles 90 mins	1.25 oz	
Fuggles 60 mins	1.25 oz	
Hallertau 30 mins	1.25 oz	
Goldings dry hops	1.00 oz	
OG	1079	
FG	1033	
ABV	6.09	
Apparent attenuation	58.23%	
IBU	36	
SRM	65	
Mash at	148° F	
Sparge at	181° F	
Boil time	90 minutes	
pitching temp	61° F	
Yeast	Wyeast 1099 Whitbread Ale	

Mini Book Series volume XXX: Let's Brew!

1915 Courage Imperial Stout

Now, don't get confused. This isn't the ancestor of the current Courage Russian Stout.

Because that was originally a Barclay Perkins beer, only being called Courage Russian Stout in the late 1960's. This is Courage's own Imperial Stout, which like so many soldiers, didn't survive WW I.

Imperial just used to be the name given to very strong Stouts, usually with an OG north of 1100°. This doesn't quite reach level, but it's still no wimp of a beer. The No. 4 invert and large percentage of roasted malts, makes a pitch black beer.

While the colour might be high, the bitterness is low. 39 IBUs is bugger all for an Imperial Stout. I'd expect more than double that.

1915 Courage Imperial Stout		
pale malt	12.25 lb	56.32%
brown malt	4.25 lb	19.54%
black malt	2.75 lb	12.64%
No. 4 invert	2.50 lb	11.49%
Fuggles 90 mins	1.50 oz	
Fuggles 60 mins	1.50 oz	
Hallertau 30 mins	1.75 oz	
Goldings dry hops	1.00 oz	
OG	1094	
FG	1040	
ABV	7.14	
Apparent attenuation	57.45%	
IBU	39	
SRM	74	
Mash at	148° F	
Sparge at	181° F	
Boil time	90 minutes	
pitching temp	58° F	
Yeast	Wyeast 1099 Whitbread Ale	

1946 Fullers P

I was most surprised when I saw P – the brewhouse name for their Porter – appearing in post-WW II Fullers brewing records. I hadn't seen any other evidence of London Porter making it past the war. But things weren't quite what they seemed.

In the early 1930's, Fullers brewed two black beers: P (Porter) and BS (Brown Stout). Both would have been served on draught, as Stout – and to a lesser extent Porter – were still standard draught beers in London. Porter had an OG of around 1041° and Stout 1056°. Three analyses from 1932 and 1933 in the Truman Gravity Book show that P, when bottled, was being sold as Stout.

Oddly for a London brewer, Fullers seems to have discontinued BS sometime in the 1930's, leaving just the weaker P. Which seems to have been a mostly, if not exclusively bottled beer. The name it was marketed under, was one of the favourites for lower-gravity, sweet versions: Nourishing Stout.

Turning to the beer itself, the grist is notable for one thing: an absence of brown malt They dropped it sometime between 1921 and 1925. London brewers were remarkably loyal to brown malt, with Whitbread using it at Chiswell Street right up until it closed in the mid-1970's. The only coloured malt in this grist is black malt.

I've made some changes to the sugars employed. A proprietary sugar called PEX I've replaced by No. 2 invert. I've substituted No. 4 invert for something called Special Dark. Not 100% the same as the original, but about as close as I can get using standard ingredients.

For a dark beer of such modest strength, it's reasonably heavily hopped, only slightly less so than their Pale Ales. Surprisingly heavily hopped, I should say, given it's clearly intended to be a sweet beer.

This type of Stout was very popular in the immediate post-war years, but gradually faded from view as its drinkers aged and died. By the time I started drinking in pubs in the early 1970's, sweet, bottled Stout was only drunk by the granny or grandad in the corner. You'd never see anyone south of 50 drinking it.

How many beers of this type are still brewed? Mackeson and Sweetheart Stout are the only two I can think of. Maybe this could be a new frontier for innovative brewers: weak and sweet. There's only so far you can innovate by throwing in more hops.

1946 Fullers P		
pale malt	4.25 lb	62.96%
black malt	0.75 lb	11.11%
flaked barley	0.50 lb	7.41%
No. 2 invert	0.25 lb	3.70%
No. 3 invert	0.75 lb	11.11%
No. 4 invert	0.25 lb	3.70%
Fuggles 90 min	1.00 oz	
Fuggles 30 min	1.00 oz	
OG	1030.7	
FG	1011.1	
ABV	2.59	
Apparent attenuation	63.84%	
IBU	28	
SRM	29	
Mash at	153° F	
Sparge at	176° F	
Boil time	90 minutes	
pitching temp	62° F	
Yeast	WLP002 English Ale	

1956 Lees Stout

Lees changed around their Stout recipe quite a bit in the 1950's and 1960's. But 1956 was a significant year. Because that's when they started adding lactose to it.

Usually I'll tell you how simple an old recipe is. Not in this case. Because it's a dead complicated one. Four malts, four sugars and one adjunct. Though I've simplified the sugars a bit, it's still quite a long list of ingredients.

It's a slightly odd grist, as it contains two base malts, mild malt and PA malt, the latter being the poshest type of pale malt. Strange that they'd use it in a Stout, where it wouldn't really be noticeable. There's also a pretty high percentage of crystal malt, but a relatively small amount of roast malt, just a little black malt.

The sugars in the original were black invert, HX and CDM. The first is obviously No. 4 invert, the latter two I've replaced with No. 3 invert, which is probably as close as you'll get.

What else do I need to tell you? Oh yes, the FG is a guess. As are the hop variety, Fuggles. As usual, all the brewing record tells us is that they were English.

1956 Lees Stout		
pale malt	1.75 lb	24.14%
mild malt	1.25 lb	17.24%
black malt	0.50 lb	6.90%
crystal malt 60 L	0.75 lb	10.34%
flaked oat	0.50 lb	6.90%
No. 3 invert sugar	1.25 lb	17.24%
No. 4 invert sugar	0.50 lb	6.90%
lactose	0.75 lb	10.34%
Fuggles 90 min	0.75 oz	
Fuggles 30 min	0.75 oz	
OG	1038	
FG	1015	
ABV	3.04	
Apparent attenuation	60.53%	
IBU	18	
SRM	30	
Mash at	151° F	
Sparge at	170° F	
Boil time	90 minutes	
pitching temp	60° F	
Yeast	Wyeast 1318 London ale III (Boddingtons)	

Mini Book Series volume XXX: Let's Brew!

1962 Lees Archer Stout

I've been scouring my brewing records looking for Milk Stouts. And I have to say that I've found disappointingly few.

I'm not totally sure why that is. From labels and advertisements it's clear that a high proportion of breweries had a Milk Stout in their portfolio. Most likely explanation I can think of is that an ordinary Stout had lactose added at racking time. Though I could be wrong.

Imagine my delight, then, at spotting lactose in Lees Archer Stout. I've published a recipe for Lees Stout from 1952 which didn't contain lactose. Looking through the records, I saw that they only started using it in 1956. Which seems quite late for introducing a Milk Stout.

Though it seems that they never billed it as such. The labels I've seen for Archer Stout make no mention of milk sugar. They don't even claim that it's sweet. Strange, as it contains about the same percentage of lactose as other Milk Stouts.

Archer Stout wasn't the only Lees beer to contain lactose. Their Best Mild did, too. Though, intriguingly, not their Ordinary Mild. Make of that what you will.

Turning to the beer itself, Archer Stout has quite a complicated grist, consisting of three malts, one adjunct and four sugars. The brown malt in my recipe is a substitution for something called "oak dried" malt. Brown malt seems like the best equivalent. There's also a reasonable amount of flaked oats in the recipe. So it's odd that the brewery didn't claim Archer was either an Oatmeal or a Milk Stout.

The No. 3 invert is another substitution, this time for CDM and HX. CDM I'm pretty sure was a dark sugar, based on its usage at various breweries. HX I've no idea about

I know nothing about the hops, other than that most were English with a tiny amount of Styrians, just 2 out of the total of 28 lbs. Fuggles seems a good bet for this type of beer, but, as usual, feel free to substitute any appropriate English hop.

As Lees couldn't be arsed to note down the FG, I've had to make a guess. It could be wildly wrong, though I doubt it could have been much lower. Could have been higher.

1962 Lees Archer Stout		
pale malt	2.75 lb	40.26%
brown malt	1.00 lb	14.64%
black malt	0.50 lb	7.32%
flaked oat	0.33 lb	4.83%
No. 3 invert sugar	0.75 lb	10.98%
No. 4 invert sugar	0.50 lb	7.32%
lactose	1.00 lb	14.64%
Fuggles 90 min	0.75 oz	
Fuggles 30 min	0.75 oz	
OG	1036	
FG	1014	
ABV	2.91	
Apparent attenuation	61.11%	
IBU	20	
SRM	29	
Mash at	152º F	
Sparge at	170º F	
Boil time	90 minutes	
pitching temp	60º F	
Yeast	Wyeast 1318 London ale III (Boddingtons)	

Mini Book Series volume XXX: Let's Brew!

1935 Perry Special Stout

Perry was a small brewery in a rural part of island. But they seem to have brewed a fair range of beers.

It's particularly nice to have examples of Irish Stout to compare with all the English ones. Special Stout doesn't look all that special. For a start, it's rather weak for a 1930's Stout. In the 1930's, Guinness Extra Stout had an OG of 1055°, considerably higher than this beer's. In fact, Perry Special Stout is about the same strength Guinness Porter was at the time.[8]

Looking at the really high percentage of black malt, I suspect it's the special kind that was produced in Ireland. It wasn't as dark as English black malt and was somewhere between brown and black malt in character. As I'd probably have guessed, the grist just consists of pale and black malt. Irish brewers mostly dropped brown malt in the 19th century.

1935 Perry Special Stout		
pale malt	8.00 lb	76.19%
black malt	2.50 lb	23.81%
Cluster 165 mins	1.25 oz	
Fuggles 30 mins	1.25 oz	
OG	1042	
FG	1011	
ABV	4.10	
Apparent attenuation	73.81%	
IBU	42	
SRM	53	
Mash at	150° F	
Sparge at	160° F	
Boil time	165 minutes	
pitching temp	60° F	
Yeast	Wyeast 1084 Irish ale	

---

[8] Whitbread Gravity book held at the London Metropolitan Archives, document number LMA/4453/D/02/001.

Mini Book Series volume XXX: Let's Brew!

1937 Perry XX Stout

It looks like Perry brewed more than one Stout. Special Stout, which was the equivalent of Guinness Porter and XX Stout, which was the equivalent of Guinness Extra Stout.

XX Stout doesn't have the grist that I would expect. Pale and black was the usual Irish combination. Not only does this contain brown malt, there's no black malt, with chocolate malt taking its place. Plus there's some crystal malt, too.

Have you noticed what's missing from these Irish beers? In contrast to English ones, I mean. There's no sugar. Very little sugar was used in Irish brewing. No idea why that was the case. I'm sure there was a reason. Just damned if I can think of one.

XX is the strength I would expect for an interwar Stout, 5% ABV, or so. And before you say "Oh, but it's not as highly attenuated as Guinness." I'll point out that in the 1930's Guinness only had around 75% apparent attenuation.

1937 Perry XX Stout		
pale malt	9.50 lb	77.55%
chocolate malt	1.25 lb	10.20%
brown malt	0.75 lb	6.12%
crystal malt	0.75 lb	6.12%
Cluster 145 mins	2.00 oz	
Fuggles 30 mins	2.00 oz	
OG	1052	
FG	1014	
ABV	5.03	
Apparent attenuation	73.08%	
IBU	62	
SRM	35	
Mash at	150° F	
Sparge at	170° F	
Boil time	145 minutes	
pitching temp	60° F	
Yeast	Wyeast 1084 Irish ale	

Mini Book Series volume XXX: Let's Brew!

1837 Reid DBSt

Now here's a strange thing. The very first brewing records I ever looked at were Reid's. Yet I've never published any of their Porter and Stout recipes. Just an IPA and a Pale Ale recipe in my Home Brewer's Guide to Vintage Beer.

Not so bad, now I think about it. As including a few in this book will make it a more tempting purchase. Which is the idea. I do hope to flog a few copies. Some fresh recipes should help. Some old ones, too. The initial draught was very 20th-century dominated.

This is a pretty typical early 19th-century Double Stout. It has the classic pale, brown and black malt combination that London brewers loved. It was a mix that they continued to use well into the 20th century. At least those that were still open Reid closed in 1899, after merging with Watney and Combe.

One note about the malt. In this period they were still using volume quarters. Which means the quarters were different weights for different types of malt. I've assumed 336 lbs for pale malt and 252 lbs for brown and black malt.

The hops in the original were one third 1837 season EK, two thirds 1836 season MK. I've knocked down the hopping a bit to account for those older hops. It worked out to almost 11 ozs. for an Imperial gallon batch. Which is quite a lot. Then again, they hopped everything like crazy back then.

The original mashing scheme was more complicated, with two mashes and a sparge. The tap heats for those three were 143° F, 156° F and 152.5° F, respectively. That's actually quite simple for the time. Three or four mashes were common.

action	water (barrels)	water temp.	tap temp.	time
mash	190	160° F	143° F	90
mash	100	182° F	156° F	50
mash	40	174° F	152.5° F	45

To really recreate the original you'll need patience. And a vat. The original was vatted, probably for around 12 months.

1837 Reid DBSt			
pale malt	15.75 lb	78.75%	
brown malt	3.50 lb	17.50%	
black malt	0.75 lb	3.75%	
Goldings 90 mins	3.00 oz		
Goldings 60 mins	3.00 oz		
Goldings 30 mins	3.00 oz		
Goldings dry hops	1.00 oz		
OG	1084.2		
FG	1026		
ABV	7.70		
Apparent attenuation	69.12%		
IBU	91		
SRM	33		
Mash at	152° F		
Sparge at	174° F		
Boil time	90 minutes		
pitching temp	61° F		
Yeast	Wyeast 1099 Whitbread Ale		

Mini Book Series volume XXX: Let's Brew!

1837 Reid P

Reid was one of the largest Porter breweries in the 19th century. Never the largest, but sometimes second behind Truman or Barclay Perkins. In the early 19th century, they were briefly the largest in 1907 and 1808, but their production remained fairly stable while others expanded.

Here's how the London Porter brewers ranked in the 1830's:

Largest London Porter breweries 1830 - 1839										
Brewery	1830	1831	1832	1833	1834	1835	1836	1837	1838	1839
Barclay Perkins	262,306	330,528	343,328	315,784	343,569	382,063	378,109	354,360	375,466	405,819
Whitbread	144,104	191,040	209,672	187,070	184,100	186,206	190,005	180,512	179,975	183,468
Truman	167,542	199,486	234,665	226,924	254,650	280,075	329,333	303,590	310,193	320,675
Reid	127,220	154,631	165,515	150,865	169,246	181,187	194,656	162,840	178,919	171,650

Sources:
Whitbread brewing log held at the London Metropolitan Archives, document number LMA/4453/D/09/023.
"The British Brewing Industry 1830-1980". T R Gourvish & R G Wilson, 1994, pages 610-612

This is a pretty typical Porter of the time. With the familiar combination of pale, brown and black malts. All pretty locally sourced. The pale was from Sussex, the brown from Hertfordshire. The hops were all pretty local, too: Mid Kents from the 1835 and 1836 crop.

As a third of the hops were over two years old, I've knocked the total hops down from 4.62 ozs. to 3.75 ozs. It still leaves a calculated 44 IBUs.

The mashing scheme was quite complicated: three mashes and no sparge. There was a fourth mash for a return wort.

action	water (barrels)	water temp.	tap temp.	time
mash	207	162° F	145° F	90
mash	150	180° F	164° F	50
mash	179	151° F	153° F	40

This was a beer that wasn't vatted and would have been drunk young. Or perhaps blended with Keeping porter at racking time. As with all Porter and Stout, the fermentation was quite hot, hitting a maximum temperature of 78.5° F.

1837 Reid P		
pale malt	11.75 lb	79.66%
brown malt	2.25 lb	15.25%
black malt	0.75 lb	5.08%
Goldings 90 mins	1.25 oz	
Goldings 60 mins	1.25 oz	
Goldings 30 mins	1.25 oz	
OG	1061.2	
FG	1018	
ABV	5.72	
Apparent attenuation	70.59%	
IBU	44	
SRM	30	
Mash at	150° F	
Sparge at	165° F	
Boil time	75 minutes	
pitching temp	66° F	
Yeast	Wyeast 1099 Whitbread Ale	

1837 Reid BS

It's fun finally getting around to these Reid's records. Not that the Porter recipes are that weird or exciting. Just nice to do some different ones.

This is their base level Stout. Brown Stout was the first modern Stout in the 18th century. Brown because of the base brown malt, Stout because of the strength.

I won't talk at great length about the recipe. Because it's the usual pale, brown, black malt and pale malt. And East Kent hops. Pretty standard. London Porter brewers were pretty conservative with their grists. And we're before the period foreign ingredients flooded in. When British agriculture couldn't keep up with the growth in population and thirst.

Hertfordshire malt and Kent hops. They were the backbone of London brewing through the birth and blossoming of Porter in the 1700's. And continued when to be so while Mild Ale's star rose in the middle of the 1800's. Until there just wasn't enough to brew the quantity of beer the masses required.

Getting back to the beer, the simplicity doesn't extend to the mashing scheme. Three mashes, no sparges. With a fourth mash for a return wort.

Here are the details:

action	water (barrels)	water temp.	tap temp.	time
mash	213	160° F	142° F	90
mash	114	182° F	158° F	50
mash	155	168° F	158° F	40

As you'd expect, BS spent some time in vats. It wasn't the poshest Stout, so perhaps less than a year, but at least six months.

1837 Reid BS		
pale malt	13.75 lb	77.46%
brown malt	3.25 lb	18.31%
black malt	0.75 lb	4.23%
Goldings 75 mins	3.00 oz	
Goldings 60 mins	3.00 oz	
Goldings 30 mins	3.00 oz	
Goldings dry hops	0.50 oz	
OG	1074	
FG	1023	
ABV	6.75	
Apparent attenuation	68.92%	
IBU	98	
SRM	33	
Mash at	150° F	
Sparge at	168° F	
Boil time	75 minutes	
pitching temp	65° F	
Yeast	Wyeast 1099 Whitbread Ale	

Mini Book Series volume XXX: Let's Brew!

1838 Reid EBSt

I'm guessing that the E in the name stands for export. The export version of their standard Stout.

And as was the case in them olden days, export didn't necessarily mean a stronger beer. But it did mean a more heavily hopped one. Which this certainly is. Even with age-adjusted hopping, it still weighs in over 100 IBUs

The recipe is much like all their others. Nothing to see there. Main point of interest: another complicated and weird mashing scheme. With rather low and high mashing heats in the three mashes. I don't know about you, but I can make no sense of these mashing schedules.

action	water (barrels)	water temp.	tap temp.	time
mash	220	160° F	142° F	90
mash	134	195° F	164° F	50
mash	167	179° F	167° F	40

1838 Reid EBSt		
pale malt	13.00 lb	76.47%
brown malt	3.25 lb	19.12%
black malt	0.75 lb	4.41%
Goldings 75 mins	3.25 oz	
Goldings 60 mins	3.25 oz	
Goldings 30 mins	3.25 oz	
Goldings dry hops	1.00 oz	
OG	1071.2	
FG	1020	
ABV	6.77	
Apparent attenuation	71.91%	
IBU	109	
SRM	33	
Mash at	152° F	
Sparge at	160° F	
Boil time	80 minutes	
pitching temp	62° F	
Yeast	Wyeast 1099 Whitbread Ale	

Mini Book Series volume XXX: Let's Brew!

1838 Reid KBSt

The final Reid Stout from the 1830's is the keeping version of their Brown Stout. As you would expect. The main difference with the standard version is heavier hopping.

Though not that much heavier. Mainly because the standard was pretty heavily hopped. But that's what you'd expect. These are, after all, Beers.

The hops were a mix of East Kent and Mid Kent, about two thirds from the 1837 crop, one third from 1836.

It was another three mash, no sparge brew. With a further mash and sparge for a return wort. It must have been a long brewing day.

action	water (barrels)	water temp.	tap temp.	time
mash	218	164° F	144° F	90
mash	125	190° F	160° F	50
mash	168	170° F	160° F	45

Not really much more to say. Here's the recipe:

1838 Reid KBSt		
pale malt	13.50 lb	78.26%
brown malt	3.25 lb	18.84%
black malt	0.50 lb	2.90%
Goldings 80 mins	3.50 oz	
Goldings 60 mins	3.50 oz	
Goldings 30 mins	3.00 oz	
Goldings dry hops	1.00 oz	
OG	1072	
FG	1020	
ABV	6.88	
Apparent attenuation	72.22%	
IBU	109	
SRM	28	
Mash at	152° F	
Sparge at	160° F	
Boil time	80 minutes	
pitching temp	62.5° F	
Yeast	Wyeast 1099 Whitbread Ale	

1845 Reid SS

Sometime around 1840, Reid changed their Stout range. Out went BS and DBSt, in came S, SS and SSS. No idea why they might have done that. They also changed the format of their brewing books at the same time.

The grists remained a blend of pale, brown and black malts, but the percentage of brown had fallen, replaced by more pale. One nice feature of this period Reid logs is that they give the weight per quarter of the malt. So I know that the pale was 344 lbs and the brown and black 264 lbs.

Another change was to the mashing scheme, which was reduced from three mashes to two. With the second mash far cooler than before.

action	water (barrels)	water temp.	tap temp.
mash	296	165° F	148° F
mash	226	177° F	162° F

The hopping is still pretty crazy, coming to 99 calculated IBUs. Unfortunately this period of logs has less information about the hops. All I know is they were split just about fifty-fifty between the 1843 and 1844 harvest.

There's no FG listed so I've just made a guess. I could be way wrong. In any case, as this beer was probably vatted, the real FG would be lower than at the end of primary fermentation.

1845 Reid SS		
pale malt	17.75 lb	85.54%
brown malt	2.25 lb	10.84%
black malt	0.75 lb	3.61%
Goldings 180 mins	3.00 oz	
Goldings 60 mins	3.00 oz	
Goldings 30 mins	3.00 oz	
Goldings dry hops	1.00 oz	
OG	1087.3	
FG	1028	
ABV	7.84	
Apparent attenuation	67.93%	
IBU	99	
SRM	31	
Mash at	150° F	
Sparge at	170° F	
Boil time	180 minutes	
pitching temp	57.5° F	
Yeast	Wyeast 1099 Whitbread Ale	

Mini Book Series volume XXX: Let's Brew!

1877 Reid Rg

I used to think that Rg stood for "Regular". Of course, it's really "Running".

Running Porter would be the full name. Even in the 1870's, it was still Reid's bread and butter beer. Surprisingly, they also still brewed a Keeping Porter, Crs. Most of the other London Porter breweries dropping their Keeping Porters in the early 1870's, ripping out their now redundant large vats.

London Porters were very consistent in their grists. Just pale, brown and black malt. All that varied over time were the proportions of each, with the percentage of brown malt falling as the 19th century progressed.

Reid still employed what was, by this time, quite a complicated mashing scheme, with three separate mashes and no sparge:

action	water (barrels)	water temp.	tap temp.
mash	270	164° F	142° F
mash	200	172° F	157° F
mash	100	165° F	156° F

Not sure exactly how that worked. For some reason the middle mash was always the hottest.

1877 Reid Rg		
pale malt	11.75 lb	83.93%
brown malt	1.50 lb	10.71%
black malt	0.75 lb	5.36%
Goldings 120 mins	1.25 oz	
Goldings 60 mins	1.25 oz	
Goldings 30 mins	1.25 oz	
OG	1058	
FG	1017	
ABV	5.42	
Apparent attenuation	70.69%	
IBU	47	
SRM	28	
Mash at	150° F	
Sparge at	170° F	
Boil time	120 minutes	
pitching temp	63° F	
Yeast	Wyeast 1099 Whitbread Ale	

1877 Reid Crs

I've managed to work out what most Brewhouse names mean. But I'm totally stumped by "Crs".

I know that it signifies a Keeping version, but what it stands for has me baffled. Turning to the beer itself, the recipe is different from the Running version, containing a smaller proportion of roasted malts.

The mashing scheme is also different, consisting of just two mashes:

action	water (barrels)	water temp.	tap temp.
mash	180	164° F	145° F
mash	190	178° F	156° F

Obviously, it's more heavily hopped than the Runner, it being intended for ageing. Speaking of which, it would probably have been vatted for around six months

1877 Reid Crs		
pale malt	12.25 lb	87.50%
brown malt	1.25 lb	8.93%
black malt	0.50 lb	3.57%
Goldings 150 mins	1.50 oz	
Goldings 60 mins	1.50 oz	
Goldings 30 mins	1.50 oz	
Goldings dry hops	1.00 oz	
OG	1058	
FG	1015	
ABV	5.69	
Apparent attenuation	74.14%	
IBU	58	
SRM	28	
Mash at	147° F	
Sparge at	170° F	
Boil time	150 minutes	
pitching temp	61° F	
Yeast	Wyeast 1099 Whitbread Ale	

1877 Reid S

We're moving our way slowly up the gravity scale of Reid's Porters, now we've got to the first Stout.

You can see that even the weakest Stout had a pretty decent gravity, in this case 1072°. The certainly liked their beer strong in Victorian London. Though in the late 18th century, a standard Porter had an OG in the mid-1070's.

Just like Crs, S was brewed using two mashes and no sparges. I find the latter a surprise at such a late date. Perhaps Reid was just conservative. This is the mashing scheme in detail:

action	water (barrels)	water temp.	tap temp.
mash	176	166° F	147° F
mash	155	180° F	152° F

The grist is a bog-standard combination of pale, brown and black malts. Note that the percentage of roast malts is lower than for the two Porters.

The hopping is fairly generous, but not too crazy, leaving 71 calculated IBUs.

1877 Reid S		
pale malt	15.25 lb	89.71%
brown malt	1.25 lb	7.35%
black malt	0.50 lb	2.94%
Goldings 150 mins	2.00 oz	
Goldings 60 mins	2.00 oz	
Goldings 30 mins	2.00 oz	
Goldings dry hops	1.00 oz	
OG	1072	
FG	1025	
ABV	6.22	
Apparent attenuation	65.28%	
IBU	71	
SRM	23	
Mash at	149° F	
Sparge at	170° F	
Boil time	150 minutes	
pitching temp	57° F	
Yeast	Wyeast 1099 Whitbread Ale	

Mini Book Series volume XXX: Let's Brew!

1877 Reid SS

All the London Porter brewers made several Stouts. One of the conventions for naming them went like this: Single Stout, Double Stout, Triple Stout and Imperial Stout.

Not every brewery produced the last of those. Though, unlike in the later 20th century, Imperial Stout wasn't equated with a specific beer from just one brewery.

You would expect the weakest Stout to be the best seller, but that wasn't necessarily true. In 1887, Whitbread brewed 854 barrels of S, 10,845 of SS and 15,283 of SSS.[9] Sadly, I don't have the same sort of production figures for Reid.

We're back to a three-mash, no sparge scheme:

action	water (barrels)	water temp.	tap temp.
mash	284	164° F	144° F
mash	126	176° F	154° F
mash	94	164° F	150° F

As usual, the hottest mash is the middle one.

The grist is the same as always, with just slightly different proportions of the three malts.

I assume this would have been vatted for at least a few months.

---

[9] Whitbread brewing record held at the London Metropolitan Archive, document number LMA/4453/D/09/071.

1877 Reid SS		
pale malt	17.25 lb	85.19%
brown malt	2.25 lb	11.11%
black malt	0.75 lb	3.70%
Goldings 165 mins	1.75 oz	
Goldings 60 mins	1.75 oz	
Goldings 30 mins	1.75 oz	
Goldings dry hops	1.00 oz	
OG	1085	
FG	1028	
ABV	7.54	
Apparent attenuation	67.06%	
IBU	57	
SRM	23	
Mash at	148° F	
Sparge at	170° F	
Boil time	165 minutes	
pitching temp	57° F	
Yeast	Wyeast 1099 Whitbread Ale	

1877 Reid SSS

We end this set with the strongest of Reid's Stout, SSS.

As you would expect, it's a pretty big beer, weighing in at almost 9% ABV. It was probably even stronger than that, after vatting. At this time it was probably also still mainly a draught beer. Imagine trying to session this down the pub. Actually, I can imagine that, as it's exactly what I did in Manchester a few weeks back.

We're back to a two-mash scheme. I've no idea why. They seem to randomly switch between two and three mashes. They are consistent in their lack of sparging.

action	water (barrels)	water temp.	tap temp.
mash	154	164° F	146° F
mash	107	176° F	158° F

The grist is a good bit different. Not in the type of mal used. That's still exactly the same. It's the proportions. SSS contains far more brown malt than Reid's other beers, as well as rather less black malt. I guess because it was a fairly posh beer.

1877 Reid SSS		
pale malt	18.25 lb	80.22%
brown malt	4.00 lb	17.58%
black malt	0.50 lb	2.20%
Goldings 150 mins	4.00 oz	
Goldings 60 mins	3.50 oz	
Goldings 30 mins	3.50 oz	
Goldings dry hops	1.50 oz	
OG	1096	
FG	1030	
ABV	8.73	
Apparent attenuation	68.75%	
IBU	112	
SRM	30	
Mash at	148° F	
Sparge at	170° F	
Boil time	90 minutes	
pitching temp	53° F	
Yeast	Wyeast 1099 Whitbread Ale	

1947 Shepherd Neame SS

I'm continuing my watery late 1940's Shepherd Neame beer theme. With a Stout. Possibly the least stout Stout ever brewed.

Because you need to remember what Stout originally meant: strong. And that's one thing you couldn't accuse this beer of. It's under 3% ABV. I have seen weaker ones than that. Stuff under 2% ABV. But they were Scottish Sweet Stouts, which at least had an OG over 1040°. Just a rubbish level of attenuation.

There's only one dark malt in the grist, black malt. This seems to be the biggest difference between London and provincial Stouts. The former had more complex malt bills, which always contained brown malt in addition to black.

I was surprised to see a decent quantity of oats include. In contrast to London "Oatmeal" Stouts which tiny token amounts. Though it doesn't state it implicitly in the brewing record, I'm sure they were malted oats. Why? Because of the position in the brewing record. Where the malts go, not the adjuncts.

Checking the pre-war records, I see that in 1938 they used R (presumably rolled) oats in their Stout. In rather smaller quantities. I was going to say that moving over to a larger quantity of malted oats was probably as a result of the war. Then I noticed that the practice didn't start until 1947. I believe they were trying to brew an Oatmeal Stout. Albeit a very weak one.

The sugar was proprietary stuff. No. 3 invert is just my guess at an approximation. It could possibly have been more like No. 4. Use a combination of the two if you feel like it.

1947 Shepherd Neame SS		
pale malt	2.75 lb	52.38%
black malt	0.50 lb	9.52%
malted oats	0.50 lb	9.52%
No. 3 invert sugar	1.25 lb	23.81%
malt extract	0.25 lb	4.76%
Fuggles 120 mins	0.50 oz	
Goldings 30 mins	0.50 oz	
OG	1027.1	
FG	1006.1	
ABV	2.78	
Apparent attenuation	77.49%	
IBU	15.4	
SRM	22	
Mash at	159º F	
Sparge at	170º F	
Boil time	120 minutes	
pitching temp	62.75º F	
Yeast	a Southern English Ale yeast	

Mini Book Series volume XXX: Let's Brew!

1952 Strong Black Bess Stout

It's another of my recipes this week. I realise they aren't as detailed as Kristen's, but he hasn't sent one in a while and I reckon one of my crappy recipes is better than none at all.

What style is this exactly? The style Nazis would struggle to pin it down. Too weak for a Dry Stout, not sweet enough for a Sweet Stout. And definitely not any Stout with American or Imperial in the name. Personally, I'd call it a post-WW II English Stout.

There are quite a few Stouts with similar specs from just after WW II. A gravity in the high 1030's or low 1040's, 70-80% apparent attenuation and always only sold in bottled format. But as the 1950's progressed, many began to evolve into something much sweeter and lower in ABV.

Black Bess was no exception. By 1960 its OG had fallen to 1035°, but it's FG had risen to 1015°, leaving it a puny 2.5% ABV. Not really very Stout at all. I can only assume that this change was in reaction to drinkers' expectations. Popular Milk Stouts like Mackeson must have led them to assume English Stout was sweet and weak. Ironically, it was the beginning of the 1950's that Guinness went in the opposite direction, upping its attenuation for 75% to 85%.

A few of this drier type of English Stout did cling on, for example that from Home Ales in Nottingham. A beer I'm ashamed to say I never tried, though I spent many happy hours in Home Ales pubs in various Midlands towns.

This beer has two base malts, of which two thirds was mild malt, the other third pale malt. It's common to see this in beers of the 1950's, especially darker ones. I assume mild malt was chosen for reasons of economy. And in a Stout, how much can you taste the base malt anyway? Unlike Pale Ales, where the malt needs to shine.

There's no brown malt, just black and crystal. While London brewers kept faith with brown malt until the bitter end, many regional brewers had already ditched it in the 19th century.

I'll confess to having simplified the sugars used. No.3 invert does appear in the original, but there's also an array of proprietary sugars: Dutton's CP, Durax, CWA and the enigmatic Am. The exact composition of that lot is anyone's guess. A combination of No. 2 and No. 3 probably is the closest approximation you'll get. Oh, and some caramel, too. Without it you won't get a dark enough colour.

1952 Strong Black Bess Stout		
mild malt	3.00 lb	46.15%
black malt	0.50 lb	7.69%
crystal malt 40 L	0.50 lb	7.69%
pale malt	0.50 lb	7.69%
no. 3 sugar	1.50 lb	23.08%
no. 2 sugar	0.50 lb	7.69%
Fuggles 90 min	0.75 oz	
Fuggles 60 min	0.75 oz	
OG	1036.6	
FG	1010.5	
ABV	3.45	
Apparent attenuation	71.31%	
IBU	23	
SRM	40	
Mash at	154° F	
Sparge at	175° F	
Boil time	90 minutes	
pitching temp	61° F	
Yeast	WLP007 Dry English Ale	

Mini Book Series volume XXX: Let's Brew!

1858 Tetley SP

Yorkshire isn't particularly well known for Stout, though, as in all parts of the UK, plenty was brewed there.

A brewery couldn't afford not to have at least one Stout in their range. Drinkers expected the option.

As you're probably tired of hearing me say, brewers outside London had mostly dropped brown malt from their Stout grists by the middle of the 19th century. They preferred a simpler grist of just pale and black malt. As is the case with this beer.

In terms of strength, it looks like a London Single Stout of the same period. Does SP stand for "Stout Porter". Possible. But I wouldn't bet my house on it. The bitterness level, however looks low. Reid's 1877 S has more than twice the number of calculated IBUs.

1858 Tetley SP		
pale malt	15.75 lb	92.65%
black malt	1.25 lb	7.35%
Goldings 90 mins	1.50 oz	
Goldings 30 mins	1.50 oz	
OG	1072	
FG	1024	
ABV	6.35	
Apparent attenuation	66.67%	
IBU	32	
SRM	34	
Mash at	150° F	
Sparge at	180° F	
Boil time	90 minutes	
pitching temp	60° F	
Yeast	Wyeast 1469 West Yorkshire Ale	

1858 Tetley X2P

We're working our way down through Tetley's Stouts of 1858.

It, too, has the minimalist grist of just pale malt and black malt. My guess is that brown and amber malts weren't used in non-specialist Porter breweries because they didn't want to stock too many types of malt. Especially malts that were only used in small quantities in a few beers.

Again, the level of hopping is very low for a Stout of this period I'd have expected about double the rate. The boil is also relatively short compared to London.

1858 Tetley X2P		
pale malt	14.50 lb	93.55%
black malt	1.00 lb	6.45%
Goldings 90 mins	1.25 oz	
Goldings 30 mins	1.25 oz	
OG	1066	
FG	1022	
ABV	5.82	
Apparent attenuation	66.67%	
IBU	28	
SRM	30	
Mash at	150° F	
Sparge at	180° F	
Boil time	90 minutes	
pitching temp	60° F	
Yeast	Wyeast 1469 West Yorkshire Ale	

Mini Book Series volume XXX: Let's Brew!

1858 Tetley X1P

The weakest in Tetley's range of Black Beers, my guess is that X1P was sold as Porter. For which there seems to have been a much smaller market in the provinces than in London.

If you're thinking these beers all look very similar, there's a good reason why they do. They were parti-gyled together. A pretty standard technique, especially if you were producing some beers in relatively small quantities. The glory of parti-gyling is that it allows you to create beers in batches of any size, no matter how large your kit.

The gravity is exactly the same as was typical in London at the time: 1056°. Though the colour is a little paler.

1858 Tetley X1P		
pale malt	12.25 lb	92.45%
black malt	1.00 lb	7.55%
Goldings 90 mins	1.00 oz	
Goldings 30 mins	1.00 oz	
OG	1056	
FG	1018	
ABV	5.03	
Apparent attenuation	67.86%	
IBU	24	
SRM	29	
Mash at	150° F	
Sparge at	180° F	
Boil time	90 minutes	
pitching temp	60° F	
Yeast	Wyeast 1469 West Yorkshire Ale	

1868 Tetley X3P

We've moved on ten years and there have been a few changes in Tetley's Black Beers.

The most interesting of which is the use of Saaz hops. I don't know if the Bohemian Hop Marketing Board had an export drive in the 1860's, but Saaz starts turning up in the recipes of several breweries about that time. Though a Stout seems an odd place to use a delicate and fine-flavoured hop of that sort. The bitterness, however, still looks on the low side.

The grist remains a simple combination of pale and black malt.

1868 Tetley X3P		
pale malt	15.00 lb	93.75%
black malt	1.00 lb	6.25%
Fuggles 120 mins	2.00 oz	
Saaz 30 mins	2.00 oz	
OG	1068	
FG	1034	
ABV	4.50	
Apparent attenuation	50.00%	
IBU	39	
SRM	30	
Mash at	158° F	
Sparge at	170° F	
Boil time	120 minutes	
pitching temp	66° F	
Yeast	Wyeast 1469 West Yorkshire Ale	

1868 Tetley X1P

Not much has happened to X1P over the last 10 years.

It's lost a fraction – two points - of its gravity, but the grist is still essentially the same. And obviously, as they were parti-gyled with X3P, it contains those fancy Saaz hops. Oh, and the pitching temperature has risen by 6° F.

1868 Tetley X1P		
pale malt	12.00 lb	94.12%
black malt	0.75 lb	5.88%
Fuggles 120 mins	1.75 oz	
Saaz 30 mins	1.75 oz	
OG	1054	
FG	1028	
ABV	3.44	
Apparent attenuation	48.15%	
IBU	38	
SRM	24	
Mash at	158° F	
Sparge at	170° F	
Boil time	120 minutes	
pitching temp	66° F	
Yeast	Wyeast 1469 West Yorkshire Ale	

Mini Book Series volume XXX: Let's Brew!

1850 Truman Export Keeping

The name of this beer doesn't tell the whole story. Because it wasn't just any old Keeping Porter. It's one that was destined for India.

The story of East India Porter is one that's been largely forgotten. As well as contracting brewers to make Pale Ale, the East India Company also got Porter brewed under contract. And, looking at their notices inviting tenders, it looks like the amount of Porter they bought was around double that of Pale Ale. How do I know this was a Contract Porter? There's a note on the brewing saying so.

It differs in a few ways from Truman's standard Running Porter. The OG is lower. Not a surprise for me, but perhaps for you. In the 1800's, the export versions of British beers were often weaker than the domestic versions. It's only after WW I that changed.

The big differences are in the grist and hopping. The India beer had far more brown malt, more than three times as much as the Runner:

	Export Keeping	Runner
pale malt	77.77%	90.68%
brown malt	19.05%	6.06%
black malt	3.18%	3.26%

If you're wondering why the percentages don't match exactly with the recipe below, it's because I've rounded to sensible numbers.

As for the hops, the India-bound beer had around double what the beer destined for the pub on the corner had. Pretty obvious and logical. Not too much chance of bacterial attack on the journey from Brick Lane to the rest London. Unlike the long and demanding India trip.

Almost certainly aged for six months or more in vats before racking into trade cask for shipping. Beers destined for a trip across the equator needed to be as fermented out as possible to give the nasties nothing to feed on and to prevent a Saccharomyces fermentation that could burst the barrels.

1850 Truman Export		
pale malt	10.75 lb	78.18%
brown malt	2.50 lb	18.18%
black malt	0.50 lb	3.64%
Fuggles 120 mins	3.50 oz	
Fuggles 60 mins	3.50 oz	
Fuggles 30 mins	3.50 oz	
Goldings dry hops	0.50 oz	
OG	1057	
FG	1015	
ABV	5.56	
Apparent attenuation	73.68%	
IBU	119	
SRM	26	
Mash at	158º F	
Sparge at	170º F	
Boil time	120 minutes	
pitching temp	62º F	
Yeast	Wyeast 1099 Whitbread Ale	

Mini Book Series volume XXX: Let's Brew!

1850 Truman Imperial Stout

Barclay Perkins and Courage weren't alone in producing an Imperial Stout. Fellow London brewer Truman had one, too.

It doesn't quite reach my Imperial Stout baseline of 1110°. I'll forgive them the one gravity point.

A high percentage of brown malt seems to be a characteristic of the posher Porters and Stouts. It's certainly the case here. Which, I suppose, made it logical to drop the black malt percentage.

Then there is just a whole load of hops. An almost unimaginable quantity: three quarters of a ton. For just 185 barrels. No surprise, then, that the calculated IBUs are in the impossible zone.

Two years in wood is what it deserves. Don't let it down.

1850 Truman Imperial Stout		
pale malt	19.00 lb	80.85%
brown malt	4.00 lb	17.02%
black malt	0.50 lb	2.13%
Goldings 120 mins	5.50 oz	
Goldings 60 mins	5.50 oz	
Goldings 30 mins	5.50 oz	
Goldings dry hops	0.75 oz	
OG	1099	
FG	1029	
ABV	9.26	
Apparent attenuation	70.71%	
IBU	158	
SRM	30	
Mash at	158° F	
Sparge at	175° F	
Boil time	120 minutes	
pitching temp	61° F	
Yeast	Wyeast 1099 Whitbread Ale	

1856 Truman Crimea Porter

Here' a beer with a tale behind it. Because the Easy India Company wasn't the only organisation getting Porter brewed under contract. The British government did, too. Specifically to be given to British troops serving in the Crimea.

The mortality rate due to disease was worryingly high. Leading army doctors to discuss what was the healthiest drink for the troops. A few advocated rum, but the majority was of the opinion Porter was the safest choice. They then got brewers to make a special brew for them.

Crimea Porter was very much like Truman's Running and Keeping Porters in terms of OG and grist. Unsurprisingly, the difference was in the hopping, which was 50% than Keeper and almost double the rate of Runner.

I suspect this would have been aged for a while before shipping, which would have taken another few weeks.

1856 Truman Crimea Porter			
pale malt		12.00 lb	84.21%
brown malt		1.75 lb	12.28%
black malt		0.50 lb	3.51%
Goldings 120 mins		3.25 oz	
Goldings 60 mins		3.25 oz	
Goldings 30 mins		3.25 oz	
Goldings dry hops		0.50 oz	
OG		1059	
FG		1021	
ABV		5.03	
Apparent attenuation		64.41%	
IBU		121	
SRM		23	
Mash at		156° F	
Sparge at		170° F	
Boil time		120 minutes	
pitching temp		65° F	
Yeast	Wyeast 1099 Whitbread Ale		

Mini Book Series volume XXX: Let's Brew!

1943 Whitbread Mackeson Stout

Continuing my Milk Stout series, here's an enchanting little Mackeson recipe from the middle of WW II.

Whitbread started brewing Mackeson at their Chiswell Street base in the late 1930's. Presumably because the Mackeson brewery in Hythe was struggling to keep up with demand. Eventually Whitbread brewed it at most of the breweries they controlled. The Whitbread Gravity Book of 1959 contains analyses of Mackeson brewed at four different locations: Chiswell Street, Stockport, Kirkstall and Hythe. It's an indication of how popular the beer was.

The main grist for Mackeson was exactly the same as for Whitbread's other two Stouts, London Stout and London Oatmeal Stout. You'll note the quite large proportion of flaked oats. That's got absolutely nothing to do with the fact that Mackeson shared a grist with Oatmeal Stout. It's much simpler than that – a bumper crop of oats in 1942 prompted the government to force brewers to use it in all their beers. The Oatmeal Stout element is actually the far smaller amount of malted oats. Before the war, Whitbread's Oatmeal Stout contained miniscule quantities of oats. It was all a bit of a con, really.

Unusually for Whitbread, the grist has no brown malt. Instead it's place is taken by amber malt. I can only assume this was because of a supply problem as only a few brews were made this way. Note also the lack of black malt. This was typical for Whitbread post-WW I. They dropped black malt in favour of chocolate malt in 1925 and never went back.

Note that the base in mild malt. It always makes me smile when I see homebrew Stout recipes with Maris Otter as base malt. Total waste with all the roasted malt. It was typical of breweries to use a cheaper malt as base for Porter and Stout because you weren't really going to be able ro taste it, anyway. The best base malt was reserved for Pale Ales, where it mattered.

The lactose is listed as milk sugar paste in the brewing record. Sounds lovely. There's also something called Duttson, for which I've bumped up the No. 3 invert sugar percentage. As Whitbread only used it in Stout, I'm assuming it's dark in colour.

The hops, as so often, are rather vague, just recorded as MK and Sussex. I've guessed at Fuggles, but any English hops appropriate for the period are a fair enough substitution.

1943 Whitbread Mackeson Stout		
mild malt	5.25 lb	56.33%
amber malt	0.50 lb	5.36%
chocolate malt	0.75 lb	8.05%
flaked oats	1.00 lb	10.73%
malted oats	0.07 lb	0.75%
no. 3 sugar	0.75 lb	8.05%
Lactose	1.00 lb	10.73%
Fuggles 60 min	1.00 oz	
Fuggles 30 min	0.75 oz	
OG	1046	
FG	1021	
ABV	3.31	
Apparent attenuation	54.35%	
IBU	20	
SRM	24	
Mash at	150° F	
Sparge at	170° F	
Boil time	60 minutes	
pitching temp	64° F	
Yeast	Wyeast 1099 Whitbread ale	

1947 Whitbread Stout

Stout, you may recall, originally meant strong. But, let's be honest, it's the last thing you could accuse this austerity-era Whitbread Stout of.

Though compared to Whitbread's Ales of the same period, it has an incredibly complex grist, with five different types of malt. Note the lack of black malt. Whitbread stopped using it in 1926 and went over to chocolate malt instead. So I guess that means for a style Nazi that it's neither a Porter nor Stout. The handful of malted oats was so they could package some as Oatmeal Stout. The percentage is typical of London versions.

A word on the sugar. There was also something called Duttson in the original. No real idea what that was so I've just upped the amount of No. 3 invert. As brewed the colour is way too low and it must have been colour corrected by the addition of caramel.

Just after WW II, when there were enough English hops to go around, foreign hops were a bit of a rarity. About the only ones you ever see are Czech. Presumably the Czech were exporting them to get hold of hard currency. And there would have been some pull, too, as British brewers liked Czech hops. I've just been writing some William Younger recipes from the 1860's and they're full of Saaz.

WS – Whitbread Stout – was only introduced after WW II. Or rather LS (London Stout) was rebranded as Whitbread Stout after the war. LS itself was only introduced in 1910, a new low-gravity (1055°) Stout to supplement their existing SS (1080°) and SSS (1092°). It was a bit of a con as a Stout, the gravity being only 2 degrees higher than their Porter. When SS and SSS were discontinued, LS became Whitbread's main Stout, by 1920 with a gravity reduced to 1046°.

Unusually, its gravity was raised back to just about the pre-WW I level, 1054°, in 1922. It remained in the mid-1050's until the Snowden budget of 1931, when it dropped to 1046°. Inevitably, WW II whittled away at its gravity and it ended the war at 1039°.

I'm pretty sure that at this time WS was available in both draught and bottled form. In London draught Stout remained a fairly common draught beer well into the 1950's, long after it had disappeared everywhere else in the UK, other than Northern Ireland. After the draught version was dropped, it continued as a bottled beer. WS was eventually dropped sometime between 1967 and 1970.

It was fun trying to find a style in BeerSmith for this, as it doesn't even vaguely match the specs of any Stout.

On that happy note, I'll give you the recipe.

Mini Book Series volume XXX: Let's Brew!

1947 Whitbread Stout		
mild malt	4.50 lb	61.48%
pale malt	0.75 lb	10.25%
brown malt	0.50 lb	6.83%
chocolate malt	0.50 lb	6.83%
malted oats	0.07 lb	0.96%
no. 3 sugar	1.00 lb	13.66%
Fuggles 60 min	1.5 oz	
Saaz 30 min	1.5 oz	
OG	1035.3	
FG	1010.5	
ABV	3.28	
Apparent attenuation	70.25%	
IBU	37	
SRM	65	
Mash at	148° F	
Sparge at	170° F	
Boil time	60 minutes	
pitching temp	64° F	
Yeast	Wyeast 1099 Whitbread ale	

Mini Book Series volume XXX: Let's Brew!

1948 Whitbread Extra Stout

English Stout. A topic I've banged on about at great length. This looks like another good opportunity for a little frothing at the mouth.

It shouldn't be a surprise that Whitbread brewed three Stouts after WW II. Porter and Stouts were where the roots of its success lay. In the first half of the 20th century, Black Beers were a large percentage of Chiswell Street's output. As late as 1939, 22% of the beer brewed there was Porter or Stout. Clearly an important product line for Whitbread.

Based on adverts I've seen, Whitbread sold their bottled Stout all over the UK before WW II. Then there was Mackeson. Which was a huge brand in the 1950's and 1960's. Not originally from Whitbread, but a beer they embraced. And parti-gyled with their existing Stouts. Remember I said there were three Stouts? Mackeson was at end of the line-up next to Whitbread Stout and Extra Stout.

I suspect Whitbread Extra Stout might have been an export beer. I'm really not sure. What I do know, is that it looks eerily similar to the pre-war version of another Extra Stout produced by an obscure Dublin brewery:

Guinness Stouts 1939 - 1948								
Year	Beer	Price per pint	OG	FG	ABV	App. Attenuation	colour	Acidity
1939	Extra Stout	10d	1054.5	1013.7	5.30	74.86%	1 + 10	0.07
1939	Extra Stout	10d	1054.5	1013.7	5.30	74.86%	1 + 10	0.07
1946	Extra Stout		1047	1016.1	4.00	65.74%	0.5 R + 20.5 B	0.09
1946	Extra Stout		1041.7	1010.8	4.01	74.10%	11 Brown	0.08
1947	Extra Stout	1/7d	1041.8	1010.5	4.06	74.88%	1 + 6	0.07
1947	Extra Stout	1/7d	1042.5	1009.6	4.27	77.41%	1 + 7.5	0.10
1948	Extra Stout	1/3.5d	1047.2	1012	4.57	74.58%	1 + 6.5	0.12
1948	Export Stout		1072	1019.1	6.89	73.47%	1 + 10	0.07
1948	Extra Stout	2/-	1045.2	1012.6	4.23	72.12%	1 + 9	0.04
Sources: Whitbread Gravity book held at the London Metropolitan Archives, document number LMA/4453/D/02/001. Whitbread Gravity book held at the London Metropolitan Archives, document number LMA/4453/D/02/002.								

I won't get into a long discussion of the grist and that crap. As this is the same basic recipe as Whitbread Stout. That's what parti-gyling is all about. For Mackeson, just add lactose at racking.

Almost forgot. English Stout rant. Not low-gravity, not sweet, no lactose. And that Guinness – a bit acidic. 0.04 – 0.05 was the usual level.

Mini Book Series volume XXX: Let's Brew!

1948 Whitbread Extra Stout		
pale malt	5.75 lb	50.00%
mild malt	2.75 lb	23.91%
brown malt	0.75 lb	6.52%
chocolate Malt	0.75 lb	6.52%
no. 3 invert sugar	0.75 lb	6.52%
no. 2 invert sugar	0.75 lb	6.52%
Fuggles 60 min	1.50 oz	
Saaz 30 min	1.50 oz	
OG	1055.3	
FG	1018.5	
ABV	4.87	
Apparent attenuation	66.55%	
IBU	32	
SRM	50	
Mash at	148° F	
Sparge at	170° F	
Boil time	60 minutes	
pitching temp	64° F	
Yeast	Wyeast 1099 Whitbread ale	

1954 Whitbread Mackeson Stout

Continuing my series of post-WW II Whitbread Stout recipes, we've arrived at the grandddaddy of them all: Mackeson.

Why have I jumped forward a few years? There's a very good reason. It's all to do with how Whitbread added the lactose. It wasn't added until post fermentation and doesn't appear in the brewing log at all. I think it's because of the deal Whitbread had with the excise on lactose. That effectively they didn't pay any duty on the gravity die to lactose. By adding it after fermentation, it wouldn't appear in the gravity reading taken for tax purposes before fermentation.

Normal sugar primings added at racking time were taxed. For them, tax was paid on the gravity of the sugar solution in exactly the same way as for a wort.

Getting back to my point, because of the way Whitbread added the lactose, I have no idea how much. But, I do have analyses of the finished beer. By looking at the difference in OG between that and the version in the brewing log, I can work out the quantity of lactose used. Simple, eh? The first post-war analysis I have is from 1954, so that's the year I've picked.

As for the recipe, it was the same as Whitbread Stout and Extra Stout with which it was parti-gyled. The only real change in the grist from the late 1940's Stouts is the replacement of pale malt with more mild malt. The No.2 invert is in place of a proprietary sugar called Duttsons in the log.

In the 1950's Mackeson was amazingly popular. This probably comes from around the peak of its fame. Whitbread produced the beer in just about every brewery it controlled. It's suffered a sharp decline since then but remains one of the few big bottled beer brands from the 1950's that is still on the market.

Oh. Nearly forgot. You'll need to add caramel to get that colour.

1954 Whitbread Mackeson Stout		
mild malt	6.50 lb	66.67%
brown malt	0.75 lb	7.69%
choc. Malt	0.75 lb	7.69%
no. 3 sugar	0.75 lb	7.69%
no. 2 sugar	0.25 lb	2.56%
lactose	0.75 lb	7.69%
Fuggles 75 min	0.75 oz	
Fuggles 40 min	0.75 oz	
Goldings 20 min	1.00 oz	
OG	1046.6	
FG	1019.5	
ABV	3.59	
Apparent attenuation	58.15%	
IBU	29	
SRM	50	
Mash at	148° F	
Sparge at	170° F	
Boil time	75 minutes	
pitching temp	64° F	
Yeast	Wyeast 1099 Whitbread ale	

Mini Book Series volume XXX: Let's Brew!

1973 Whitbread Mackeson Stout

Still not wrung the last drop from Milk Stout. Yet another Mackeson recipe. But quite a sad one, in a way. Because it's the last one I have from Chiswell Street.

The recipe is very different from the last one I published from 1943. Though a lot of the differences – in particular all the oats – were the result of enforced changes due to wartime restrictions, rather than voluntary.

The pale, brown and chocolate combination used here was more typical of Whitbread's 20th-century recipes. Not sure what the tiny amount of crystal malt contributes. Looks like a bit of a waste of time to me with all that roasted malt. And what about the torrefied barley? Is that there for head retention or as a cheap bulker-out?

There's no mention of lactose in the original log, as Whitbread only added it at racking time. I've no analyses of Mackeson from this period so I've just had to guess. As brewed, the OG was 1039° and FG 1015.

The hops in the original were all Worcester. Apart from the hop extract. I guess you probably won't be using that, so I've just bumped up the hops. As no variety was specified for the hops, you can you use any English hops you fancy. I've just gone with Fuggles as a conservative choice.

1973 Whitbread Mackeson Stout		
pale malt	6.25 lb	64.10%
brown malt	0.50 lb	5.13%
choc. Malt	0.75 lb	7.69%
crystal malt 60L	0.25 lb	2.56%
torrefied barley	1.00 lb	10.26%
lactose	0.75 lb	7.69%
No. 3 invert sugar	0.25 lb	2.56%
Fuggles 60 min	0.50 oz	
Fuggles 40 min	0.50 oz	
Fuggles 20 min	0.50 oz	
OG	1044	
FG	1015	
ABV	3.84	
Apparent attenuation	65.91%	
IBU	16	
SRM	25	
Mash at	150° F	
Sparge at	170° F	
Boil time	60 minutes	
pitching temp	64° F	
Yeast	Wyeast 1099 Whitbread ale	

Mini Book Series volume XXX: Let's Brew!

1868 William Younger DBS

Time for another Scottish recipe. Especially as I forgot to post a recipe last week. Apologies for that. A pure oversight on my part. Though the extra Saturday recipes I threw in mean I've still averaged more than one a week so far.

Though Scottish brewers all made Porter and Stout, it was never as important a product as for many of their English colleagues. Especially those in London. William Younger had three: Porter, Bottling Porter and DBS. The first two were both pretty weak, 1041° and 1046°, respectively. All three were brewed in small quantities, far less than most of their Scottish Ales, Strong Ales and Pale Ales.

I assume this was for a combination of factors. A limited market in Scotland for Stout. But also what they could sell in export markets. Scottish brewers were famous for Strong Ales and Pale Ales and these were what they sold to England and beyond. While in these markets London and Irish brewers controlled the Stout trade.

The grist is very different to a London Stout. There's no brown malt, something that appeared in every London Porter and Stout from the 18th century to the 1970's. But there is amber malt, something you mostly only saw in the better quality London Stouts. Whereas Irish Stouts were usually just pale and black malt.

Younger DBS is also weaker than London Stouts of the period. Truman's weakest Stout, Running Stout, had an OG of 1070°. Whitbread's, SS, an OG of 1082°. Barclay Perkins BSt 1089°.

But there's one thing that makes this brew very special. It also appears in the personal brewing book of Carl Jacobsen, son of Carlsberg's founder. A couple of years later he was brewing his own beer called DBS back in Copenhagen. With an OG of 1077°, his was a bit stronger than Younger's. And the grist was a little different:

    2 pale
    9 amber
    1 patent
    3 brown

Quaint that Jacobsen still listed the grain quantity in Imperial quarters. I was more shocked to see that even in 1932 Carlsberg Porter, the successor to DBS, still contained 21% brown malt. Who would have expected that?

Nothing left but the recipe itself . . .

1868 William Younger DBS		
pale malt	12.25 lb	81.67%
amber malt	1.75 lb	11.67%
black malt	1.00 lb	6.67%
Poperinge 90 min	2.75 oz	
Goldings 60 min	2.50 oz	
Saaz 20 min	2.50 oz	
OG	1062	
FG	1014	
ABV	6.35	
Apparent attenuation	77.42%	
IBU	85	
SRM	31	
Mash at	150° F	
Sparge at	185° F	
Boil time	120 minutes	
pitching temp	62° F	
Yeast	WLP028 Edinburgh Ale	

Mini Book Series volume XXX: Let's Brew!

1939 William Younger Btlg DBS

Moments like this are always exciting. When I can link together a pair of obsessions. In this case, my most current pair: Scottish beer and Milk Stout.

Like Brown Ale, Milk Stout is a tricky bugger to pin down. Because there's rarely a brewing record with the name Milk Stout on it. The explanation is much the same is for Brown Ale. It's because it wasn't a beer brewed specifically, but was another beer tinkered with. Presumably brewers added lactose to their standard Stout at racking time. It's what Whitbread did with Mackeson, so why wouldn't everyone else?

Then you have William Younger. Who liked lactose so much, they used it in several of their beers, even ones not usually associated with it like Mild and Scotch Ale. But they did throw it into their Stouts, too.

You may think that this looks a little strong for a Milk Stout. That's because in its later days, Milk Stout had all the alcoholic punch of an arthritic granny. But that hadn't always been the case. Before WW II, Milk Stouts could be surprisingly strong. For example, in 1929, Mackeson Milk Stout had an OG of $1060°$[10].

The grist is typical crazy William Younger. Though, for the period, the proportion of grits is quite low. They had used over 40% at times.

A fair dose of English hops leaves it with a respectable level of bitterness. Probably more than you'd expect in a Milk Stout. Though I'm not sure this was marketed as such. Younger did have one in their portfolio, I know because I've seen labels, but I don't know if it was this particular beer. Dry hopping also seems odd for a Milk Stout. But, hey, this is William Younger. They did lots of crazy things.

---

[10] Whitbread Gravity book held at the London Metropolitan Archives, document number LMA/4453/D/02/001.

Mini Book Series volume XXX: Let's Brew!

1939 William Younger DBS Btlg		
pale malt	9.50 lb	64.41%
black malt	0.50 lb	3.39%
crystal malt 60L	0.50 lb	3.39%
grits	2.75 lb	18.64%
caramel	0.50 lb	3.39%
lactose	1.00 lb	6.78%
liquorice	0.25 oz	
Fuggles 90 min	1.00 oz	
Fuggles 60 min	1.00 oz	
Fuggles 30 min	1.00 oz	
Goldings dry hops	0.50 oz	
OG	1066	
FG	1023	
ABV	5.69	
Apparent attenuation	65.15%	
IBU	34	
SRM	30	
Mash at	155° F	
Sparge at	160° F	
Boil time	150 minutes	
pitching temp	60.5° F	
Yeast	WLP028 Edinburgh Ale	

Mini Book Series volume XXX: Let's Brew!

IV Strong Ale

Mini Book Series volume XXX: Let's Brew!

1949 Adnams XXXX

This is the last in the set of Adnams beers from 1949/1950 and is the strongest of the lot. Though that isn't saying all that much.

As a young man, I can remember noticing that breweries in Southeast of England often had a beer called Old Ale of around 4.5%. Beers that looked and tasted suspiciously like a strong Mild. It's taken a while, but when I finally got to look at brewing records my suspicions were confirmed. Harveys, King & Barnes and Adnams all brewed beers of this type.

I was more used to Northern Old Ales like Old Tom or Owd Roger, beers that were considerably stronger. It obviously confuses the hell out style guideline writers as they only document the stronger type. Personally, I'm a big fan of the weaker type as they resemble pre-1931 Mild Ale. It's a cheeky way of getting a taste of the past.

So you shouldn't be surprised that Adnams Old Ale has a grist that is essentially the same as that of XX Mild Ale. Quite an interesting grist it is, too, with a couple of types of dark malts in the form of amber and crystal. As I've mentioned several drillion times, these types of dark beer were mostly coloured with sugar and caramel.

Which isn't to say that XXXX doesn't contain No. 3 invert and caramel. I suspect drinkers wouldn't have been impressed had Adnams tried to sell a Mild coloured with chocolate or black malt. Because, as I now realise, No. 3 invert is the signature flavour of Dark Mild. That's why most American versions, which try to get colour from dark malts, just don't taste right.

Proper Dark Mild. Give it a try. It might change your life. Mine changed in 1976 when the Cardigan Arms installed handpulls.

1949 Adnams XXXX		
mild malt	8.75 lb	80.82%
amber malt	0.50 lb	4.62%
crystal malt 80L	0.50 lb	4.62%
no. 3 invert sugar	1.00 lb	9.24%
caramel	0.08 lb	0.70%
Fuggles 90 min	1.00 oz	
Goldings 60 min	1.00 oz	
Goldings 30 min	1.00 oz	
OG	1051	
FG	1015.5	
ABV	4.70	
Apparent attenuation	69.61%	
IBU	37	
SRM	20	
Mash at	148° F	

Mini Book Series volume XXX: Let's Brew!

Sparge at	170° F
Boil time	120 minutes
pitching temp	59° F
Yeast	WLP025 Southwold

Mini Book Series volume XXX: Let's Brew!

1953 Adnams Tally Ho

Now Scotland is out of the way I can return to that most exciting of decades, the 1950's.

This is a beer you've probably heard of, if you're British, as it's still being brewed. I always thinks that makes things more fun. Though my guess is that the recipe has changed a bit over the last 60 years. If only because the strength has dropped a little over the years.

Back in the early 1950's, this was about as strong as British beer got. I'm not sure if it was available on draught back then. It might possibly have been, as a winter seasonal. Even in my younger days beers like Marstons Owd Roger would appear in a pin on the bar when the weather turned cold.

Adnams were a bit of an oddity in that they didn't use any unmalted adjuncts, just malt and sugar. The vast majority of UK breweries were enthusiastic users of adjuncts, mostly in the form of flaked maize. They were pretty simple with their sugars, too, using numbered inverts rather than proprietary sugars. Which makes like easier both for me and for you.

The recipe here is much the same as their XX Mild Ale and XXXX Old Ale: medium malt (which I've interpreted as mild malt), amber malt, crystal malt, No. 3 invert sugar and a bit of caramel. Amber malt is an unusual ingredient in this period. You don't see it much in the 20th century and it's usually reserved for Stouts.

As always, the hop varieties are a guess, A pretty conservative one and Fuggles and Golding accounted for around 75% of UK-grown hops at the time.

1953 Adnams Tally Ho		
mild malt	13.00 lb	75.76%
amber malt	1.25 lb	7.28%
crystal malt 80 L	1.25 lb	7.28%
no. 3 invert sugar	1.50 lb	8.74%
caramel	0.16 lb	0.93%
Fuggles 120 min	1.50 oz	
Fuggles 60 min	1.50 oz	
Goldings 30 min	1.50 oz	
Goldings dry hops	0.25 oz	
OG	1080	
FG	1016.1	
ABV	8.45	
Apparent attenuation	79.88%	
IBU	47	
SRM	32	
Mash at	150° F	
Sparge at	170° F	
Boil time	120 minutes	
pitching temp	58° F	
Yeast	WLP025 Southwold	

Mini Book Series volume XXX: Let's Brew!

1891 Barclay Perkins KK

Here's another recipe that will feature in volume II of Strong! Though who knows when that will come out. It's behind vol. II of Scotland! in the queue. The queue of books I have to finish, that is. I've several in various states of completion. I still plan a huge update of Decoction! when I can be arsed.

It's amazing to think that this KK was an everyday drinking beer. One of the standard features of a late Victorian London bar. Also amazing to think that in the 20th century draught Burton, which is what this is, went from on sale everywhere in London to totally forgotten in just a couple of decades (1955 to 1975).

Even I wouldn't be able to put away many pints of a beer this strong. Victorians must have been made of stronger stuff. Or just total pissheads. Having read plenty of newspaper reports of drunken disorder, I suspect the latter is true.

The grist is typical of Barclay Perkins grists after the 1880 Free Mash Tun Act: 75% malt, the rest split evenly between an adjunct and sugar. Initially, they preferred flaked rice as an adjunct but switched to flaked maize around 1900. My guess would be because of the price. Flaked maize was used by most breweries in England, an exception being Whitbread which only used malt and sugar. Many Scottish brewers preferred their maize in the form of grits.

The hops are an interesting mix of English and German. As is often the case, the foreign hops are named by variety, while the English hops only mention the region where they were grown. In this case Mid Kent. So they could be Fuggles, but my money would be on something classier, such as a form of whitebine. Of which Goldings are the most easily available modern variety.

At this time KK was almost certainly aged for a couple of months before sale. Probably in trade casks, i.e. the cask in which it would be shipped to the customer. This seems to have been the usual practice for K Ales. While Stouts still tended to be aged in vats.

You'll note that this Burton is still relatively pale. That changed around 1900, when, like X Ale, KK started to become darker. Don't ask me why. I have no hard evidence, just half-arsed guesses.

1891 Barclay Perkins KK		
Mild malt	11.00 lb	69.84%
crystal malt 60L	0.75 lb	4.76%
flaked rice	2.00 lb	12.70%
No. 2 invert sugar	2.00 lb	12.70%
Hallertau 90 min	3.50 oz	
Goldings 60 min	2.75 oz	
Goldings 30 min	2.75 oz	
Goldings dry hops	1.00 oz	
OG	1074	
FG	1019	
ABV	7.28	
Apparent attenuation	74.32%	
IBU	106	
SRM	13	
Mash at	152° F	
Sparge at	168° F	
Boil time	90 minutes	
pitching temp	60° F	
Yeast	Wyeast 1098 British ale - dry	

Mini Book Series volume XXX: Let's Brew!

1891 Barclay Perkins KKK

Since I've already given you the recipe for KK, I may as well let you have the one for its big brother, KKK, too.

Not that it's very different. Just a little bit more of everything than the KK. But the same basic grist of 75%, 12.5% flaked rice and 12.5% No. 2 invert sugar. I can tell this is going to be a short post. That's already pretty much everything I need to say.

I know something I can tell you. Unusually, Barclay Perkins continued to brew really strong K Ales after WW I. In the 1920's they brewed a beer called KKKK, which had an OG of 1079°. It was only available in the winter and from adverts I've seen, appeared to be served from a pin on the bar.

I've just had a look at my spreadsheet of Barclay Perkins brewing records and was surprised to see that KKK, which was discontinued during WW I, did reappear in the early 1920's, and with an OG of 1082°, just about at pre-war strength. And, with batch sizes of a little over 100 barrels, it was being brewed in decent quantities. Unlike Fuller's OBE, a similar beer, of which there were usually fewer than 10 barrels brewed at a time.

I'm not sure in which form KKK was sold. Probably on draught, as was most beer in the 1890's. That's really about the start of bottled beer as a real mass-market product.

That's me done. I told you it would be short.

1891 Barclay Perkins KKK		
Mild malt	12.50 lb	69.44%
crystal malt 60L	0.75 lb	4.17%
flaked rice	2.50 lb	13.89%
No. 2 invert sugar	2.25 lb	12.50%
Hallertau 90 min	3.75 oz	
Goldings 60 min	3.25 oz	
Goldings 30 min	3.25 oz	
Goldings dry hops	1.00 oz	
OG	1085	
FG	1024	
ABV	8.07	
Apparent attenuation	71.76%	
IBU	112	
SRM	15	
Mash at	152° F	
Sparge at	168° F	
Boil time	90 minutes	
pitching temp	60° F	
Yeast	Wyeast 1098 British ale - dry	

1909 Barclay Perkins KK

Do you know the era I'd most like to travel back to? For beer sampling purposes. Just before WW I. Variety and lots of strong beers.

By the Edwardian age, London-brewed Burton was turning to the dark side. Not the foggiest idea why. Before 1880, they were 100% pale malt. After the Free Mash Tun Act they start to change. More choice of ingredients. And though sugar had been legal since 1847, brewers hadn't used it much. When they did start using it, they acquired far more control over the colour of their beer.

This is the little brother of the unacceptably-named KKK. Which was much the same, but 15 gravity points stronger. By this time Barclay Perkins had dropped KKKK and brewed only two Burton Ales.

The grist is typical of the period 1880 – 1914. Pale and crystal malt, maize and sugar. A Pale Ale grist would have been much the same, just without crystal malt. 10% and 10-15% sugar was pretty standard.

For once the hop additions aren't a guess. Barclay Perkin occasionally listed them. One of the odd features of brewing logs is that foreign hop varieties are usually named, while only the region or grower is given for UK hops. In this case, EK or East Kent and MK Mid Kent. I've interpreted that as Goldings for EK, Fuggles for MK.

It looks a cracking beer. Plenty of hops, but plenty of body, too. Hang on. Wasn't this, or something similar, the recipe for Pretty Things KK? I believe it was.

1909 Barclay Perkins KK		
pale malt	10.75 lb	72.27%
crystal malt	0.50 lb	3.36%
flaked maize	1.50 lb	10.08%
caramel	0.125 lb	0.84%
No. 3 invert sugar	2.00 lb	13.45%
Fuggles 90 mins	3.00 oz	
Hallertau 60 mins	3.00 oz	
Goldings 60 mins	3.00 oz	
Goldings dry hops	1.25 oz	
OG	1073	
FG	1021.1	
ABV	6.87	
Apparent attenuation	71.10%	
IBU	112	
SRM	38	
Mash at	153° F	
Sparge at	170° F	
Boil time	90 minutes	
pitching temp	60° F	
Yeast	Wyeast 1099 Whitbread Ale	

1913 Boddington CC

Boddington had some confusing names for their beers. B, BB and CC. No idea what they stand for. The first two are Mild Ales, the last one a Strong Ale.

Is it connected with the legendary C Ale, a type of Strong ale specific to Manchester? I've no clue, if I'm being honest. It would be nice to think that there is, but why would you go from two C's to one? The implication would be that it was weaker. Because that's how beer naming usually went. And that's not normally the impression you'd want to give with a Strong Ale.

Boddington's CC was brewed until WW II, but discontinued, never to return, in 1941. They did brew a Strong Ale after WW II, but that was simply called SA in the brew house. I think you can guess what the initials stood for.

The recipe is classic 20th century English: pale malt, flaked maize, sugar and colouring. It strikes me that breweries, especially smaller ones like Boddington, tried to use as few types of malt as possible. In the run up to WW I, Boddington only used two: pale and black. The latter being used in tiny quantities and only in Stout.

As you may have noticed, this beer is quite heavily hopped. To be honest, other than the Cluster, the varieties are a guess. All that's listed is the name of the grower, not even the region where they were grown. Feel free to substitute them.

While I'm mentioning guesses, the sugar is, too. The logs reveal nothing about the sugar type at all. It could be anything, but invert sugar is the most likely. As I'm pretty sure this beer was dark, No. 3 invert is the obvious choice.

1913 Boddington CC			
pale malt		11.50 lb	86.34%
flaked maize		0.75 lb	5.63%
caramel		0.07 lb	0.53%
No. 3 invert sugar		1.00 lb	7.51%
Cluster 145 mins		0.75 oz	
Fuggles 90 mins		1.00 oz	
Fuggles 60 mins		0.50 oz	
Fuggles 30 mins		0.50 oz	
Goldings dry hops		0.50 oz	
OG		1062	
FG		1020	
ABV		5.56	
Apparent attenuation		67.74%	
IBU		75	
SRM		20	
Mash at		158° F	
Sparge at		168° F	
Boil time		165 minutes	
pitching temp		61.5° F	
Yeast	Wyeast 1318 London ale III (Boddingtons)		

Mini Book Series volume XXX: Let's Brew!

1939 Boddington CC

There's a story behind this recipe. One with a happy ending.

When I was in Manchester a few years back I went to photograph some Boddingtons records. I was really disappointed that all they had were a couple of books from the 1980's. Then Boak and Bailey posted something about the difference between Boddie's Bitter in the 1960's and the 1980's. I immediately emailed them asking where they'd found the 1960's brewing log.

It turns out there are a lot more Boddington's brewing books. A full set from 1900, in fact. Which is brilliant news. It turns out they were in the process of moving when I visited the archive and not everything was available. I'm already penciling in a trip to Manchester.

Boddington had weird beer names before WW I. A was Pale Ale, BB was Mild Ale and CC was their Strong Ale. I can't really detect any logic there. It's been suggested that their CC might be the origin of "C" Ale, a strong beer exclusively brewed in the Manchester area. Could be true. I haven't got a better explanation.

This is probably the quickest I've gone from getting hold of a record to publishing a recipe. I haven't had my hands on it a week yet. I was so excited I had to rush it out.

The only unusual feature of the grist is the presence of wheat malt. In this period they put it every one of their beers. Could be a head retention thing. In their Stout it made up 12% of the grist. Which is quite a lot. Don't think I've ever seen that much in a British beer.

Otherwise it's a typical 20th-century Strong Ale or Mild: pale malt base, a touch of crystal malt, flaked maize and sugar. If you'd shown me just the recipe I would have said it was a London-brewed Burton.

I'm not sure if there was a draught version at this date. It's possible that it was only available in bottled format.

That's me done, time for the recipe.

Mini Book Series volume XXX: Let's Brew!

1939 Boddington CC		
pale malt	7.75	62.63%
crystal malt	1.50 lb	12.12%
flaked maize	1.50 lb	12.12%
wheat malt	0.75 lb	6.06%
caramel	0.125 lb	1.01%
No. 3 invert sugar	0.75 lb	6.06%
Cluster 90 mins	0.75 oz	
Fuggles 90 mins	0.75 oz	
Fuggles 60 mins	1.50 oz	
Goldings 30 mins	1.50 oz	
Goldings dry hops	0.50 oz	
OG	1056	
FG	1015.5	
ABV	5.36	
Apparent attenuation	72.32%	
IBU	63	
SRM	37	
Mash at	149° F	
Sparge at	162° F	
Boil time	90 minutes	
pitching temp	62° F	
Yeast	Wyeast 1318 London ale III (Boddingtons)	

Mini Book Series volume XXX: Let's Brew!

1914 Courage XX

Courage is another brewery whose records I've not paid sufficient attention to. Not sure why that is. Especially considering all the research I've done into London brewing.

Their Horsleydown brewery was odd in the first half of the 20th century in that it only brewed Ales and Porter. No Pale Ales. They were supplied by another brewery they owned in Alton, Hampshire.

XX was Courage's draught Burton Ale. I know it's hard to imagine now that drinkers would be knocking back pints of beers of maybe 7% ABV. Or maybe not, if you're the crafty type. That seems to come in strengths similar to those before WW I. Speaking of which, this was brewed in October, just a couple of months after war broke out. When it was too early for it to have had any impact on brewing.

Burtons were pale in the 19th century but around 1900, at a time when something similar was happening to London Mild, it started to turn dark. Why is one of beer's great mysteries. This beer isn't a dark brown, but is on the way there. It may have been darker than the recipe indicates as it could have been darkened with caramel at racking time.

The colour derives mostly from the No. 3 invert, which makes up 12% of the grist. Other than that, it's all pale malt. The hops are a combination of US and Kent. Which was pretty typical in the decades before WW I.

1914 Courage XX		
pale malt	14.75 lb	88.06%
No. 3 invert sugar	2.00 lb	11.94%
Cluster 120 mins	2.00 oz	
Goldings 60 mins	2.00 oz	
Goldings 30 mins	2.00 oz	
Goldings dry hops	1.00 oz	
OG	1079	
FG	1033	
ABV	6.09	
Apparent attenuation	58.23%	
IBU	73	
SRM	14	
Mash at	152° F	
Sparge at	170° F	
Boil time	120 minutes	
pitching temp	60° F	
Yeast	Wyeast 1099 Whitbread Ale	

Mini Book Series volume XXX: Let's Brew!

1955 Flowers SA

Nearly done. But just think, you'll be able to turn your pub shed into a mid-1950's Flowers tied house. With the full, authentic beer range.

I think I can work out what SA stands for in this case: Strong Ale. I know. I'm a genius. Actually, I'm an idiot. Because the beer is really Shakespeare Ale. At least I've seen labels for that. It's probably deliberate, having the initials SA.

Strong beers started to make a comeback in the early 1950's, after years of restrictions during and immediately after WW II. Gravities in the 1070's were quite popular. Across the North you see strong, bottled Old Ales with that sort of gravity. And in London Barclay Perkins brought back KKKK as a winter special on draught.

Sometimes, as with Fullers OBE, these beers were simply stronger versions of Dark Mild. Not in the case of Flowers. The grist of SA is quite different to Flowers Brown Ale (BX) and XXX Mild. Both of those contain lactose. It's also the only beer, other than BX, to contain any crystal malt. I keep banging on about this: crystal malt wasn't that common an ingredient in the past.

Not only was SA the strongest beer in Flowers portfolio, it was also by far the most heavily hopped, more than twice as much as the next. Even taking the gravity into account, it's the most heavily hopped: almost 9 lbs per quarter to IPA's 7.5 lbs. Though as the attenuation is fairly low, there will be plenty of malt and body to balance out the hops.

It should be dark brown in colour. You'll need to adjust with caramel to get the right shade as with the grist given it will come out way too pale.

1955 Flowers SA		
pale malt	12.15 lb	77.64%
crystal malt 60 L	0.75 lb	4.79%
No. 3 invert	0.75 lb	4.79%
malt extract	2.00 lb	12.78%
Fuggles 90 min	2.00 oz	
Goldings 60 min	2.00 oz	
Goldings 30 min	2.00 oz	
OG	1075.4	
FG	1027	
ABV	6.40	
Apparent attenuation	64.19%	
IBU	68	
SRM	21	
Mash at	145° F	
Sparge at	160° F	
Boil time	90 minutes	
pitching temp	59° F	

1946 Fullers BO

BO – not the most inspiring name for a beer. It stands for Burton Old and was Fullers draught Burton Ale.

In the late 1940's, Burton was still a regular draught beer in London. The war hadn't been kind to Fullers version, with the gravity falling from 1055.5° in 1939 to 1039° in 1946. Though the gravity was back up to 1049.5° by 1958.

You may spot something familiar. Because BO was parti-gyled with X, they share a recipe. So really this beer is nothing more than a strong Mild. Though not really *that* strong of a Mild.

The same remarks apply about the sugars in the grist as for X Ale. I've substituted No. 2 and No. 3 invert for PEX and intense. Not sure how close that will get me to the original. But I'm pretty sure you can trundle down the shop and buy either of those proprietary sugars.

Not sure I've anything else to say. SO how about just finishing with the recipe?

1946 Fullers BO		
pale malt	6.75 lb	75.38%
flaked barley	1.50 lb	16.75%
glucose	0.33 lb	3.69%
No. 2 invert	0.1875 lb	2.09%
No. 3 invert	0.1875 lb	2.09%
Fuggles 90 min	1.00 oz	
Fuggles 30 min	0.75 oz	
OG	1039	
FG	1011	
ABV	3.70	
Apparent attenuation	71.79%	
IBU	24	
SRM	25	
Mash at	155° F	
Sparge at	165° F	
Boil time	90 minutes	
pitching temp	61° F	
Yeast	WLP002 English Ale	

Mini Book Series volume XXX: Let's Brew!

1958 Fullers Old Burton Extra

OBE, Fullers Strong Burton Ale, was discontinued during WW II, but reappeared in the 1950's. Though it never returned fully to its former strength.

The late 1930's version had an OG of 1069 and over 6% ABV. Which was pretty strong for a draught beer – which is what OBE was – between the wars. On the other hand, it was brewed in tiny quantities. The largest batches were a little under 10 barrels, the smallest just two. To put that into context, their big-sellers had batch sizes of 300 or 400 barrels. The post-war version was brewed in slightly larger batches. 27.25 barrels of this beer were brewed.

It's another very simple recipe: pale malt, flaked maize and sugar. In addition to No. 2 sugar, the original contained two proprietary sugars: PEX and CDM. The PEX I've replaced with No. 2 sugar, the CDM with No. 3. The hops I've interpreted as Fuggles, were just listed as Kent in the brewing record. It seems a reasonable enough guess.

To get the right colour, you'll need to add caramel. With just the listed ingredients it will come out way too pale.

1958 Fullers OBE		
pale malt	8.50 lb	80.95%
flaked maize	1.00 lb	9.52%
no. 2 sugar	0.75 lb	7.14%
no. 3 sugar	0.25 lb	2.38%
Fuggles 90 min	1.00 oz	
Fuggles 60 min	0.50 oz	
Goldings Varieties 30 min	0.50 oz	
OG	1049.4	
FG	1013.3	
ABV	4.78	
Apparent attenuation	73.08%	
IBU	26	
SRM	30	
Mash at	149° F	
Sparge at	165° F	
Boil time	90 minutes	
pitching temp	62° F	
Yeast	WLP002 English Ale	

Mini Book Series volume XXX: Let's Brew!

1958 Fullers Strong Ale

Another Fullers beer from the late 1950's, this time a strong bottled beer. Though you may find the recipe rather familiar.

Everyone knows how Fullers proudly uphold the tradition of parti-gyling to this day, brewing Chiswick, London Pride, ESB and Golden Pride from one basic recipe. Back in the day, they did something similar with their dark beers. From that recipe they brewed X (or Hock) their Mild, OBE, their draught Burton and SA, a bottled Strong Ale. In reality a Mild Ale, a strong Mild Ale and a very strong Mild Ale.

I used to think that strong Mild had died on the Somme, but, as ever, reality is far more complicated. Southern Old Ales – like the one Harveys still brew – were really strong Milds. And many stronger dark bottled Ales, like Fullers SA, were stronger versions still. It made a lot of sense to brew this way. The market for stronger beers was relatively small. If your brew length was several hundred barrels, as at Fullers, it made sense to parti-gyle a small-batch beer with something else. This particular brew produced 53 barrels of SA, 9.74 of OBE and 277 of Mild.

I can't really say much about the recipe, as it's essentially identical to the last. And that you'll need a good dose of caramel to get the right colour.

1958 Fullers Strong Ale		
pale malt	12.00 lb	80.00%
flaked maize	1.25 lb	8.33%
no. 2 sugar	1.25 lb	8.33%
no. 3 sugar	0.50 lb	3.33%
Fuggles 90 min	1.50 oz	
Fuggles 60 min	0.75 oz	
Goldings Varieties 30 min	0.75 oz	
OG	1072.4	
FG	1016.1	
ABV	7.45	
Apparent attenuation	77.76%	
IBU	35	
SRM	30	
Mash at	149° F	
Sparge at	165° F	
Boil time	90 minutes	
pitching temp	60° F	
Yeast	WLP002 English Ale	

Mini Book Series volume XXX: Let's Brew!

1951 Lees "C" Ale

Here's a classic – and very geographically specific – type of Strong Ale: a Manchester "C" Ale.

I was so pleased when I found this tucked away in the Lees brewing records. I'd come across mentions of "C" Ale a couple of years previously and had wondered what the hell it was. Some sort of stronger bottled beer, but I had no real details. Lees records told me it was very like a London Burton, but bottled rather than draught. So dark, 5%-ish ABV, reasonably hopped, dark in colour.

In the middle decades of the 20th century several Manchester breweries produced a "C" Ale. I've seen labels from four different breweries: Lees, Groves & Whitnall, Cornbrook and Openshaw. There may well have been others. As to what the name means and who first brewed it – I've no idea. And it seems to have disappeared just as mysteriously as it emerged. I'm not being very informative, am I? I could make something up, but I've sort of made a point of not doing that. I'll leave that to you.

Getting back to cold, hard facts, I am sure of the OG. The FG is a guess because the brewers at Lees couldn't be bothered to enter it in this period. Which is a bit irritating. At least they filled most of the rest in. Apart from the pitching temperature. That, too, is a reasoned guess.

Lees were quite adventurous for 1950's British brewers in that they used some dark malts. Unlike most brewers who preferred to use sugar, other than in Stout. This has a touch of black malt and some crystal. The log just says "invert", but I think the No. 3 variety is a reasonable guess. What I've listed as cane sugar was "Barbados syrup" in the original. Sounds like some sort of unrefined sugar to me.

There's very little detail on the hops in the brewing record, save that they were from the 1949 crop and cost £27 per cwt. I happen to know that the average price of that year's crop was 26 10s per cwt.[11] So these are hops of average quality. Fuggles is definitely the way to go. Goldings would probably have cost more. And those two hops made up 90-95% of English hop production back then.

---

[11] 1955 Brewers' Almanack, page 63.

1951 Lees "C" Ale		
pale malt	8.25 lb	75.00%
black malt	0.125 lb	1.14%
crystal malt	0.63 lb	5.68%
enzymic malt	0.25 lb	2.27%
glucose	0.50 lb	4.55%
No. 3 invert sugar	0.75 lb	6.82%
cane sugar	0.50 lb	4.55%
Fuggles 90 min	1.25 oz	
Fuggles 30 min	1.00 oz	
OG	1053	
FG	1014	
ABV	5.16	
Apparent attenuation	73.58%	
IBU	28	
SRM	28	
Mash at	150° F	
Sparge at	170° F	
Boil time	90 minutes	
pitching temp	60° F	
Yeast	Wyeast 1318 London ale III (Boddingtons)	

Mini Book Series volume XXX: Let's Brew!

1954 Lees Golden Brew

Yes, the 1950's are still alive and kicking. At least here.

I hope you're enjoying these solo recipes. I know Kristen throws in more brewing notes. But these are better than nothing. Which is what the alternative is.

I must admit that I've an ulterior motive in starting this series of 1950's recipes. Two ulterior motives, really. Not sure I'm ready to tell you them both yet. That's just the secretive sort of twat I am. I've started to accumulate so much stuff from the 1950's that I feel a book coming along. It seems ages since my last.

Not totally worked out all the details yet. I'll probably cover 1945 to 1960. It's a fairly interesting period. It's when the beers I drank as a young man coalesced into the form I recognise. The working title is "Victory!". Though that may change.

Right, on with Golden Brew. It ties in quite nicely with some of the stuff I've written about the Strong beers of the 1950's. It seems to have appeared at the classic time for post-war strong beers: the 1953 Coronation. The colour, too, as it belongs to the new breed of pale Strong Ales or Barley Wines. Though just checking back on Gold Label, that only seems to have become pale in 1955.

This is a dead, dead simple recipe. Pale malt and sugar and that's it. This is going to be quick. The sugars are a combination of invert and proprietary sugars. I've simplified it down to No. 2 invert. Once again, I've no idea of the hop varieties. Anything English you fancy, really.

Er, that's it.

1954 Lees Golden Brew		
pale malt	13.25 lb	82.81%
No. 2 invert	2.75 lb	17.19%
Northern Brewer 90 min	2.00 oz	
Goldings 30 min	1.00 oz	
OG	1078	
FG	1020	
ABV	7.67	
Apparent attenuation	74.36%	
IBU	41	
SRM	11	
Mash at	150° F	
Sparge at	170° F	
Boil time	90 minutes	
pitching temp	60° F	
Yeast	Wyeast 1318 London ale III	

Mini Book Series volume XXX: Let's Brew!

1992 Maclay Scotch Ale

It's been a bit odd since I finished writing the book. I keep thinking that I should be doing something. It's a bit like the vague worry that remains after exam season is over.

Especially weird has been not writing any recipes. I'd been throwing them together like crazy for a couple of weeks. Now it's just back to one or two a week.

One thing I debated with myself was the cut-off date for the recipes. The book nominally covers 1840 to 1970, but I do have some Maclay recipes that are later than that. Should I include those? Eventually, the decision was made for me. I decided that the book gad to be published by last Saturday at the very latest. When that deadline fell, I hadn't got to the later Maclay recipes.

Not being one to waste material, I've assembled this 1990's Maclay recipe anyway. Partly because it's a bit of an oddity: a beer called Scotch Ale. Let me explain, Scottish brewers didn't usually have beers called Scotch Ale in their home market. What was sold as Scotch Ale in England and beyond was called Strong Ale in Scotland.

Now you might expect a beer with a name like this to have a long history. It doesn't. Maclay only introduced it sometime between 1985 and 1992. In their later years Maclay went recipe crazy. In addition to their tried and trusted Pale Ale recipe, they started brewing beers single-gyle: TPA, an Old Ale, Oat Malt Stout and Scotch Ale. It must have been scary to any old hands in the brewery.

This is a pretty strange beer for a Scotch Ale. It's a bit weak, though I guess Younger's No. 3 was a similar strength. But that was a bit of an oddity. It has an extremely simple grist of just pale and crystal malt. My guess is that it was also darkened with caramel after primary fermentation.

With about 4.5 lbs of hops per quarter of malt, the hopping is at the same level as their Pale Ales, though, this being a bit stronger, it contained more hops in absolute terms. The varieties are a guess. I only know for certain that the hops were English.

1992 Maclay Scotch Ale		
pale malt	11.00 lb	93.62%
crystal malt 60 L	0.75 lb	6.38%
Fuggles 90 min	0.75 oz	
Fuggles 60 min	0.75 oz	
Goldings 30 min	0.75 oz	
OG	1050	
FG	1016	
ABV	4.50	
Apparent attenuation	68.00%	
IBU	28	
SRM	8	
Mash at	148/157° F	
Sparge at	165° F	
Boil time	90 minutes	
pitching temp	65° F	
Yeast	WLP028 Edinburgh Ale	

Mini Book Series volume XXX: Let's Brew!

1952 Strong SSB

I suppose I may as well finish off the full Strong range now I've started. For want of a better idea.

Kristen still seems too busy to bother with recipes so you'll have to put up with me again. I hope you're not too disappointed.

This is one of the Strong beers which appeared in both bottled and draught form. Was it available on draught all year? I ask the question because it looks quite like draught Old Ales some Southern brewers had (and still do) as Winter specials.

Here are some examples I remember from my younger drinking days:

Draught Southern Old Ales in 1981		
Brewer	Beer	OG
Brakspear	Old or XXXX	1043
Burt	4X	1040
Gale	XXXXX (Winter Brew)	1045
Harvey	XXXX	1043
Hook Norton	Old Hookey	1049
King & Barnes	XXXX	1047.5
Palmer	Tally Ho	1047
Tolly Cobbold	Old Strong	1047
Source: 1982 Good Beer Guide		

You can see that SSB fits in nicely with this bunch.

In many cases – I'm thinking Harveys – these beers look like a stronger version of the brewery's Dark Mild. And I'm sure many were parti-gyled with Mild. There was no parti-gyling in this case, but the recipes for XXX Mild and SSB are pretty similar. The only significant differences being that SSB contained a little crystal malt and was dry hopped. And was darker, too. XXX wasn't all that dark Just about dark enough to count as Dark Mild. Maybe.

As with all Strong's beers other than the posher Pale Ales, most of the base was mild malt. Though all their beers contained some PA (Pale Ale) malt. There's a whole load of sugar, too, over 20% of the grist.

I've gone with a Fuggles and Golding combination for the hops. As a relatively expensive beer, I'd expect it to be finished with good quality hops. But that's just a guess. The brewing Just specifies Kent and Worcester. I do know that a majority of the hops grown in Worcestershire were Fuggles so my guess isn't totally random.

Don't think I've anything else to say. Other than we've still PA and SPA to come.

1952 Strong SSB		
mild malt	4.25 lb	47.22%
PA malt	2.50 lb	27.78%
crystal malt 60L	0.25 lb	2.78%
no. 3 sugar	0.50 lb	5.56%
table sugar	0.75 lb	8.33%
candy sugar	0.375 lb	4.17%
malt extract	0.375 lb	4.17%
Fuggles 90 min	0.75 oz	
Fuggles 60 min	0.75 oz	
Goldings 30 min	0.75 oz	
Goldings dry hops	0.25 oz	
OG	1045.4	
FG	1014	
ABV	4.15	
Apparent attenuation	69.16%	
IBU	30	
SRM	19	
Mash at	151° F	
Sparge at	160° F	
Boil time	90 minutes	
pitching temp	60° F	
Yeast	WLP007 Dry English Ale	

Mini Book Series volume XXX: Let's Brew!

1853 Reid KK

Reid were a slightly odd bunch, who dropped their Ales and reverted to brewing just Porter in the 1860's or 1870's. Which was exactly the time when Ales were starting to overtake Porter in terms of popularity.

As was the rule in London, Reid brewed two sets of Ales, Mild Ales designated by X's and Stock Ales denoted by K's. The equivalent K and X Ales were very similar, except the former were much more heavily hopped. Which makes sense, as they would need the protection of the extra hops to help them survive the months of maturation before sale.

KK was a style of beer that was long popular in London. In the 20th century it was generally known as Burton and was a standard draught beer in the capital's pubs until the 1960's. After which it slipped into obscurity incredibly quickly. The only example today is Young's Winter Warmer.

Pale malt and a shitload of Goldings. It's a classic combination.

1853 Reid KK		
pale malt	18.75 lb	100.00%
Goldings 90 mins	3.00 oz	
Goldings 60 mins	3.00 oz	
Goldings 30 mins	3.00 oz	
Goldings dry hops	1.00 oz	
OG	1083	
FG	1019	
ABV	8.47	
Apparent attenuation	77.11%	
IBU	92	
SRM	8	
Mash at	149° F	
Sparge at	165° F	
Boil time	90 minutes	
pitching temp	55.5° F	
Yeast	Wyeast 1099 Whitbread Ale	

Mini Book Series volume XXX: Let's Brew!

1853 Reid KKK

One step up from KK was, logically enough KKK.

Never brewed in quite the same quantities as it weaker sibling, KKK was popular enough to survive the 19th century. But not WW I. Beers of its strength were just too expensive after the war. The tax alone on a beer of 1075° (which is about how strong it would have been) in the 1920's was 6d a pint. At a time when the cheapest Mild was just 4d a pint in the public bar.

The beer itself is just like KK, but with a bit more of everything. Higher OG, more hops, more alcohol.

Having undergone ageing of probably at least six months, the finished beer would have expressed a Brettanomyces character. That was, after all, what drinkers expected in a Stock Ale. I'd stick a beer of this strength away for 12 months with Brettanomyces to give it plenty of time to work its wonders.

1853 Reid KKK		
pale malt	21.25 lb	100.00%
Goldings 90 mins	3.50 oz	
Goldings 60 mins	3.50 oz	
Goldings 30 mins	3.50 oz	
Goldings dry hops	1.00 oz	
OG	1094	
FG	1021	
ABV	9.66	
Apparent attenuation	77.66%	
IBU	99	
SRM	8	
Mash at	148° F	
Sparge at	165° F	
Boil time	90 minutes	
pitching temp	56° F	
Yeast	Wyeast 1099 Whitbread Ale	

1853 Reid KKKK

The strongest X and K Ales, XXXX and KKKK had both disappeared by 1900. In London, at least.

Though between the wars Barclay Perkins brewed one. It was a winter seasonal and, if the adverts are to be believed, was dispensed from a pin on the bar. Something you still saw in the 1970's. Marston's Old Ale was usually served that way. I wonder if anywhere still does that?

KKKK is, as you would expect, an absolute monster of a beer. Over 11% ABV and more than 100 calculated IBUs. The perfect beer for a lunchtime session.

As with all Stock Ales, this would have been aged. In the case of a beer this strong, probably at least 12 months.

1853 Reid KKKK		
pale malt	26.25 lb	100.00%
Goldings 120 mins	5.00 oz	
Goldings 60 mins	5.00 oz	
Goldings 30 mins	5.00 oz	
Goldings dry hops	1.50 oz	
OG	1116	
FG	1032	
ABV	11.11	
Apparent attenuation	72.41%	
IBU	128	
SRM	10	
Mash at	148° F	
Sparge at	165° F	
Boil time	120 minutes	
pitching temp	56° F	
Yeast	Wyeast 1099 Whitbread Ale	

1954 Tennant's Gold Label

As promised, here's a recipe for Gold Label when it was still brewed in Sheffield by Tennant.

Having read a little about this early version, I really wish I'd got to try it. Sounds like it was cracking beer when brewed by the original method. Should you wish to give the recipe – and ageing a go – I'd be happy to drop by and help you drink the result.

As Frank Priestley, a former brewer there, remarked, all the ingredients were pale in colour. Pale malt, flaked maize and No. 1 invert sugar. There's also a little enzymic malt, but you can leave that out. It wouldn't have impacted the flavour of the beer at all, just helped the mash.

At three hours, the boil is extremely long for the period. Porter brewers boiled weaker worts for three or four hours in the early 19th century, but by the end of WW II fuel restrictions had reduced most boil times to around 90 minutes.

In the 1950's very few beers were anything like as strong as Gold Label. Out of 1400-odd beers from 1952 to 1959 in my gravity table, only 11 have an OG over $1090°$: Bass No. 1, Barclay's Russian Stout, Benskins Colne Spring Ale, Lacons Audit Ale, Mitchell & Butler Strong Ale, Tennant Gold Label, Tennant No. 1 Barley Wine, Truman No. 1 Burton Barley Wine, Watney Stingo plus two Scotch Ales which were probably for the Belgian market. Tennant were very unusual in having two beers in this class.

From Priestley's book, I know that Gold Label was aged in wooden hogsheads for six to twelve months then blended before bottling. Unfortunately, I don't know if it was bottle conditioned. My guess would be no, but I could be wrong. Brewing this up sounds like a nice little project for me and a brewer. Who wouldn't want to sample a beer like this?

1954 Tennant's Gold Label		
pale malt	15.75 lb	67.74%
enzymic malt	0.25 lb	1.08%
flaked maize	4.75 lb	20.43%
No. 1 invert sugar	2.50 lb	10.75%
Fuggles 120 min	2.75 oz	
Goldings 90 mins	1.25 oz	
Goldings 60 mins	1.25 oz	
Goldings 30 mins	1.25 oz	
Goldings dry hops	0.25 oz	
OG	1109	
FG	1024	
ABV	11.24	
Apparent attenuation	77.98%	
IBU	63	
SRM	17	
Mash at	149° F	
Sparge at	165° F	
Boil time	180 minutes	
pitching temp	56° F	
Yeast	Wyeast 1099 Whitbread ale	

Mini Book Series volume XXX: Let's Brew!

1877 Truman K4

Truman didn't just use their Burton brewery for brewing Pale Ales. They also made Burton Ales there.

There's been a fair bit of confusion in the beer world about Burton Ale. I partly blame allied who, when they released a cask version of Double Diamond, decided to call it Burton Ale. Even though it was a Pale Ale. A Burton Pale Ale to give it its full name.

I can also understand that Pale Ale is the type of beer most associated with Burton. So if you hear something called Burton Ale, it's natural to assume it's a Pale Ale. Unless you know the history of brewing in Burton. Then you'll be aware that Burton was a famous brewing town even before the first Pale Ale was brewed there in the 1870s.

The beers that made Burton originally famous were strong, dark Ales. This type of beer continued to be brewed there after the arrival of Pale Ale, though in the 19th century they had become strong, pale-coloured Ales. The most famous being Bass No. 1, the first beer marketed as a Barley Wine.

K4 is an example of a Burton Ale. Like Bass, Truman numbered their Ales. In their case from 1 to 9. Annoyingly, I don't have examples of 1 to 3 from the 1877 brewing book. Making 4 the strongest one I have. Though with an OG of over 1080°, it's not exactly puny.

There's not a great deal to it: 100% pale malt, American and Kent hops. Combined, they create a golden-coloured beer with a heft bitter bite. Though that would have worn off a little by the time the beer was sold. Because, as the K indicates, the was a Keeper, which would have been aged for at least six months before being sent out.

1877 Truman K4		
pale malt	18.75 lb	100.00%
Cluster 180 mins	4.50 oz	
Goldings 90 mins	2.25 oz	
Goldings 30 mins	2.25 oz	
Goldings dry hops	0.50 oz	
OG	1083	
FG	1028	
ABV	7.28	
Apparent attenuation	66.27%	
IBU	123	
SRM	8	
Mash at	152° F	
Sparge at	170° F	
Boil time	180 minutes	
pitching temp	54° F	
Yeast	Wyeast 1099 Whitbread Ale	

Mini Book Series volume XXX: Let's Brew!

Mini Book Series volume XXX: Let's Brew!

1883 Truman S4 x

Truman's 19th-century Burton brewing records have lots of variations of some numbered Ales.

In addition to S4 x, there's also CS4 and L4 R. I've no real idea what all the letters stand for, except that S = Stock and R = Runner. It's a bit enigmatic.

How has 4 changed since 1877? It's a little weaker, down four gravity points. And much less bitter, with only about half the calculated IBUs. That's mostly as a result of half the hops being German rather than American.

British brewer regularly used the posher types of Continental hops, usually from Bavaria or Bohemia. They had little option but to use foreign hops as British growers couldn't produce enough to meet demand. They bought hops from just about every country that produced them.

Being a Stock Ale, this would have been aged. Six months or so would be my guess. Which would leave the FG lower than that indicated below, which is the racking gravity.

1883 Truman S4 x		
pale malt	17.75 lb	97.26%
No. 1 invert sugar	0.50 lb	2.74%
Fuggles 180 mins	2.50 oz	
Spalter 60 mins	2.00 oz	
Spalter 30 mins	2.00 oz	
Goldings dry hops	1.00 oz	
OG	1079	
FG	1029	
ABV	6.61	
Apparent attenuation	63.29%	
IBU	63	
SRM	7	
Mash at	152° F	
Sparge at	170° F	
Boil time	180 minutes	
pitching temp	54° F	
Yeast	Wyeast 1099 Whitbread Ale	

1887 Truman S3

It doesn't to take a genius to work out that S3 was one step up, strength-wise, from S4.

The recipes of the two beers are pretty similar, except for the hopping. S3 has all English hops, all Worcester hops, to be exact. It's probably not a deliberate recipe change, just a reflection of which hops were available.

Other than that, S3 is pretty much just a beefed up version of S4. Albeit with a greater proportion of sugar in the grist.

1887 Truman S3		
pale malt	17.75 lb	92.21%
No. 1 invert sugar	1.50 lb	7.79%
Fuggles 180 mins	3.50 oz	
Fuggles 90 mins	3.50 oz	
Fuggles 30 mins	3.50 oz	
Goldings dry hops	1.00 oz	
OG	1087	
FG	1028	
ABV	7.81	
Apparent attenuation	67.82%	
IBU	94	
SRM	8	
Mash at	151° F	
Sparge at	170° F	
Boil time	180 minutes	
pitching temp	54° F	
Yeast	Wyeast 1099 Whitbread Ale	

1887 Truman S5

The weakest of Truman's Burton-brewed beers to come in a stock version was S5.

You're probably thinking "These beers are all really a bit similar, aren't they?" and you'd be right. They are. Just slightly different strength versions of the same thing. A bit like the range of cask Bitters a brewery might make nowadays.

Three to six months ageing would be my bet.

1887 Truman S5		
pale malt	16.25 lb	97.01%
No. 1 invert sugar	0.50 lb	2.99%
Fuggles 180 mins	2.50 oz	
Fuggles 60 mins	2.00 oz	
Fuggles 30 mins	2.00 oz	
Goldings dry hops	1.00 oz	
OG	1074	
FG	1021	
ABV	7.01	
Apparent attenuation	71.62%	
IBU	65	
SRM	6	
Mash at	151° F	
Sparge at	170° F	
Boil time	180 minutes	
pitching temp	56° F	
Yeast	Wyeast 1099 Whitbread Ale	

1914 Truman S3

Brewed just a few weeks after the outbreak of WW I, this version of S3 is still as powerful a beer as its Victorian predecessors.

But it didn't survive much longer. S3, along with most of Truman's other numbers Ales, was a casualty of the war. Only S1, S4 and R7 were brewed after the war.

Though while the strength of S3 might still have been unchanged, the hopping wasn't. This version contained significantly fewer hops than that from 1887, leaving the calculated IBUs almost halved. Which would have been pretty noticeable, had you been able to drink the two side by side.

1914 Truman S3		
pale malt	11.25 lb	55.56%
Munich malt 20L	5.75 lb	28.40%
flaked maize	1.75 lb	8.64%
No. 3 invert sugar	1.50 lb	7.41%
Cluster 120 mins	1.00 oz	
Fuggles 60 mins	2.25 oz	
Fuggles 30 mins	2.25 oz	
Goldings dry hops	1.00 oz	
OG	1091	
FG	1022	
ABV	9.13	
Apparent attenuation	75.82%	
IBU	52	
SRM	18	
Mash at	150° F	
Sparge at	170° F	
Boil time	120 minutes	
pitching temp	55° F	
Yeast	Wyeast 1099 Whitbread Ale	

Mini Book Series volume XXX: Let's Brew!

V Lager

Notes on Lager recipes

In most of the Lager recipes, rather than detailing the mashing scheme, I've just written "Munich method" of "Kulmbacher method". Rather than repeating the same complicated instructions in more than one recipe, I've listed them all here.

Munich method

This is a description of the Munich method, taken from "Handbuch der Chemischen Technologie: Die Bierbrauerei" by Dr. Fr. Jul. Otto, published in 1865, pages 120 to 122.

> For 100 pounds of malt, 800 pounds of water are used. [Not sure what sort of pounds. I would assume around 1 pound = 0.5 kg.]
>
> Half to two-thirds of the water is cold and used to dough in. The rest is brought to the boil in the kettle. After doughing in, the mash is left to rest for 3 or 4 hours. If warm water is used for doughing in, the mash should not be left to rest.
>
> When the water has boiled it is added to the mash. The temperature should rise to 30-37.5° C.
>
> When this temperature has been reached, about a third of the thicker part of the mash is transferred to the kettle and boiled for 30 minutes. (Boiling the first thick mash.)
>
> The thick mash is returned to the mash tun and mashed for 15 minutes, so that the thinner and thicker parts completely separate. The temperature should now be 45-50° C.
>
> As soon as this is finished a third of the mash, again the thicker part, is transferred to the kettle and boiled for 30 minutes. (Second thick mash.)
>
> The second thick mash is returned to the mash tun and mashed. The temperature should now be 60-62.5° C.
>
> Now a portion of the thin mash is transferred to the kettle (enough to raise the temperature of the mash to 75° C when returned to the mash tun) and boiled for 15 minutes. (Lauter mash.)
>
> The Lauter mash is returned to the mash tun and there's another round of mashing. The temperature should now be 75° C. The mash is left to rest for 90 minutes.
>
> After the wort has been drawn off, more water is brought to the boil (30 - 60 pounds for 100 pounds of grain) and poured over the grains. The resulting wort is either added to the main wort or used to make Nachbier (Small Beer), which in Munich is called Scheps.

Mini Book Series volume XXX: Let's Brew!

The Bohemian method

This is taken from "Schule der Bierbrauerei" pages 306-308.

In Bohemia decoction mashing is carried out differently to in Bavaria and provides an interesting practical example of dispensing with the last starch rest.

Before discussing this method in more detail we first need to learn more about the division of the brewing water. For 100 kg of malt 750 kg of water is required. Of this amount, a quarter is used for the Nachguß (sparge) and the rest for mashing, except for one thirtieth, which is used to dilute the first wort. Of the remaining mash water, four fifths is used for Ausschütten (pouring) and one fifth for the following temperature rises (Zubrühen). The 750 kg are divided like this:

435 kg pouring
108 kg warming
19 kg diluting the first wort
188 kg sparge

The water required for pouring [Ausschütten] is boiled in the kettle (a highly wasteful and unnecessary practice; rational brewers heat just a little water and put cold water into the mash tun) and put into the mash tun where it is allowed to cool (to 33° C in summer, 40° C in winter). The warming [Zubrühen] water is now put into the kettle and brought to the boil.

The ground malt is added to the cooled water in the mash tun and mashed well for 5 or 6 minutes, after which the boiling Zubrühen water is added and stirred in well. Then about a third of the mashed grains are moved to one side of the mash tun and transferred to the kettle as thick mash. There it is careful brought to the boil (to prevent burning or boiling over) and simmered for 30 minutes. The foam that accompanies saccharification then appears. As soon as this foam starts to disappear and the pale colour of the wort starts to turn brownish-yellow (as a result of the transformation of proteins) the thick mash is considered to have boiled long enough and is returned to the mash tun. There it is mixed in well. Now another thick mash is assembled, but from another side of the mash tun (why "from another side?" Hasn't it been mashed properly?) put into the kettle, boiled for 20 to 24 minutes (why not again until the appearance of signs of saccharification, as with the first thick mash?) and returned to the mash tun. Finally there is a third thick mash which is boiled for 20 minutes.

Through the three boils, the temperature in the mash tun is raised to 71-75° C. The remaining one thirtieth of the mashing water is now put into the kettle.

The wort is run off into the underback until it becomes clear. The cloudy wort (which is full of starch) is added to the boiling water in the kettle and boiled for several minutes (whereby the starch is gelatinised). It is returned to the mash tun, but without disturbing the sediment which has already settled. Then the saccharification is left to complete.

If, however, the intended complete saccharification can ever take place is doubtful, since, as Balling has shown, the temperature in the mash tun is already over 75° C after the third thick mash and is now raised even further.

Triple Decoction

This description is taken from Olberg, Johannes (1927) Bömisches Bier in Moderne Braumethoden, pp 59-61, A. Hartleben, Wien & Leipzig. It describes the process used in Bohemia between the two world wars:

Per 100 kg of malt 260-270 litres of water are used for mashing and 200 for sparging. Meaning it was a thin mash.

Mashing in is at 35° C. Part of the mash is transferred to the kettle and raised to 65° C for saccharification then brought to the boil in the kettle and boiled for 15 minutes. When this is added back to the main mash the temperature is raised to 52° C.

A second thick mash is boiled in the kettle for 10 minutes and when returned to the main mash the combined temperature should be 65° C.

Now the lauter mash is boiled in the kettle for 15 minutes which when added back to the main mash raises the temperature to mash out at 75° C. The wort is run off after a rest of 35 to 40 minutes.

Sparge water should be at 75° C or a temperature such that when the wort is drawn off it's at most 70-75° C. If the water is hotter it can dissolve starch from the grains and this can a haze, albeit slight.

The Kulmbach method of decoction

Another Bavarian method of decoction from Otto (("Handbuch der Chemischen Technologie: Die Bierbrauerei" by Dr. Fr. Jul. Otto, published in 1865, page 128).

As soon as the water in the kettle reaches 50° C, as much as is needed is put into the mash tun to dough in.

After an hour, when the rest of the water has come to the boil in the kettle, this is added to the mash. The temperature of the mash should be 53.75 - 56.25° C. A small amount of water should remain in the kettle so that the temperature of the mash is correct. Or a small amount of cold water is added to the mash. When, after resting, the wort in the mash tun has cleared, this is run off and boiled in the kettle. After just a few minutes boiling, this Lauter mash is added back to the tun and mashed for 45 minutes. The temperature of the mash should be 71.25 - 72.5° C.

Usually a small quantity of wort is left in the kettle and boiled with all the hops for 10 to 12 minutes (hopfenrösten).

The mash in the tun is left to rest for 90 minutes, then it is drawn off and added to the kettle where it interrupts the rösten.

The wort from the first lot of cold water poured over the grains is usually used for topping up the kettle.

Double decoction

This description is taken from Dickscheit's "Leitfaden für den Brauer und Mälzer", Leipzig, 1953, pages 64 – 66, a brewing text book from the DDR.

Double decoction is the most widely used method in Germany. It is suitable for the production of pale beers and is more rational as it uses less coal and time. Beers brewed by double decoction are paler than those made using triple decoction. The mashing temperatures are 50, 70 and 76° C. When using poorly modified malt a rest at the start temperature, 50° C, is recommended. As an example, this is a method of double decoction employed by Schönfeld in the Hochschulbrauerei in Berlin. This method is typified by the care which is taken.

Duration of the process 3 hours and 5 minutes.

Mash in at 35° C (95° F)	5 minutes
Warm whole mash to 52° C (126° F)	20 minutes
Rest whole mash at 52° C (126° F) (protein rest)	15 minutes
Draw off first mash and without a rest bring to the boil	30 minutes
Boil first mash	10 minutes
The rest of the mash remains at 52° C (126° F)	40 minutes
Mash at 70° C (158° F)	25 minutes
Rest whole mash at 70° C (158° F) (saccharification rest)	30 minutes
Draw off second mash and without a rest bring to the boil	15 minutes
Boil second mash	10 minutes
Mash at 76° C (169° F) and mash out	20 minutes

Bohemian double decoction

A slightly different version of double decoction performed in Czechoslovakia. This description is taken from Olberg, Johannes (1927) Bömisches Doppelbier in Moderne Braumethoden, pp 59-61, A. Hartleben, Wien & Leipzig.

The mashing scheme is a double thick mash where the temperature rises quickly from 50 to 65° C. Mashing in is at 35° C. The first thick mash ids taken off and the temperature raised, either through adding boiling water or fire, depending on whether you prefer to mash in thick or thin, to 50, 65 and 70° C at which last temperature saccharification takes place. Then the first thick mash is boiled for 10 minutes and raises the temperature of the total mash to 56° C when mixed back in. With the second thick mash, which boils for 15 minutes, mash out at 75° is achieved. The whole mash is then left to rest for 35 to 40 minutes and then the wort is run off. In order to create a fine flavour only mellow malt is used which means it lies loose in the tun with only being stirred twice.

The sparge water need to be hot enough so that when the wort is run off it is between 70 and 75° C, so must be not less than 75° C, but not more than 80° C, as this could lead to problems with clarity.

Mini Book Series volume XXX: Let's Brew!

1866 Munich Bock

Let's make one thing clear from the start. This recipe wasn't taken from a brewing record, but assembled from information in brewing text books.

As with most older recipes it's pretty. Well. The ingredients are pretty simple. The mashing scheme certainly isn't.

The attenuation on this beer isn't that bad for a Munich beer of the period. I've taken the OG and FG from an analysis of Munich Bock in 1866.

1866 Munich Bock		
Munich malt 20L	17.75 lb	100.00%
Saaz 60 min	5.25 oz	
OG	1074	
FG	1024	
ABV	6.61	
Apparent attenuation	67.57%	
IBU	58	
SRM	22	
Mash Munich method		
Boil time	90 minutes	
pitching temp	48° F	
Yeast	WLP833 Bock Lager	

Mini Book Series volume XXX: Let's Brew!

1896 Munich Lagerbier

Dark Lagerbier was the staple of Munich in the 19th century. Though this beer dates from just about when that was starting to change.

Until the 1890's, the Munich brewers had refused to brew Pale Lager. They worried it would devalue their brand. The city was so renowned for beers on the dark side, that it gave its name to a dark style: Münchener.

Though things were a bit vaguer back then. Any Lager brewed in Munich was likely to be called a Münchener, though now the name is associated with a beer of Lagerbier or Export strength. Come to think of it, it's odd that this is called Lagerbier as it's really at Märzen strength, being 14.5° Plato. I guess they had different ideas back then.

1896 Munich Lagerbier		
Munich malt 20L	14.00 lb	100.00%
Hallertau 60 mins	2.50 oz	
OG	1058	
FG	1022	
ABV	4.76	
Apparent attenuation	62.07%	
IBU	33	
SRM	19	
Mash Munich method		
Boil time	90 minutes	
pitching temp	48° F	
Yeast	WLP830 German Lager	

Mini Book Series volume XXX: Let's Brew!

1869 Vienna Märzen

This is such an important beer in the history of brewing. Because in the 1860's it was Dreher's Vienna Lager which first spread the word of bottom-fermentation around Europe.

Despite what most people think, Pilsner wasn't the first type of Lager brewed in most countries. In the case of those very early to the game, like Carlsberg in Copenhagen, it was Munich-style Dark Lager. In places which only picked up on Lager in the 1860's, it was usually the Vienna style.

The OG and FG I've taken from an analysis. The other details come from brewing test books.

1869 Vienna Märzen		
pilsner malt 2 row	12.00 lb	82.76%
Caravienne	2.50 lb	17.24%
Saaz 60 min	3.25 oz	
OG	1062	
FG	1019	
ABV	5.69	
Apparent attenuation	69.35%	
IBU	36	
SRM	9	
Mash Bohemian method		
Boil time	90 minutes	
pitching temp	48° F	
Yeast	WLP820 Octoberfest/Marzen Lager	

1870 Bohemian Summer Beer

Another very important type of Lager. This is the ancestor of Světlý Ležák, the style of beer most associated with the Czech Republic. Though not actually the most popular style within the country. The nation's favourite tipple is in fact 10° Pale Lager.

In the 19th century, there were two main styles of Lager in Bohemia. Winter Beer, which was consumed in the winter, was only lagered for a few weeks. Summer Beer, which was brewed in the winter but drunk in the summer, was stronger and lagered for longer. In the case of a 10° Plato beer like this, around three months.

It's strange that this comparatively obscure local style should eventually, in the guise of Pilsner, totally dominate the beer world.

1870 Bohemian Summer Beer		
pilsner malt 2 row	10.75 lb	100.00%
Saaz 60 min	2.00 oz	
Saaz 30 min	2.00 oz	
OG	1047	
FG	1012	
ABV	4.63	
Apparent attenuation	74.47%	
IBU	44	
SRM	3	
Mash Bohemian method		
Boil time	90 minutes	
pitching temp	48° F	
Yeast	WLP800 Pilsner Lager	

1888 Bohemian Export

This is a stronger type of Bohemian Lager which, at 15° Plato, would now be described as Speciální Pivo.

It's not a complicated recipe, just pilsner malt and Saaz hops. Which is pretty much what pale Czech Lagers are about. It's a bit better attenuated than most late 19th-century Lagers. That seems to be one of the defining features of early Bohemian Lagers. Perhaps because they had better quality malt than in Bavaria.

Braník in Prague used to brew a 14° beer in the 1980's that was pretty similar to this. A very nice drop it was. Too. Maybe not quite as bitter as this one, but still very nice.

1888 Bohemian Export		
pilsner malt 2 row	13.50 lb	100.00%
Saaz 60 min	2.50 oz	
Saaz 30 min	2.50 oz	
OG	1060	
FG	1015	
ABV	5.95	
Apparent attenuation	75.00%	
IBU	45	
SRM	4	
Mash Bohemian method		
Boil time	90 minutes	
pitching temp	48° F	
Yeast	WLP800 Pilsner Lager	

1929 Bohemian Lagerbier

This is the type of beer usually associated with the Czech Republic: a Pale Lager of around 5% ABV.

I could also call this by its Czech name, Světlý Ležák, though that is rather harder for most to pronounce. It literally translates as Pale Lagerbier.

The mashing scheme, a triple decoction, is pretty damn complicated. I doubt I could be arsed to go through the process myself. Very time consuming. I'm not going to get involved in any argument about whether there's any point to decoction mashing with modern malts. I'll leave that to the experts.

The key to this type of beer is good quality, very pale, two-row barley and good Czech hops. Not complicated, is it? Followed by three months lagering at about 1° C. Should produce a lovely drinking beer (as opposed to a stare at and sip beer).

1929 Bohemian Lagerbier		
pilsner malt 2 row	10.75 lb	100.00%
Saaz 120 mins	1.00 oz	
Saaz 90 mins	1.00 oz	
Saaz 45 mins	2.00 oz	
OG	1048	
FG	1012	
ABV	4.76	
Apparent attenuation	75.00%	
IBU	52	
SRM	3	
Mash triple decoction		
Boil time	120 minutes	
pitching temp	41° F	
Yeast	WLP800 Pilsner Lager	

1929 Bohemian Schankbier

While the stronger Lagerbier is the type of beer usually associated with the Czech Republic, this is actually the most popular style in the country itself.

10° or, to give it its official name, Výčepní Pivo, which literally means "draught beer". Or Schankbier, which is the German term. It's pretty much the weedier younger brother of Lagerbier, brewed in much the same way and with the same sort of ingredients. And with a shorter lagering time of just three months.

I wouldn't blame you if you skipped the triple decoction and just went for an infusion mash. It's probably what I would do.

1929 Bohemian Schankbier		
pilsner malt 2 row	9.00 lb	100.00%
Saaz 120 mins	0.75 oz	
Saaz 90 mins	0.75 oz	
Saaz 45 mins	1.50 oz	
OG	1040	
FG	1010	
ABV	3.97	
Apparent attenuation	75.00%	
IBU	41	
SRM	3	
Mash triple decoction		
Boil time	120 minutes	
pitching temp	41° F	
Yeast	WLP800 Pilsner Lager	

1929 Bohemian Doppelbier

Right. So we've already seen Světlý Ležák and Výčepní Pivo. Now we're onto what is nowadays called Speciální Pivo in the modern Czech Republic.

Braník, my favourite of the Prague breweries, used to brew a cracking 14° Světlé. Which sometime in the later 1980's was downgraded to 13°. A shame. Of course, nothing like as bad as when they totally shut the brewery. If you wanted to pigeonhole this in an "official" style, I suppose Helles Märzen would do at a pinch. Though Czech Speciální Pivo tends to hoppier than German Märzen.

The very late hop addition is such a modern touch. Presumably purely for the aroma of those classy Saaz hops. But there are a stack of hops for a Lager.

Looks like a lovely beer. Brew it and send me some.

1929 Bohemian Doppelbier		
pilsner malt 2 row	12.75 lb	100.00%
Saaz 120 mins	2.00 oz	
Saaz 45 mins	3.50 oz	
Saaz 5 mins	0.50 oz	
OG	1056	
FG	1020	
ABV	4.76	
Apparent attenuation	64.29%	
IBU	68	
SRM	4	
Mash Bohemian double decoction		
Boil time	90 minutes	
pitching temp	41° F	
Yeast	WLP800 Pilsner Lager	

1879 Kulmbacher Export

In the early days of Lager brewing outside its traditional central European home, several regional Bavarian styles were imitated abroad. One of these was Kulmbacher.

Even Heineken used to brew this style of strong, hoppy and very dark Lager. But for some reason it quickly fell out of fashion and is today virtually unknown as a style. Which is a shame as I'm sure its bold flavours would go down well with modern drinkers. You could think of it as a Münchener on steroids.

1879 Kulmbacher Export		
Munich malt 20L	15.25 lb	96.83%
Carafa III	0.50 lb	3.17%
Hallertau 60 mins	3.50 oz	
Hallertau 30 mins	3.50 oz	
OG	1065	
FG	1018	
ABV	6.22	
Apparent attenuation	72.31%	
IBU	80	
SRM	30	
Mash Kulmbach method		
Boil time	90 minutes	
pitching temp	48° F	
Yeast	WLP830 German Lager	

Mini Book Series volume XXX: Let's Brew!

1911 Heineken Bok

Unlike the generic recipes earlier, this one comes from a brewing record. Though not a full brewing record.

Because, while it does have details of the ingredients and the fermentation, there's nothing about mashing or boiling. Which is a bit of a bummer. So those bits are just guesses.

Apart from the shit attenuation, this isn't a million miles away from a modern Dutch Bok. Reddish in colour, malty and without a huge amount of bitterness. It is a lovely beer. I know because I've drunk it. Coronado in San Diego brewed the recipe a couple of years ago. Dangerously drinkable would be my description.

There's still a Heineken Bok, though 20 years or so ago they changed it to a Tarwe (wheat) Bok. I've heard rumours that the current Amstel Bok recipe is closer to the original Heineken one. I can believe that. Or rather, would like to. Amstel Bok is my favourite Heineken beer by a long way. And stupidly cheap. I get stuck into it every Autumn.

This was a beer brewed in Heineken's Rotterdam brewery, located on the not very might river Rotter. It wasn't far from where I used to live in Rotterdam. I used to walk past the one remaining bit – offices I think – on my way back from town.

1911 Heineken Bok		
pilsner malt 2 row	12.50 lb	80.33%
Munich malt 20L	2.75 lb	17.67%
Carafa III	0.31 lb	1.99%
Saaz 60 min	1.50 oz	
OG	1067.5	
FG	1029.5	
ABV	5.03	
Apparent attenuation	56.30%	
IBU	16	
SRM	17	
Mash double decoction		
Boil time	90 minutes	
pitching temp	48° F	
Yeast	WLP830 German Lager	

Mini Book Series volume XXX: Let's Brew!

1911 Heineken Gerste

In the early 20th century Heineken brewed three Dark Lagers: a Bok a Münchener and Gerste.

Of the three, Gerste was by far the most popular. In fact, it was the most popular of all the beers brewed in Heineken's Rotterdam brewery, accounting for more than half of what they brewed.

What was Gerste? Literally, it just means barley. There was a popular top-fermenting Dutch style with the same name. That was Oranjeboom's biggest seller and Heineken seem to have introduced their bottom-fermenting version to compete with it. It was cheaper than their other Lagers, possibly because it underwent little or no lagering.

Gerste seems to have disappeared around WW I. In the 1920's its place in Heineken's range was taken by Donker Lagerbier, a cheap Lager of 9.2° Plato.

1911 Heineken Gerste		
pilsner malt 2 row	10.50 lb	96.42%
Carafa III	0.39 lb	3.58%
Hallertau 60 mins	1.50 oz	
OG	1048	
FG	1019	
ABV	3.84	
Apparent attenuation	60.42%	
IBU	20	
SRM	16	
Mash double decoction		
Boil time	90 minutes	
pitching temp	48° F	
Yeast	WLP830 German Lager	

Mini Book Series volume XXX: Let's Brew!

1911 Heineken Beiersch

Beiersch, one of the first Lagers Heineken brewed, was pretty much a posher version of Gerste.

In style, it's a Münchener, which was the type of Lager many early bottom-fermenting breweries outside central Europe started with. In Holland, it was one of the Lager breweries' standard range until the 1950's, when it slowly died out. Which is a shame. Though the Poesiat & Kater brewery in Amsterdam has recently brewed one.

Much like the German original, this beer is malty and only lightly hopped. Just the sort of thing I like to drink myself. Which is one of the reasons I'm publishing the recipe. Hint, hint.

1911 Heineken Beiersch		
pilsner malt 2 row	10.50 lb	95.45%
Carafa III	0.50 lb	4.55%
Hallertau 90 mins	1.50 oz	
OG	1053	
FG	1017	
ABV	4.76	
Apparent attenuation	67.92%	
IBU	20	
SRM	19	
Mash double decoction		
Boil time	90 minutes	
pitching temp	48° F	
Yeast	WLP830 German Lager	

1911 Heineken Pils

Here's a beer that you possibly have heard of. It is one of the biggest sellers in Europe.

As with any beer that's been around for more than five minutes, Heineken Pils has undergone several recipe changes. One of the most obvious differences between this and the modern version is the OG: which is a good bit higher in the older version. While the rate of attenuation is much higher in the modern version.

One thing both versions do have in common is that they are all-malt. Though for most of the intervening period Heineken Pils did contain adjuncts.

The hopping rate is far lower than in the original Bohemian versions. It wouldn't surprise me if the current version was about as bitter. As relatively low hopping rates are common across all the Heineken beers, I assume they were catering to Dutch tastes.

1911 Heineken Pils		
pilsner malt 2 row	11.75 lb	100.00%
Saaz 60 min	2.00 oz	
OG	1053	
FG	1014	
ABV	5.16	
Apparent attenuation	73.58%	
IBU	24	
SRM	3.7	
Mash double decoction		
Boil time	90 minutes	
pitching temp	48° F	
Yeast	WLP830 German Lager	

Mini Book Series volume XXX: Let's Brew!

1911 Heineken Lagerbier

As well as expensive beers like Pils and Beiersch, Heineken also had some more attractively priced products.

Just as you had Gerste as a cheap Dark Lager, so you had Lagerbier as a low-budget Pale Lager. You can see all Heineken's prices here:

Heineken wholesale prices 1904 - 1914	
beer type	cents per litre
Gerstebier	8
Lager	8
Rotterdamsche Gerste	11
Münchener	14
Export	14
Beiersch (donker)	13
Pilsner (licht)	13
Bock	15
Source: 1904-1914 - "Korte Geschiedenis der Heineken's Bierbouwerij Maatschappij N.V. 1873 - 1948" (p.218)	

The Gerste whose recipe is a few pages back was the more expensive Rotterdamsche Gerste. You can see that this beer, as just 8 cents a litre, was one of Heineken's cheapest.

Its successor, Licht Lagerbier was brewed in the interwar years but looks like it was killed off by WW II. After the German occupation, the gravities of Heineken's beers rapidly fell and by October 1943 it had an OG of just 3.9° Plato (1016°).

It's another very uncomplicated recipe, just pilsner malt and hops.

1911 Heineken Lagerbier		
pilsner malt 2 row	8.25 lb	100.00%
Hallertau 90 mins	1.25 oz	
OG	1037	
FG	1011	
ABV	3.44	
Apparent attenuation	70.27%	
IBU	19	
SRM	3	
Mash double decoction		
Boil time	90 minutes	
pitching temp	48° F	
Yeast	WLP830 German Lager	

Mini Book Series volume XXX: Let's Brew!

1933 Oranjeboom Pils

Oranjeboom was a large Rotterdam brewery. One that for a while in the late 19th century was larger than Heineken.

When I first moved to Rotterdam in 1987 the brewery, located on the south side of the Maas, was still in operation. Though not for long. It was closed and then erased from the face of the earth. Much like the Oranjeboom brand, which has pretty much disappeared.

The document I'm using for the Oranjeboom recipes isn't a complete brewing record. It only lists the ingredients and fermentation details. So all the other details are just my guess.

It's another very simple recipe, just lager malt and flaked maize. At least I think it's flaked maize. It's some sort of adjunct, indicated by an "r" in the record. Which I think stands for "raw", as in unmalted grain. It could also be unmalted barley.

Like all the Dutch beers I've seen the hopping is very light. Especially for a style like Pils, which is supposed to be hop-accented.

1933 Oranjeboom Pils		
lager malt	9.25 lb	90.24%
flaked maize	1.00 lb	9.76%
Hallertau 90 mins	0.75 oz	
Saaz 30 mins	0.25 oz	
OG	1046	
FG	1014	
ABV	4.23	
Apparent attenuation	69.57%	
IBU	13	
SRM	3	
Mash double decoction		
Boil time	90 minutes	
pitching temp	48° F	
Yeast	WLP830 German Lager	

1933 Oranjeboom Munchener

Before WW II the dark Munich style of Lager was still quite popular in Holland, though it was a minority taste.

If you thought the Pils wasn't very hoppy, take a look at this baby: just 12 calculated IBUs.

No adjuncts in this grist, just lager malt, caramel malt and caramel. The latter presumably to get the right colour. At least I assume it's some sort of caramel. It isn't totally clear what it is in the brewing record. But, judging by the quantities used and the beers it was used in, caramel seems the most likely option.

You might be surprised to heart that I've adjusted the FG down from 1023. I've assumed it would have attenuated more during lagering.

1933 Oranjeboom Munchener		
lager malt	9.50 lb	91.70%
caramel malt 120 L	0.75 lb	7.24%
caramel 1000 SRM	0.11 lb	1.06%
Hallertau 90 mins	0.50 oz	
Saaz 30 mins	0.50 oz	
OG	1048	
FG	1019	
ABV	3.84	
Apparent attenuation	60.42%	
IBU	12	
SRM	16	
Mash double decoction		
Boil time	90 minutes	
pitching temp	48° F	
Yeast	WLP830 German Lager	

1933 Oranjeboom Licht Gerste

Judging by the number of entries in the brewing book, Licht Gerste must have been one of Oranjeboom's favourite beers, almost as popular than Pils. I'd love to know when they stopped brewing it. Probably around WW II.

Though it was originally a top-fermenting beer I'm sure that by this point it was being bottom fermented.

The small amount of caramel malt is just enough to colour it distinctively darker than Pils. It would have been towards the dark end of the Bitter spectrum in colour.

Other than that, it's a very uncomplicated recipe. Producing what must have been a pretty light and inoffensive beer. I've adjusted the finishing gravity down from 1010. Though I doubt this particular beer was lagered.

1933 Oranjeboom Licht Gerste		
lager malt	7.25 lb	93.55%
caramel malt	0.50 lb	6.45%
Hallertau 90 mins	0.50 oz	
Spalt 30 mins	0.50 oz	
OG	1034	
FG	1008	
ABV	3.44	
Apparent attenuation	76.47%	
IBU	13	
SRM	8	
Mash double decoction		
Boil time	90 minutes	
pitching temp	48° F	
Yeast	WLP830 German Lager	

1933 Oranjeboom Gerste

I'm not going to have much to say about this beer. It's pretty much like the last one, but coloured darker with caramel.

It was brewed in far smaller quantities than the paler version. This should give you some idea of the quantities of each beer Oranjeboom brewed:

Beer	no. of brews
Licht Gerste	15
Gerste	3
Munchener	1
Pils	20
Bok	3
Stout	1

Once again I've adjusted the FG down, this time from a very high 1017. I know that both this and Licht Gerste were declared as 3.5% ABV (it's on the label) so lowering it seems logical.

1933 Oranjeboom Gerste		
lager malt	6.50 lb	92.33%
caramel malt	0.50 lb	7.10%
caramel	0.04 lb	0.57%
Hallertau 90 mins	0.50 oz	
Spalt 30 mins	0.50 oz	
OG	1033	
FG	1010	
ABV	3.04	
Apparent attenuation	69.70%	
IBU	13	
SRM	10	
Mash double decoction		
Boil time	90 minutes	
pitching temp	48° F	
Yeast	WLP830 German Lager	

Mini Book Series volume XXX: Let's Brew!

1933 Oranjeboom Stout

Until surprisingly recently, Stout was a standard beer in most Dutch Lager brewers' ranges. Though the first examples of Dutch Stout predate Lager-brewing in Holland, later versions were almost always made by bottom-fermentation.

Stout was usually one of the strongest beers made by brewery, either slightly stronger or slightly weaker than their Bok. They were almost always the most bitter beer. Which makes sense if you remember that Stout was originally a Beer.

Getting on to this particular beer, I have to admit that there's a good bit of guesswork in the recipe. I've assumed that the sugar used must be very dark, something similar to No. 4 invert. Without that, the colour would be way too pale. Pretty sure it wasn't achieved with caramel as that is specified for some other beers, but not this one.

1933 Oranjeboom Stout		
lager malt	12.25 lb	87.50%
caramel malt	0.50 lb	3.57%
No. 4 invert sugar	1.25 lb	8.93%
Hallertau 90 mins	1.50 oz	
Spalt 30 mins	1.50 oz	
OG	1066	
FG	1020	
ABV	6.09	
Apparent attenuation	69.70%	
IBU	31	
SRM	26	
Mash double decoction		
Boil time	90 minutes	
pitching temp	48° F	
Yeast	WLP830 German Lager	

Mini Book Series volume XXX: Let's Brew!

1933 Oranjeboom Bok

Every Dutch Lager brewery has always produced a Bok a seasonal special. Though exactly which season it was sold has changed over the years.

Originally Lent was Bokbier season. But breweries, wanted to get the jump on their competition kept releasing them earlier and earlier. When the season had moved as far back as October, the brewers organisation said enough was enough and stepped in. They started setting a date every year for the release of Bok. They still do. Though some of the new brewers, who aren't part of the organisation, ignore it and release their Boks earlier.

Looking at older recipes, it doesn't seem that Dutch Bok has changed that much over the years. The gravity and colour are both very much the same. Though that might be because of the rules defining limits for those two attributes: and autumn Bok has to be dark and at least 16° Plato.

This looks like a typical malty Bok, though not as ridiculously sweet as the current Grolsch Bok, which is sweetened with all sorts of shit.

1933 Oranjeboom Bok		
lager malt	14.00 lb	93.71%
caramel malt	0.75 lb	5.02%
caramel	0.19 lb	1.27%
Hallertau 90 mins	1.00 oz	
Spalt 30 mins	0.75 oz	
OG	1068	
FG	1022	
ABV	6.09	
Apparent attenuation	67.65%	
IBU	19	
SRM	20	
Mash double decoction		
Boil time	90 minutes	
pitching temp	48° F	
Yeast	WLP830 German Lager	

Mini Book Series volume XXX: Let's Brew!

1956 Amstel Gold

I was surprised to discover that Amstel Gold had been around since at least the 1950's. My guess for its birth would have been in the 1970's.

It's a bit of a tricky one to classify. RateBeer calls it an Imperial Pils, which is pretty clueless. It's closer to a Heller Bock, really, though a little too weak. Maybe the Pils definition isn't so far off as it's called P Gold in the brewing record. As opposed to straight P, which was their Pils.

The recipe is not just a scaled-up version of their Pils, though. As Gold contains sugar rather than the raw grain of the Pils. It's also ever so slightly more heavily hopped than the Pils, though it's still far from being a very bitter beer.

A month or two of lagering would probably help smooth it out. Though I doubt Amstel lagered it for very long in the 1950's. Maybe a couple of weeks.

1956 Amstel Gold		
lager malt	11.50 lb	92.00%
glucose	1.00 lb	8.00%
Hallertau 90 mins	0.75 oz	
Hallertau 60 mins	0.50 oz	
Saaz 30 mins	0.50 oz	
OG	1059	
FG	1015	
ABV	5.82	
Apparent attenuation	74.58%	
IBU	20	
SRM	3.5	
Mash double decoction		
Boil time	90 minutes	
pitching temp	43° F	
Yeast	WLP830 German Lager	

Mini Book Series volume XXX: Let's Brew!

1956 Amstel Pils

Amstel Pils is the preferred tipple of both my sons. Their hierarchy seems to go: Amstel, Heineken, Grolsch. Not my order of preference, but hey, I'm an old git.

Mind you Alexie seemed quite keen on La Chouffe when he was a toddler. I'd give him a sip when he asked, thinking, like most kids, he'd hate the taste of beer. Unfortunately, he quite liked it. If I wasn't careful he'd gulp down half a glass.

Amstel Pils is another very simple beer: just lager malt and raw grain. Now I'm not 100% sure that raw grain was maize. It's the most likely bet, as it was usually the cheapest. But it could also have been unmalted barley or another grain. The brewing record isn't very clear.

Pale, light-bodied and not very hoppy. Sounds lovely.

1956 Amstel Pils		
lager malt	7.25 lb	70.73%
flaked maize	3.00 lb	29.27%
Hallertau 90 mins	0.50 oz	
Hallertau 60 mins	0.50 oz	
Saaz 30 mins	0.50 oz	
OG	1046	
FG	1010	
ABV	4.76	
Apparent attenuation	78.26%	
IBU	18	
SRM	3	
Mash double decoction		
Boil time	90 minutes	
pitching temp	43° F	
Yeast	WLP830 German Lager	

Mini Book Series volume XXX: Let's Brew!

1956 Amstel Oud Bruin

I can guarantee you that no-one you know has ever brewed a Dutch-style Oud Bruin. Because it's one of the world's most obscure beer styles. And one that the style guideline writers haven't noticed.

That said, it's not the world's most inspiring style. On my first trip to Holland, I can remember getting all excited in a Deventer bar when the barman told me that, in addition to the standard draught Pils, they also had a bottled dark beer. It looked the part in the glass, but I was horrified when I tasted it: thin and gum-achingly sweet.

I'm not really selling the style, am I? It doesn't have a long history. Though there was a style of beer called Oud Bruin that went back centuries (and which was closer to the Belgian style), this type was only invented in the 1930's. Supposedly by northern Lager brewers who wanted to wean drinkers in the south of Holland off the sweet, dark, top-fermenting beers still brewed down their way.

Several Lager brewers still produce Oud Bruin, but only in tiny quantities. When I wanted to buy some (for scientific purposes) the only one I could find was Heineken. I've heard rumours that some breweries just water down, colour and sweeten their Pils to make it, rather than brewing it from scratch.

Surprisingly, it's one the bitterest Amstel beers.

1956 Amstel Oud Bruin		
lager malt	6.75 lb	89.46%
black malt	0.125 lb	1.66%
Candi sugar dark 275 SRM	0.67 lb	8.88%
Hallertau 90 mins	0.50 oz	
Hallertau 60 mins	0.50 oz	
Hallertau 30 mins	0.50 oz	
OG	1034	
FG	1010	
ABV	3.18	
Apparent attenuation	70.59%	
IBU	21	
SRM	18	
Mash double decoction		
Boil time	90 minutes	
pitching temp	43° F	
Yeast	WLP830 German Lager	

1927 Barclay Perkins Export

My favourite Barclay Perkins was the first of the large London brewers to spot the potential of Lager.

I suspect it all kicked off during WW I, when supplies of continental Lager were cut off. You might think "So what?" no-one drank Lager back then. But that's not true. Both Pale and Dark Lager were popular enough to be specifically mentioned in a London publicans' price-fixing agreement:

"The new scale of prices as fixed by the Licensed Victuallers' Central Protection Society of London is:

	half pint	Glass
Mild ale	3.5d.	-
Bitter	5d.	4d.
Stout	5d.	5d.
Burton	6d.	5d.
Mild and Bitter	4.5d.	3.5d .
Stout and Mild	5d.	4d.
Mild and Burton	5d.	4d.

Other prices: Small Bass 7d.; Guinness 8d.; London stout (screws) 5d.; pale ale (screws) 5d.; barley wine nips 6d.; lager, light or dark, 8d."
Weekly Dispatch, April 8th 1917.

During the war they conducted various experiments in brewing Lager, kicking off on March 10th 1915 when they brewed an experimental Dark Lager with a decoction mash. They must have got the taste for Lager brewing because when the war was over they built a dedicated Lager brewery. This came on stream in 1921.

Initially they brewed three beers: Export, Dark and Munich. The latter doesn't seem to have lasted long, though it might just have been renamed Special Dark. In 1922 a draught Lager was added.

Of all Barclay Perkins Lagers, Export was the one that hung around the longest, still being brewed in 1962. Not sure how much longer it lasted than that. At some point in the 1960's the Barclay's branded Lagers were discontinued, presumably so they could concentrate on Harp.

The 1928 iteration is a simple beer: pilsner malt, corn grits, Saaz and English hops. The cereal mash of the grits was used like a decoction, raising the temperature of the mash to 156° F.

This is the full mashing scheme:

mash in	117° F	75 minutes
raise to	158° F	6 minutes
raise to	170° F	5 minutes
hold at	165° F	30 minutes
Sparge at	175° F	

At around 13° Plato, it's about the same strength as a continental Export of the day. Though I notice in a notebook about the Lager brewery it's called Export pilsener, not just Export. Though I wouldn't put too much faith in a British brewery's correct use of Lager type names.

1927 Barclay Perkins Export		
pilsner malt 2 row	9.00 lb	78.26%
corn grits	2.50 lb	21.74%
Saaz 60 min	2.00 oz	
Goldings 30 min	1.00 oz	
OG	1051	
FG	1014	
ABV	4.89	
Apparent attenuation	72.55%	
IBU	32	
SRM	3	
Mash at	158° F	
Sparge at	175° F	
Boil time	90 minutes	
pitching temp	48° F	
Yeast	Wyeast 2042 Danish lager	

Mini Book Series volume XXX: Let's Brew!

1925 Barclay Perkins Dark Lager

You might be surprised to learn that Barclay Perkins brewed a Dark Lager for several decades.

In fact, their first experiments with Lager during WW I seem to have been of the darker kind. It's not that odd. The Munich type of Dark Lager was still pretty popular and not just in Bavaria. It was brewed in several European countries, especially in Scandinavia.

The grist is quite different from their Export, in that there are no grits. And two coloured malts, crystal and black. That doesn't look hugely authentic to me. Surely there should be some Munich malt in there? Though I guess outside Bavaria, that probably wasn't how Dark Lager was brewed.

Without the grits, the mashing scheme is quite different:

mash in	123° F	75 minutes
raise to	140° F	10 minutes
raise to	156° F	10 minutes
raise to	170° F	
hold at	170° F	35 minutes
Sparge at	170° F	

Surprisingly, it comes out more bitter than the Export, probably because of the American hops.

1925 Barclay Perkins Dark Lager		
pilsner malt 2 row	10.75 lb	81.13%
crystal malt 60 L	2.25 lb	16.98%
black malt	0.25 lb	1.89%
Cluster 90 min	0.75 oz	
Saaz 60 min	1.50 oz	
Goldings 30 min	0.75 oz	
OG	1058	
FG	1020	
ABV	5.03	
Apparent attenuation	65.52%	
IBU	37	
SRM	19	
Mash at	156° F	
Sparge at	170° F	
Boil time	90 minutes	
pitching temp	48.5° F	
Yeast	Wyeast 2042 Danish lager	

Mini Book Series volume XXX: Let's Brew!

1932 Barclay Perkins Draught Lager

Introduced a year after the Lager brewery opened, Draught Lager was another beer that was around for a long time.

Introduced in 1922, it must have been one of the earliest draught Lagers brewed in the UK. Initially, it had a surprisingly low OG of 1034°. Far weaker than their other Lagers. In July 1923, it was raised to the more reasonable level of 1044°.

Interestingly, unlike their other pale Lager, the draught was all malt. No idea why there are no grits in this one.

They were a bit strange sometimes with their Lager. For example, in the brewing book this recipe comes from, which covers 1930 to 1934, in the latter part of the book there is no water treatment. Whereas in the earlier part gypsum is added. This particular beer had 30 lbs gypsum added to around 200 barrels of water.

The mashing scheme was pretty typical for Barclay Perkins Lagers:

mash in	125° F	60 minutes
raise to	158° F	10 minutes
raise to	170° F	
hold at	170° F	45 minutes
Sparge at	175° F	

The temperature was raised through the application of steam.

1932 Barclay Perkins Draught Lager		
lager malt	9.50 lb	100.00%
Hallertau 90 min	0.88 oz	
Saaz 60 min	0.67 oz	
Saaz 30 min	0.67 oz	
OG	1043.5	
FG	1011	
ABV	4.30	
Apparent attenuation	74.71%	
IBU	29	
SRM	3	
Mash at	155° F	
Sparge at	160° F	
Boil time	90 minutes	
pitching temp	48° F	
Yeast	Wyeast 2042 Danish lager	

Mini Book Series volume XXX: Let's Brew!

1939 Barclay Perkins Sparkling Beer

Just before the start of WW II Barclay Perkins introduced a new Lager, Sparkling Beer.

It seems to have been a beer destined solely for the export trade as it doesn't appear in any of their pub price lists. Empty Sparkling Beer cans, left by British troops during WW II, occasionally turn up in the Libyan desert. Oh yes, it was also a very early canned beer.

It's a bit of a tricky one to classify style-wise. They were always pretty vague on labels and cans, just calling it "Beer". It wasn't even mentioned that it was aa Lager. Being amber in colour, a style Nazi would probably plump for Vienna Lager. It's on the bitter side for that, really, at 39 IBUs.

Luckily, I don't have to worry about forcing Sparkling Beer into a style pigeonhole. So let's just call it beer and be done with it.

It's not a complicated recipe, just pilsner malt, crystal malt and Saaz hops. I wouldn't mind trying it myself. Though without the pasteurisation the original would have undergone.

1939 Barclay Perkins Sparkling Beer		
pilsner malt 2 row	9.50 lb	88.37%
crystal malt 80l	1.25 lb	11.63%
Saaz 90 min	1.25 oz	
Saaz 60 min	1.25 oz	
Saaz 30 min	1.25 oz	
OG	1048	
FG	1014	
ABV	4.50	
Apparent attenuation	70.83%	
IBU	39	
SRM	10	
Mash at	158° F	
Sparge at	175° F	
Boil time	90 minutes	
pitching temp	45° F	
Yeast	Wyeast 2042 Danish lager	

Mini Book Series volume XXX: Let's Brew!

1942 Barclay Perkins Export

Barclay Perkins continued to brew their Lagers during WW II. In fact the war, which isolated the UK from most of the Europe's Lager producers, probably boosted their sales.

Though as brewing ingredients aren't always used immediately, they were still using continental hops three years into the war. This beer contained hops from two countries occupied by the Germans: Saaz and Belgian Saaz.

British brewers definitely had a liking for Saaz and didn't just use it in Lagers. It crops up in quite a few 19th-century William Younger Pale Ales.

The war hasn't had much impact on the recipe, which is still lager malt and grits. Though it has knocked down the OG by 8 points to 1043°.

The mashing scheme hasn't changed much, either:

mash in	110° F	86 minutes
raise to	154° F	20 minutes
raise to	168° F	
hold at	168° F	45 minutes
Sparge at	175° F	

1942 Barclay Perkins Export		
lager malt	7.25 lb	74.36%
grits	2.50 lb	25.64%
Goldings 120 mins	0.75 oz	
Saaz 30 mins	0.75 oz	
OG	1043	
FG	1009	
ABV	4.50	
Apparent attenuation	79.07%	
IBU	19	
SRM	3	
Mash at	154° F	
Sparge at	175° F	
Boil time	120 minutes	
pitching temp	41.5° F	
Yeast	Wyeast 2042 Danish lager	

1942 Barclay Perkins Draught Lager

It's interesting to note that even during WW II, Barclay's Draught Lager remained all malt.

I'd love to know how many pubs actually had it on draught. That and their other Lagers. Because it wasn't just Draught that was sold on draught. I know that from a price list dated April 1942. In the section for draught beers it lists three Lagers:

Export	8/6 per gallon
Home Light	7/5
Dark	9/3

For comparison purposes, X Ale (Ordinary Mild) was 5/8 and XLK (Ordinary Bitter) 6/11.

I'd love to know exactly what casks it came in. I know that they were 11 gallons and 5.5 gallons. Which implies they were some sort of continental design, because that's the equivalent of 50 and 25 litres.

I'm sure that they were served on top pressure, because the price list also includes CO2 cylinders.

If I'm ever in wartime London, I must remember to look for Barclay's Dark Lager on draught. Somewhere must have sold it, otherwise it would be in the price list.

Here's the original mashing scheme:

mash in	123° F	55 minutes
raise to	156° F	20 minutes
raise to	170° F	
hold at	170° F	40 minutes
Sparge at	175° F	

Which is pretty much the same as what they always did.

1942 Barclay Perkins Draught Lager		
lager malt	8.00 lb	100.00%
Fuggles 105 mins	0.50 oz	
Goldings 60 mins	0.50 oz	
Saaz 30 mins	0.25 oz	
OG	1036	
FG	1008	
ABV	3.70	
Apparent attenuation	77.78%	
IBU	17	
SRM	3	
Mash at	156° F	
Sparge at	175° F	
Boil time	105 minutes	
pitching temp	45.5° F	
Yeast	Wyeast 2042 Danish lager	

Mini Book Series volume XXX: Let's Brew!

1941 Barclay Perkins Dark Lager

It's a demonstration of how much more interesting British Lager used to be that Barclay Perkins brewed a Dark Lager for so long.

Ironically, it was when Lager started to become popular that the range of Lagers brewed was trimmed down to basically just Pilsner. Or a sort of watery Pilsner.

The war seems to have had an impact on the recipe, because some of the malt looks like straightforward pale malt, not lager malt. Not only that, it's pale malt from Newark, because it's listed as "Gilstrap", which was one of the large Newark maltsters.

It's still got a very respectable OG for a wartime beer: 1056°. In fact, it was stronger than anything else Barclay Perkins brewed, other than Russian Stout which was aa tad stronger at 1056.5°

This is the original mashing scheme:

mash in	129° F	30 minutes
raise to	158° F	30 minutes
raise to	170° F	
hold at	170° F	35 minutes
Sparge at	175° F	

1941 Barclay Perkins Dark Lager		
lager malt	6.75 lb	51.92%
pale malt	3.50 lb	26.92%
crystal malt 80 L	2.50 lb	19.23%
roast barley	0.25 lb	1.92%
Goldings 90 mins	0.75 oz	
Saaz 30 mins	0.75 oz	
OG	1056	
FG	1017	
ABV	5.16	
Apparent attenuation	69.64%	
IBU	16	
SRM	20	
Mash at	158° F	
Sparge at	170° F	
Boil time	90 minutes	
pitching temp	46° F	
Yeast	Wyeast 2042 Danish lager	

Mini Book Series volume XXX: Let's Brew!

1953 Barclay Perkins Export

In the early 1950's, Barclay Perkins was still brewing its full range of four Lagers: Export, Draught, Dark and Sparkling Beer.

These were the final years of the brewery's independence. They were bought out by Courage in 1955 and most brewing stopped three years later. With one exception: Lager. The specialist Lager plant in the Park Street complex continued to brew until the early 1970's. Which leaves me wondering: did Courage partly buy Barclay Perkins to get hold of the Lager brewery?

The grist of Export has a new addition: flaked maize. Which is a bit odd. Why include two forms of maize? Wouldn't it have been simpler to just use whichever was cheaper? I assume that would be the grits. And I'd be wrong. The brewing record handily includes prices. The flaked maize was 190/- per quarter, the grits 199/6. While the two types of malt were 220/- and 225/- per quarter.

While we're discussing prices, the Saaz hops were almost double the price of the Goldings: 1200/- per cwt. as opposed to 650/-. Maybe that's why Lager was always so expensive.

Here's the original mashing scheme:

mash in	122° F	105 minutes
raise to	154° F	30 minutes
raise to	168° F	
hold at	168° F	50 minutes
Sparge at	165° F	

1953 Barclay Perkins Export		
lager malt	7.25 lb	72.50%
grits	2.25 lb	22.50%
flaked maize	0.50 lb	5.00%
Goldings 120 mins	1.00 oz	
Saaz 30 mins	0.75 oz	
OG	1045	
FG	1008.5	
ABV	4.83	
Apparent attenuation	81.11%	
IBU	22	
SRM	3	
Mash at	154° F	
Sparge at	165° F	
Boil time	120 minutes	
pitching temp	46.5° F	
Yeast	Wyeast 2042 Danish lager	

Mini Book Series volume XXX: Let's Brew!

Mini Book Series volume XXX: Let's Brew!

1953 Barclay Perkins Sparkling Beer

Looking up Sparkling Beer on the internet, it seems to have been sold to a lot of British merchant ships. In canned form.

It doesn't ever appear to have been officially sold in the UK, though one source on the web has a docker in Liverpool recalling buying cans from seamen.

The recipe has changed from the pre-war one, which was all malt. This includes both grits and flaked maize. A combination that still has me scratching my head. Why on earth use both? I've never come across this at any other brewery. It's always either the one or the other.

The OG is a few degrees lower than in 1939, but an increased degree of attenuation means that the ABV is higher.

Here's the original mashing scheme:

mash in	122° F	105 minutes
raise to	154° F	30 minutes
raise to	168° F	
hold at	168° F	50 minutes
Sparge at	165° F	

1953 Barclay Perkins Sparkling Beer		
lager malt	7.25 lb	70.73%
crystal malt 80 L	1.75 lb	17.07%
grits	1.00 lb	9.76%
flaked maize	0.25 lb	2.44%
Goldings 120 mins	1.00 oz	
Saaz 30 mins	1.00 oz	
OG	1045	
FG	1008	
ABV	4.89	
Apparent attenuation	82.22%	
IBU	24	
SRM	12.5	
Mash at	154° F	
Sparge at	165° F	
Boil time	120 minutes	
pitching temp	46.5° F	
Yeast	Wyeast 2042 Danish lager	

1953 Barclay Perkins Dark Lager

It's interesting to note that Barclay Perkins' Lagers were mostly fairly strong in the early 1950's.

At a time when average OG was 1037°, Export, Dark and Sparkling Beer were all well over 1040°. Only Draught, at 1034°, was below the average.

The recipe is much as it always was: lager malt, crystal malt and a little roast barley for colour. Speaking of which, one of the most satisfying aspects of assembling the Barclay Perkins Lager recipes is that the colours calculated by BeerSmith pretty much exactly match those in the brewing records. I must be doing something right.

The original mashing scheme:

mash in	124° F	105 minutes
raise to	154° F	30 minutes
raise to	168° F	
hold at	168° F	50 minutes
Sparge at	165° F	

And the recipe:

1953 Barclay Perkins Dark Lager		
lager malt	8.50 lb	77.27%
crystal malt 80 L	2.25 lb	20.45%
roast barley	0.25 lb	2.27%
Goldings 120 mins	1.00 oz	
Saaz 30 mins	0.75 oz	
OG	1048	
FG	1009.5	
ABV	5.09	
Apparent attenuation	80.21%	
IBU	22	
SRM	18	
Mash at	154° F	
Sparge at	165° F	
Boil time	120 minutes	
pitching temp	46.5° F	
Yeast	Wyeast 2042 Danish lager	

1953 Barclay Perkins Draught Lager

As mentioned earlier, Draught was the only Barclay Perkins Lager below average strength in the early 1950's.

Draught remained an all-malt beer, but there was a change in the grist: an addition of amber malt. That was quite a surprise when I spotted it. Usually brewers are trying hard to keep the colour as light as possible in pale Lagers. Amber malt is definitely going to make it darker. Though, as you can see in the recipe, it was still pretty pale.

This looks very much like the type of Lager that came to dominate the UK market: pale, not very bitter three and a bit percent ABV. At least it had some Saaz hops in it.

The original mashing scheme:

mash in	123° F	60 minutes
raise to	156° F	20 minutes
raise to	170° F	
hold at	170° F	55 minutes
Sparge at	165° F	

And recipe:

1953 Barclay Perkins Draught Lager		
lager malt	7.50 lb	96.77%
amber malt	0.25 lb	3.23%
Goldings 120 mins	0.50 oz	
Goldings 60 mins	0.50 oz	
Saaz 30 mins	0.50 oz	
OG	1034	
FG	1007	
ABV	3.57	
Apparent attenuation	79.41%	
IBU	21	
SRM	3	
Mash at	156° F	
Sparge at	165° F	
Boil time	120 minutes	
pitching temp	46.5° F	
Yeast	Wyeast 2042 Danish lager	

Mini Book Series volume XXX: Let's Brew!

1959 Lees Lager

I never imagined that I'd write so many recipes for crappy, post-WW II British Lagers. It's strange what life will throw at you.

Towards the end of the 1950's, before really strong national Lager brands had been established, many regional brewers brought out ones of their own. Mostly, they didn't last all that long. Either the brewers were bought up by one of the big boys, or they bought in a Lager from one of them. Other than Sam Smiths, I can't think of a regional that still has their own Lager.

Lees doesn't. But that doesn't mean that they don't brew one. They do: Carlsberg under licence. Surprisingly, they brew more of it than any of their own beers.

Just for variety, this recipe includes flaked rice. Possibly for the same reasons as late 19th-century German brewers: it helped to keep the colour and body light.

I have to admit that the yeast and pitching temperature are a guess. It's quite possible that this beer was fermented warm with their standard yeast. It's the way many regional brewers, who couldn't afford to invest in the specialist equipment needed to brew a true Lager, worked.

At 1037°, this is reasonably strong for a standard Lager. Many weren't much over 1030°. It's also surprisingly bitter, boasting 40 calculated IBUs.

1959 Lees Lager		
lager malt	6.50 lb	83.87%
flaked rice	0.50 lb	6.45%
no. 1 sugar	0.75 lb	9.68%
Fuggles 90 mins	1.50 oz	
Styrian Goldings 30 mins	1.50 oz	
OG	1037	
FG	1008	
ABV	3.84	
Apparent attenuation	78.38%	
IBU	40	
SRM	4	
Mash at	146° F	
Sparge at	170° F	
Boil time	90 minutes	
pitching temp	48° F	
Yeast	Wyeast 2042 Danish lager	

1964 Eldridge Pope Konig Lager

Another Lager from a regional brewery. One I think may have been typical.

Because, even though it was fermented with Carlsberg yeast, it was at a top-fermenting temperature. Be interesting to see how Lager-like a beer that would leave you with. Especially as I'm sure that this beer wasn't lagered.

It's another Lager with rice in the grist. Brewers seem to have preferred rice to maize as their Lager adjunct. The sugar in the original is something called Solexona. No idea what that was, but I assume it must have been pretty pale in colour. So I've substituted No. 1 invert.

It looks fairly typical for a UK Lager, with both a modest gravity and bitterness.

1964 Eldridge Pope Konig Lager		
lager malt	6.75 lb	93.10%
No. 1 invert sugar	0.50 lb	6.90%
Styrian Goldings 90 mins	0.75 oz	
Hallertau 30 mins	0.75 oz	
OG	1034	
FG	1007	
ABV	3.57	
Apparent attenuation	79.41%	
IBU	22	
SRM	3	
Mash at	148° F	
Sparge at	165° F	
Boil time	90 minutes	
pitching temp	59° F	
Yeast	Wyeast 2042 Danish lager	

Mini Book Series volume XXX: Let's Brew!

1888 Tennent's Lager Beer

Now here's a beer that you might have heard of: Tennent's Lager. Even I've drunk this.

Well, a later version. Just a few years back in the curry house on Sauchiehall Street in Glasgow. It was pretty dismal, if I'm honest. I couldn't even finish my pint. Which is saying something, if you know me.

They don't seem to have Tennent's brewing records at the Scottish Brewing Archive. But they do have a document that lists the ingredients used and OG. Which is enough for me to knock together a rough recipe.

This is from the early days of Tennent's Lager brewery, which they brought in German engineers to build at great expense. So I'm surprised it didn't end up like most early British Lager breweries: bankrupt. Though I suppose they did still have their original brewery and weren't 100% dependent on the Lager trade.

Like most Lagers, it's way more lightly hopped than other British beers of the time. Must have come as a shock – or relief – to drinkers weaned on much more bitter beers.

1888 Tennent's Lager Beer		
lager malt	10.00 lb	75.47%
flaked rice	3.25 lb	24.53%
Hallertau 90 mins	0.75 oz	
Hallertau 60 mins	0.75 oz	
Saaz 30 mins	0.75 oz	
OG	1057	
FG	1017	
ABV	5.29	
Apparent attenuation	70.18%	
IBU	25	
SRM	3.5	
Mash double decoction		
Boil time	90 minutes	
pitching temp	48° F	
Yeast	WLP830 German Lager	

1940 Whitbread Lager

This is a strange one. Whitbread, for no apparent reason, made one brew of Lager in the summer of 1940.

I can guess what the motivation might have been. With the Nazis just having taken over most of Europe, foreign supplies of Lager would have dried up. And I know from a Whitbread sales ledger that they imported and sold Tuborg, Carlsberg and Artois Lager. I suppose this was intended as a replacement for them.

In terms of OG, it looks very similar to Carlsberg Pils of the day. So perhaps that's what it was intended to replace.

Unlike London rivals Barclay Perkins, Whitbread didn't have a dedicated Lager plant at their Chiswell Street home. In fact, this is the only example I have of a Lager ever being brewed at Chiswell Street. Which probably explains why they made such a poor fist of it.

Other than the Saaz hops and the colour, there's nothing very lagery about it. An infusion mash was employed, the base was pale malt and, most importantly, it was fermented with their standard yeast at a warm temperature. That might explain why there was only one brew.

1940 Whitbread Lager		
pale malt	7.00 lb	80.00%
no. 1 sugar	1.75 lb	20.00%
Goldings 90 mins	0.50 oz	
Goldings 60 mins	0.50 oz	
Saaz 30 mins	0.25 oz	
OG	1043	
FG	1008	
ABV	4.63	
Apparent attenuation	81.40%	
IBU	17	
SRM	6	
Mash at	148° F	
Sparge at	170° F	
Boil time	90 minutes	
pitching temp	63° F	
Yeast	Wyeast 1099 Whitbread Ale	

Mini Book Series volume XXX: Let's Brew!

1969 Truman LL

I was so pleased to find this beer. Because it's an example of a short-lived type of beer: a regional brewery's own brand of Lager.

The first British Lagers were mostly brewed in specialist breweries. Either standalone enterprises like the Wrexham Lager Brewery and the Red Tower Lager Brewery. Or a specialist plant within a larger brewery – examples being Tennent in Glasgow and Barclay Perkins in London. There were only a handful of such specialist plants in the first half of the 20th century.

When Lager started to take off in the late 1950's, just about everyone wanted to get in on the act and market their own brand of Lager. These were usually just brewed on the standard kit and weren't even necessarily bottom fermented. As the 1960's and 1970's progressed, most of these regional Lagers disappeared, replaced by national or international brands. Only weird breweries like Sam Smiths have persisted.

Truman's London Lager – which is what I assume LL stands for – was such a beer. And true to tradition, it was replaced by an international brand, Tuborg, which Truman's brewed under licence.

Here's a selection of the Lagers from regional breweries in the 1950's and 1960's:

Mini Book Series volume XXX: Let's Brew!

British regional Lagers 1954 - 1962

Year	Brewer	Beer	Price per pint d	OG	FG	ABV	App. Attenuation	colour
1954	Steel Coulson	Lager Beer	30	1032	1004.3	3.60	86.56%	11
1955	Tennent	Lager	30	1036.1	1007.7	3.69	78.67%	9
1957	McEwan & Younger	"MY" Export Lager		1035.2	1007.3	3.62	79.26%	13
1960	Greene King	Lager		1034.9	1006.4	3.56	81.66%	9.5
1960	Lees	Lager		1037.0				
1960	Mitchell & Butler	Export Lager	32	1039.7	1010	3.71	74.81%	7.5
1960	Tennant Bros.	Lager	31.875	1035.2	1006.8	3.55	80.68%	8.5
1960	Tollemache	Kroner Lager		1033.4	1007.5	3.24	77.54%	7
1961	Flowers	Lager	30	1044	1011.3	4.09	74.32%	12
1961	Greene King	Lager	36	1036	1005.8	3.78	83.89%	7.5
1961	Hall & Woodhouse	Brock Lager	36	1033.9	1004.1	3.73	87.91%	10
1961	Lacons	Lager	34	1034.9	1007.1	3.48	79.66%	8
1961	Phipps	Stein Lager	36	1034.8	1005.5	3.66	84.20%	7.5
1961	Tennant Bros.	Lager	33	1036	1007.6	3.55	78.89%	7.5
1961	Tollemache & Cobbold	Kroner Lager	36	1033.1	1005.7	3.42	82.78%	9.5
1961	Charrington	Pilsner Lager	32	1036.3	1008.1	3.66	77.69%	8
1961	Eldridge Pope	König Pilsener	36	1038.6	1007.3	3.91	81.09%	8
1961	McEwan	MY Export Lager	42	1032.9	1010.1	2.85	69.30%	10
1962	Flowers	Lager	48	1044.9	1011.6	4.16	74.16%	8

Sources:
Whitbread Gravity book held at the London Metropolitan Archives, document number LMA/4453/D/02/002.
Lees brewing records held at the brewery.

Tennent's Lager is the only one to still exist. M & B and Charrington, which both ended up in Bass Charrington, had their Lagers replaced by Carling Black Label and Tennent's. Flowers, which ended up in Whitbread, had their Lager replaced by Heineken. Not sure what happened at the smaller regionals, but I'd be very surprised if any still brewed their own Lager.

Back to Truman's Lager. It's not a very complicated grist, just lager malt, sugar and flaked barley. Unlike all their other beers of the time, it doesn't use English hops, but ones described as "Styrian", which I presume means Styrian Goldings. The level of hopping is extremely low. So more of a Helles than a Pilsner.

I'm not sure about the mashing. It looks like a step mash, with strike heats of 125° F and 170° F. Not sure what that equates to in terms of initial heats. The fermentation, though cooler than for their other beers, still hit a maximum temperature of 60° F, which looks too warm for a true Lager. Though it was crashed down to 41° F just before racking.

Looks like a great example of a pseudo-Lager. Or semi-Lager. Though I'm not sure why exactly you'd want to brew one, other than for academic purposes.

Mini Book Series volume XXX: Let's Brew!

1969 Truman LL		
lager malt	6.25 lb	83.33%
flaked barley	0.75 lb	10.00%
cane sugar	0.50 lb	6.67%
Styrian Goldings 90 min	0.25 oz	
Styrian Goldings 60 min	0.25 oz	
Styrian Goldings 30 min	0.25 oz	
OG	1034.6	
FG	1008.9	
ABV	3.40	
Apparent attenuation	74.28%	
IBU	11.5	
SRM	4	
Mash at	125° F	
Sparge at	170° F	
Boil time	120 minutes	
pitching temp	53° F	
Yeast	Wyeast 2042 Danish lager	

Mini Book Series volume XXX: Let's Brew!

VI Brown Ale

Mini Book Series volume XXX: Let's Brew!

1955 Fullers Old Harry

While I'm on my whole 1950's thing, I thought I'd throw in some recipes, too. It's thirsty work doing all this number shuffling.

This is an odd beer. On the label, it's billed as a "Extra Brown Ale". Which I suppose it sort of is. Though it could equally be called a Burton. The base brew is X Ale, or Hock, Fullers standard Mild. Because obviously this was a parti-gyle. That's just the way Fullers operated. And the quantity of Old Harry being brewed was quite small - just 60 barrels, along with 480 barrels of X. Still, that's a huge volume compared to OBE in the 1930's. I don't think I've seen a batch bigger than five or six barrels.. The smallest are only one or two barrels.

I was a bit surprised by the lack of crystal malt in the recipe. I would have expected that. Instead it's just pale malt, flaked maize and sugar.

A word about the sugar. The original is No. 2 Invert, PTX and Intense. I'm not totally sure what the composition of the latter two was. I know Intense was pretty dark, probably a mix of invert sugar and caramel. PTX I haven't a clue about. So I've specified No. 3 invert and caramel as a substitute. It should get you somewhere in the right area.

There are no details of the hops, other than that they are English. A Fuggle's/Goldings combination seems a fair enough guess. Feel free to use any English hops that take your fancy.

Brown Ale is another one of those terms used inconsistently. As you'll see when I finally get my arse in gear and look at my Brown Ale analyses. There a couple of pretty different variations.

1955 Fullers Old Harry		
pale malt	7.75 lb	73.81%
flaked maize	1.00 lb	9.52%
No.2 invert	1.25 lb	11.90%
No.3 invert	0.50 lb	4.76%
caramel	1.00 oz	
Fuggles 90 min	0.75 oz	
Goldings 60 min	0.75 oz	
Goldings 30 min	0.75 oz	
OG	1051	
FG	1015	
ABV	4.76	
Apparent attenuation	70.59%	
IBU	30	
SRM	24	
Mash at	150° F	
Sparge at	166° F	
Boil time	90 minutes	
pitching temp	61° F	
Yeast	Wyeast 1968 London ESB or White Labs WLP002 English Ale	

1963 Manns Brown Ale

I'm so pleased that Boak & Bailey sent me the Watney Quality Control Manual. Because it means that I have a detailed recipe for the classic Manns Brown Ale.

If you're unaware, Manns was the first modern Brown Ale, first brewed around 1900. It took the style a while to take off, but in the 1920s it became all the rage. Soon every brewery was making one. Or, in most cases, fiddling with their Mild Ale to create one. For that reason Brown Ales are frustratingly rare in brewing records. They only turn up when a brewery really made one as a specific brew of its own.

You can't accuse this recipe of being simple. You have to wonder what the point is of the tiny amount of malt extract. While there are several ingredients there for the colour. Caramel is always a tricky one. But as I know the colour of the finished beer, I could work out how dark in needed to be.

I had to laugh about the colour. BeerSmith tells me that 27 SRM is too dark for the style. The original is not true to style, according to the BJCP.

There's one other ingredient you'll need to add for full authenticity. The manual says that up to 11% "sterile breakings" can be blended in after primary fermentation. That means all sorts of muck, like returned beer that has been pasteurised. Small wonder Watney ended up with a reputation for shit beer.

1963 Manns Brown Ale		
Mild Ale malt	5.50 lb	69.53%
crystal malt 60L	0.75 lb	9.48%
torrefied barley	0.75 lb	9.48%
black malt	0.125 lb	1.58%
malt extract	0.125 lb	1.58%
No. 3 invert sugar	0.33 lb	4.17%
caramel 1000 SRM	0.33 lb	4.17%
Fuggles 60 mins	1.00 oz	
OG	1035	
FG	1013	
ABV	2.91	
Apparent attenuation	62.86%	
IBU	14	
SRM	27	
Mash at	156° F	
Sparge at	165° F	
Boil time	50 minutes	
pitching temp	60° F	
Yeast	WLP023 Burton Ale	

Mini Book Series volume XXX: Let's Brew!

1956 Shepherd Neame DB

You might have noticed that I've never published many Brown Ale recipes. There's a good reason for that.

No, it isn't that I hate the style. It's much simpler than that: Brown Ales rarely show up in brewing records. Barclay Perkins DB and Whitbread DB are exceptions. Because they were both brewed single-gyle to unique recipes. The conclusion I've come to is that most breweries just tweaked their Mild for bottling. So they don't show up in the records.

When I do find a Brown Ale in the logs, I'm always keen to publish the recipe. Even when, as in this case, it's a complicated parti-gyle. Though it isn't that obvious from the recipe, this was parti-gyled with Abbey Ale. The reason the recipes are so different, is that Abbey Ale was mostly put together from the first wort, while the No. 3 sugar went into the second.

The colour of the finished beer might well have been darker than indicated below. Colour corrections with caramel were common in British brewing.

I was going to say that this was one of the few recipes that fits the BJCP style parameters hard-coded in BeerSmith. Then I noticed that it was outside the gravity range, which starts at 1033°. That's so wrong. Loads and loads of Brown Ales were weaker than that. It should really start at 1027°.

Overall, this looks like a typical 1950's Brown Ale: weak, sweet and with lots of sugar in it.

1956 Shepherd Neame DB		
pale malt	3.00 lb	56.60%
wheat malt	0.25 lb	4.72%
no. 3 sugar	2.00 lb	37.74%
malt extract	0.05 lb	0.94%
Fuggles 105 mins	0.50 oz	
Goldings 60 mins	0.25 oz	
Goldings 30 mins	0.25 oz	
OG	1029.4	
FG	1010.7	
ABV	2.50	
Apparent attenuation	64.29%	
IBU	15	
SRM	12	
Mash at	153° F	
Sparge at	170° F	
Boil time	105 minutes	
pitching temp	61.25° F	
Yeast	a Southern English Ale yeast	

Mini Book Series volume XXX: Let's Brew!

1959 Watneys Brown Ale

Now here's a special treat: a beer from the legendary Watneys. Unfortunately, they're legendary for all the wrong reasons. Maybe notorious would be a better word.

I thought I'd never get to write any Watney recipes. Because their brewing records don't appear to have been preserved. However those of one of the breweries they took over, Usher's of Trowbridge, have. And they brewed some Watney brands in addition to their own beers.

Watney acquired a terrible reputation in the 1970's for producing crap beer. Their name got so bad, that they eventually removed it from the exterior of their pubs. As a brand, Watney became unusable.

CAMRA was to a great part responsible. Watney produced no cask beer for many years and were an obvious target. Grotney was what they called them. And with good reason: their beer was crap.

John Keeling told me how when he worked at Wilson's, another Watney subsidiary, the Cream Stout they produced was for a large part made up of ullage - returned beer - pasteurised and coloured up with caramel. It sounded disgusting. I now realise that this wasn't an isolated example.

Because the Watney's Dairy Maid Stout, Brown Ale and XX Mild brewed at Ushers are exactly the same. There's all sorts of drecky beer added at racking time to the stuff that was breed and fermented.

In the case of Brown Ale, this was added to the 734 barrels brewed the normal way:

    BB 30 barrels
    Bottoms 40 barrels
    RB 93 barrels
    finings 9 barrels

That's 172 barrels, in total. Bottoms is the sludgy stuff left behind in vessels. RB I assume stands for returned beer, or ullage. Not sure what BB is, but it's definitely not Best Bitter.

I can't imagine that lot improved the quality of the finished beer.

The recipe below is for the beer as brewed. If you want to go all authentic, I suggest collecting dregs and the gunk left after racking, filtering it, boiling it for a while to kill any bugs, then add it to the beer when you rack. Not that I would recommend such scummy practice.

The recipe itself doesn't look too bad. A mild malt base, a bit of crystal for body and roast barley for colour. At about the standard gravity for Brown Ale back then, around 1030°.

Mini Book Series volume XXX: Let's Brew!

1959 Watneys Brown Ale		
MA malt	5.50 lb	81.06%
crystal malt	0.33 lb	4.86%
flaked maize	0.33 lb	4.86%
roast barley	0.25 lb	3.68%
No. 2 invert	0.25 lb	3.68%
caramel	0.125 lb	1.84%
ginger	pinch	
Fuggles 45 min	1.00 oz	
OG	1031	
FG	1007	
ABV	3.18	
Apparent attenuation	77.42%	
IBU	14.5	
SRM	30	
Mash at	152° F	
Sparge at	170° F	
Boil time	45 minutes	
pitching temp	60° F	
Yeast	WLP023 Burton Ale	

Mini Book Series volume XXX: Let's Brew!

1954 Whitbread Double Brown

I thought for a minute that I'd finished with Whitbread's beers of the 1950's. Then remembered that I hadn't done the Brown Ales. Or the ordinary Mild. Without them, how would you recreate a 1950's Whitbread pub?

I'll admit to having a bit of a thing about Double Brown. It is a fascinating beer. A type of Brown Ale which has been forgotten. Sadly, in my opinion as it looks like a cracking beer. Dark, but quite hoppy and a good bit stronger than most post-WW II Brown Ales.

It was introduced in 1932, when it had a very respectable gravity of 1058°. And a grist very different from Whitbread's Mild Ales. A more expensive grist, using pale ale malt as its base, as did their, er, Pale Ales. At 10 lbs of hops per quarter of malt, it was one of their most heavily hopped beers, ranking above PA (6lbs per quarter) and just behind IPA (11 lbs per quarter). Two things are clear: it wasn't a cheap drink and it wasn't based on Mild.

DB managed to survive WW II, though its OG did drop to the low-1040's. By 1950, it was almost back to its pre-war strength, at 1055°. But it wasn't to last long. DB was discontinued either in late 1955 or early 1956. And Whitbread concentrated on their other Brown Ale, Forest Brown. A watery beer based on Best Ale, Whitbread's standard Mild.

You can't accuse the recipe of being over-complicated. There's just the base malt, a smidgin of chocolate malt and some No.3 invert sugar. There was a small amount of a proprietary sugar which I've replaced by more No. 3. The hops were a combination of Kent, Mid Kent and Sussex. I've assumed they were all Fuggles, but feel free to swap some for Goldings.

Whitbread went in for very short boils after WW II and this beer is no exception, being boiled for just 60 minutes.

1954 Whitbread Double Brown		
pale malt	9.00 lb	82.76%
chocolate malt	0.125 lb	1.15%
no. 3 invert sugar	1.75 lb	16.09%
Fuggles 60 min	1.25 oz	
Fuggles 40 min	1.25 oz	
Fuggles 20 min	1.50 oz	
OG	1053	
FG	1014.5	
ABV	5.09	
Apparent attenuation	72.64%	
IBU	42	
SRM	30	
Mash at	150° F	
Sparge at	168° F	
Boil time	60 minutes	
pitching temp	62° F	
Yeast	Wyeast 1099 Whitbread ale	

1954 Whitbread Forest Brown

The next Whitbread Brown Ale is much more typical of the 1950's. Weak, sweet and spun out of a Mild recipe. Every brewery in the country had a beer along these general lines.

And very popular beers they were, too. Mostly off the back of poor draught beer quality rather than on their own merits. Falling gravities had left many landlords struggling to keep their draught beer in decent condition. Bottled beer was more reliable, but also quite a bit more expensive. The answer? Mix bottled Brown Ale and draught Mild. Not as dodgy as pure draught, but cheaper than a pint of bottled beer.

Forest Brown wasn't originally a Whitbread brand. It came from the Forest Hill Brewery, which Whitbread bought in the 1920's. Bottling was the reason of the purchase. Because Whitbread had insisted on sticking with bottle conditioning past WW II, which was quite unusual. Especially as Whitbread had an unusually large trade in bottled beer. When they finally decided to move into artificially carbonated beer, they brought in the expertise by buying the Forest Hill Brewery, which were quite big in that type of beer.

Forest Brown long outlived the brewery that spawned it. It was still Whitbread's principal Brown Ale when I was drinking in the 1970's and 1980's. Not that I ever tried it. Mostly because I rarely drank in Whitbread pubs, as they had pretty much eradicated cask in their pubs in the Midlands and the North. And I didn't drink Brown Ale.

You'll see that the grist is quite different from Double Brown. Both beers have a similar amount of No. 3 invert, but the malts are completely different, Forest Brown having a base of mild malt with a fair whack of crystal, while Double Brown is PA malt with just a touch of chocolate. Unsurprisingly, given its far lower gravity, the hopping in Forest Brown is much lighter.

1954 Whitbread Forest Brown		
mild malt	5.50 lb	80.00%
crystal malt	0.38 lb	5.45%
no. 3 invert sugar	1.00 lb	14.55%
Fuggles 60 min	0.50 oz	
Fuggles 40 min	0.50 oz	
Goldings 20 min	0.50 oz	
OG	1032.4	
FG	1009.5	
ABV	3.03	
Apparent attenuation	70.68%	
IBU	18	
SRM	25	
Mash at	147° F	
Sparge at	168° F	
Boil time	60 minutes	
pitching temp	65° F	
Yeast	Wyeast 1099 Whitbread ale	

Mini Book Series volume XXX: Let's Brew!

1968 Whitbread Forest Brown

This is an unusual one. Two recipes for the same beer from the same year. Just brewed at different breweries.

I'll explain how this came about. I was visiting the Wimbledon Brewery on Saturday to chat with my old mate Derek Prentice. I was especially interested in the two Truman's brewing books he keeps in his office. One covers most of WW I and it was fun pointing out what GA meant (Government Ale) and why it appeared at a specific time in 1917. The other is from 1969 and that contained the biggest shock: a beer called FB.

"That's Forest Brown," Derek said, "we used to brew it for Whitbread."

That was news to me. And quite a surprise as Whitbread owned more than a dozen breweries at the time. It seems odd that they'd get a London rival to brew one of their core products for them. Were they that short of capacity? Anyway, the beer was fermented at Truman then picked up by a Whitbread tanker and taken off for bottling. They were brewing a fair amount of it a Truman, going by the number of entries in the brewing book. And 500 barrels at a time.

I immediately realised this was a great opportunity. A chance to compare the beer brewed in two different places.

My first guess, having looked at the Truman version, was that it was pretty close to the original. For a start, unlike the other Truman beers it contained no adjuncts, just malt and sugar. And it was fermented with the Whitbread yeast. How wrong I was.

I'd forgotten that Whitbread started using adjuncts in 1963. At first just in their Pale Ales, but later in just about everything. Including Forest Brown. Which got me wondering about when exactly Truman started brewing Forest Brown. Because looking back through the Whitbread brewing books, their recipe appears remarkably similar to the Whitbread one from early 1964. Looks to me like Whitbread changed the recipe, but never told Truman.

See for yourself:

	1964 Whitbread FB	1968 Truman FB	1968 Whitbread FB
pale malt		79.48%	68.46%
flaked barley			13.69%
mild malt	78.97%		
crystal malt	7.70%	8.57%	7.82%
no. 3 invert sugar	10.91%	9.87%	
no. 1 invert sugar			7.17%
Hays M	2.41%		
Duttson CDM		2.08%	2.85%

That Truman were using an old recipe might also explain the colour difference, as Whitbread also darkened the colour in 1965.

Talking of colour, Duttson CDM must be pretty dark. Because when spun through BeerSmith both the Truman and Whitbread versions come out way too pale. Which is why I've substituted N. 4 invert for it. I suspect the letters stand for something like "Caramel Dark Mix".

As usual, the hop varieties are a bit of a guess. The 1968 Whitbread version has WGV and some that are just listed as MK. The Truman version only list the grower, though one is Whitbread so I guess it's probably WGV. Even though the hopping and boil times differ, BeerSmith calculates both to be 19 IBUs.

Believe it or not, this is actually on the strong side for a 1960's Brown Ale. 1027° – 1030° is a more typical gravity range. Interestingly, Truman always achieved better attenuation than Whitbread. The lowest OG for Whitbread's version in the 1960's (in the photos I have) is 1008.3°. The highest Truman's is 1007.3°. Not sure what that tells us.

1968 Whitbread Forest Brown		
pale malt	5.00 lb	68.97%
crystal malt 80 L	0.50 lb	6.90%
flaked barley	1.00 lb	13.79%
no. 1 sugar	0.50 lb	6.90%
no. 4 sugar	0.25 lb	3.45%
Fuggles 60 mins	0.25 oz	
Goldings 60 mins	0.25 oz	
Goldings 40 mins	0.50 oz	
Goldings 20 mins	0.50 oz	
OG	1032.1	
FG	1008.3	
ABV	3.15	
Apparent attenuation	74.14%	
IBU	19	
SRM	25	
Mash at	150° F	
Sparge at	170° F	
Boil time	60 minutes	
pitching temp	64° F	
Yeast	Wyeast 1099 Whitbread ale	

1969 Truman Whitbread Forest Brown		
pale malt	5.75 lb	80.42%
crystal malt 80 L	0.50 lb	6.99%
no. 3 invert sugar	0.75 lb	10.49%
no. 4 invert sugar	0.15 lb	2.10%
Fuggles 75 mins	0.50 oz	
Fuggles 60 mins	0.50 oz	
Goldings 30 mins	0.50 oz	
OG	1033	
FG	1005.5	
ABV	3.64	
Apparent attenuation	83.33%	
IBU	19	
SRM	17	
Mash at	144° F	
Sparge at	180° F	
Boil time	75 minutes	
pitching temp	62° F	
Yeast	Wyeast 1099 Whitbread ale	

Mini Book Series volume XXX: Let's Brew!

VII North America

Mini Book Series volume XXX: Let's Brew!

1833 Vassar Double Ale

Vassar was a successful Ale brewery in Poughkeepsie, New York. So successful in fact, that the owner was able to use some of the money he earned from it to found Vassar College.

If I'd just been shown their brewing records and given no other information, I would have guessed that they were from an English country brewery. They're quite a contrast from the later Amsdell records, which show a clear influence from German brewing. While Vassar's are English through and through.

Vassar didn't brew a huge range, just a couple of different strength Ales, either in Pale or Amber form. Sadly, I can't use any of the Amber Ale recipes because they're brewed from 100% amber malt. And diastatic amber malt doesn't currently exist.

Not really very much to say about Double Ale, other than that it's dead strong and quite hoppy. It looks quite similar to a London XXXX Ale of the 1830's. Like one of my all-time favourite reconstructions, 1832 Truman XXXX Ale.

1833 Vassar Double Ale		
pale malt	24.75 lb	100.00%
Cluster 180 mins	1.75 oz	
Cluster 60 mins	1.75 oz	
Cluster 30 mins	1.75 oz	
Cluster dry hops	0.50 oz	
OG	1107	
FG	1036	
ABV	9.39	
Apparent attenuation	66.36%	
IBU	72	
SRM	8	
Mash at	156° F	
Sparge at	170° F	
Boil time	180 minutes	
pitching temp	61° F	
Yeast	WLP051 California V	

1833 Vassar Single Ale

Parti-gyled with Double Ale was Single Ale. How more English could you get than that?

Which means Single Ale is exactly the same as Double Ale, just with a bit less of everything. That's painted myself into a corner. Nowhere to go. Let's just leave it at that.

1833 Vassar Single Ale		
pale malt	14.75 lb	100.00%
Cluster 180 mins	1.00 oz	
Cluster 60 mins	1.00 oz	
Cluster 30 mins	1.00 oz	
Cluster dry hops	0.25 oz	
OG	1064	
FG	1020	
ABV	5.82	
Apparent attenuation	68.75%	
IBU	53	
SRM	5	
Mash at	156° F	
Sparge at	170° F	
Boil time	180 minutes	
pitching temp	66° F	
Yeast	WLP051 California V	

1834 Vassar Pale Double Stock Ale

Vassar also brewed a Stock version of their Double Ale. Which is about the same as a London KKKK Ale.

So the same recipe as ordinary Double Ale, just with more hops. This is the problem with early 19th-century recipes. There's really not very much to say about them.

My guess is that original would have been aged for six to twelve months. Giving Brettanomyces plenty of time to work its wonderful magic.

1834 Vassar Pale Double Stock Ale		
pale malt	21.75 lb	100.00%
Cluster 75 mins	2.50 oz	
Cluster 60 mins	2.50 oz	
Cluster 30 mins	2.50 oz	
Cluster dry hops	1.00 oz	
OG	1094	
FG	1033	
ABV	8.07	
Apparent attenuation	64.89%	
IBU	96	
SRM	7	
Mash at	156° F	
Sparge at	170° F	
Boil time	75 minutes	
pitching temp	61° F	
Yeast	WLP051 California V	

Mini Book Series volume XXX: Let's Brew!

1893 Labbatt Pale Ale

A sign of the continuing influence of British brewing in North America is the appearance of locally-brewed Pale Ales in the 19th century.

Labbatt's Pale Ale isn't a million miles away from a UK-brewed version of the same date. Though the gravity is a little lower. A typical English Pale Ale had an OG of 1055-1060° in the 1890's. Which shouldn't be a real surprise, as that's what they were trying to emulate.

The hops are a total guess. I reckoned that they'd most likely be using locally-grown hops, so Cluster and British Columbian Goldings seem the obvious choice. But as I've no real idea, feel free to use any period-appropriate hops.

1893 Labbatt Pale Ale		
pale malt	11.50 lb	100.00%
Cluster 120 mins	1.50 oz	
BC Goldings 60 mins	1.25 oz	
BC Goldings 30 mins	1.25 oz	
OG	1049.9	
FG	1012.5	
ABV	4.95	
Apparent attenuation	74.95%	
IBU	63	
SRM	5	
Mash at	150° F	
Sparge at	176° F	
Boil time	120 minutes	
pitching temp	58° F	
Yeast	Wyeast 1099 Whitbread Ale	

1893 Labatt IPA

It wasn't just vanilla Pale Ale that was brewed in North America, IPA was popular, too.

Everyone has heard of the legendary Ballantine's IPA from New Jersey. But IPA was also brewed north of the border in Canada.

As with the Pale ale, this is a little weaker than the Burton style of IPA, which was usually 1060-1065°. This is basically just a slightly beefed-up version of Labatt's Pale Ale. Higher OG, more hops.

Not really much more to be said.

1893 Labatt IPA		
pale malt	12.75 lb	100.00%
Cluster 120 mins	2.00 oz	
BC Goldings 60 mins	1.50 oz	
BC Goldings 30 mins	1.50 oz	
BC Goldings dry hops	1.00 oz	
OG	1055.4	
FG	1012.5	
ABV	5.68	
Apparent attenuation	77.44%	
IBU	77	
SRM	5	
Mash at	150° F	
Sparge at	176° F	
Boil time	120 minutes	
pitching temp	58° F	
Yeast	Wyeast 1099 Whitbread Ale	

Mini Book Series volume XXX: Let's Brew!

1893 Labatt Brown Stout

Porter was the world's first truly international beer style, being brewed on just about every continent in the 19th century. North America was no exception.

Even before the independence of the USA, Porter was being brewed in the British colonies. Canada was no exception. And it has continued right through until today.

Labatt Brown Stout looks very much like a provincial English Stout of the same period, in that it has a grist of just pale malt and black malt. London Stouts, on the other hand, always included brown malt as well. For A London Stout, it would be a bit weak, but it's about the same strength as a provincial Stout.

The hops are a guess, but Canadian hops seem the most likely.

1893 Labatt Brown Stout		
pale malt	13.25 lb	89.83%
black malt	1.50 lb	10.17%
BC Goldings 120 mins	1.50 oz	
BC Goldings 60 mins	1.50 oz	
BC Goldings 30 mins	1.50 oz	
OG	1068	
FG	1015	
ABV	7.01	
Apparent attenuation	77.94%	
IBU	64	
SRM	38	
Mash at	150° F	
Sparge at	176° F	
Boil time	120 minutes	
pitching temp	58° F	
Yeast	Wyeast 1099 Whitbread Ale	

1904 Amsdell Burton

As a special treat for the week of the 4th July, I'm publishing an American recipe for once.

I didn't come up with the idea myself. It was a suggestion of a reader. And a very good suggestion it was. I just wish it had come a few days earlier.

This recipe has an interesting history. I originally wrote it for my book The Home Brewer's Guide to Vintage Beer. There was initially a chapter at the end on American beers. Then I changed my mind, deciding I'd like to save those for a later book. Which obviously hasn't happened do far. One day, one day.

Getting back to the beer itself, Burton was a style that never really caught on in the US. Beers with the name pop up every now and again in the Northeast, but with nothing like the frequency of IPA, Porter or Stock Ale. The most famous example, Ballantine Burton, was only ever brewed a few times and wasn't available for purchase, being given by the brewery as a Christmas gift.

In terms of strength, this looks more like a Bass No. 1 type Burton Ale than the London draught beer (usually called KK). That would have had an OG of about $1075°$ in this period. Even the stronger London KKK would have been weaker than this beer.

Amsdell's Burton does have much in common with London Burton. The brown colour and heavy hopping, for a start. Plus the combination of pale malt, maize and sugar. Not seen black malt in a London version of this period, though.

I've made one slight adjustment to the recipe, changing grits to flaked maize. If you fancy having a go at a cereal mash, feel free to use grits as in the original. I assume most of you would rather not bother.

Almost forgot. Amsdell was a largish Ale brewery in Albany, New York.

1904 Amsdell Burton		
pale malt 6 row	15.25 lb	72.62%
Black malt	0.25 lb	1.19%
fructose	1.50 lb	7.14%
Caramel		
Flaked corn	4.00 lb	19.05%
Cluster 90 min	4.00 oz	
Cluster 30 min	4.00 oz	
OG	1094	
FG	1028	
ABV	8.73	
Apparent attenuation	70.21%	
IBU	113	
SRM	20	
Mash at	148° F	
Sparge at	180° F	
Boil time	90 minutes	
pitching temp	60° F	
Yeast	Wyeast 1098 British ale - dry	

Mini Book Series volume XXX: Let's Brew!

1905 Amsdell India Pale Ale

Amsdell was a large brewery in the brewing town of Albany, New York, one of the biggest centres of Ale brewing before Prohibition.

Originally, they brewed in a very English way, but by the early 20th century the influence of German brewing was obvious, with the gravity being measured in Balling a European techniques like kräusening being employed.

In contrast to Labatt, Amsdell's IPA was stronger than was usual in the UK at the time. One of the reasons I suspect people in the USA think IPA is/was a strong beer, is because it was a strong beer in the USA. A separate tradition developed which, for some reason, seems to have led to IPA becoming stronger. I'd love to know why, but probably never will.

As was common in the USA, there are grits in the grist. It was never that popular as an adjunct in the UK, apart from at William Younger, who loved the stuff. About the only other place I can recall seeing it used in Britain is in some Barclay Perkins Lagers.

The hopping is rather lighter than would have been the case in the UK, but it still calculates out to a respectable 56 IBUs.

1905 Amsdell IPA		
pale malt	9.50 lb	60.32%
grits	3.25 lb	20.63%
glucose	3.00 lb	19.05%
Cluster 60 mins	1.50 oz	
Cluster 40 mins	1.50 oz	
Cluster 20 mins	1.50 oz	
BC Goldings dry hops	0.50 oz	
OG	1078	
FG	1029	
ABV	6.48	
Apparent attenuation	62.82%	
IBU	56	
SRM	4	
Mash at	152° F	
Sparge at	170° F	
Boil time	60 minutes	
pitching temp	56° F	
Yeast	WLP051 California V	

Mini Book Series volume XXX: Let's Brew!

1900 Amsdell Winter Stock

Stock Ale is another style whose roots can be traced directly back to Britain. Though there seem to have been some changes on the way.

For a start, this is weaker than, for example, a bottom-level London-brewed Burton Ale, such as the Barclay Perkins KK earlier in this book. Less hoppy, too. The BP KK has a gravity of 1074 and over 100 IBUs. This looks a bit puny in comparison.

And whereas London Burtons were mostly aged in trade casks, this beer was vatted. It says in the log: "Pumped Oct 23 to vat No. 3 with 50 lbs hops and 12 lbs sulphite soda." If they bothered transferring it to a vat, then it was probably aged for at least 3 months, if not longer.

The recipe is much like most of Amsdell's recipes: pale malt, grits and glucose. Which, in its way, is quite similar to UK recipes, which were typically pale malt, invert sugar and an adjunct, usually flaked maize.

Interesting that the boil times at Amsdell were pretty short. At this period in the UK, 90 minutes was about as short as boils got.

1900 Amsdell Winter Stock		
pale malt	8.75 lb	72.92%
grits	3.25 lb	27.08%
glucose	1.25 oz	
Cluster 45 mins	2.00 oz	
Cluster 30 mins	2.00 oz	
Cluster dry hops	0.4 oz	
OG	1062	
FG	1026	
ABV	4.76	
Apparent attenuation	58.06%	
IBU	57	
SRM	4	
Mash at	154° F	
Sparge at	170° F	
Boil time	45 minutes	
pitching temp	56° F	
Yeast	WLP051 California V	

Mini Book Series volume XXX: Let's Brew!

1900 Amsdell Winter XX

X Ales were one of the mainstays of American Ale breweries in the 19th century. With their origin obviously lying with English X Ales.

The term Mild Ale doesn't seem to have been used much in the USA. "Present Use", a slightly old-fashioned term in the UK by 1900, was used to signify the same thing. But mostly they were just called Ales. Usually XX or XXX, for some reason. X Ale, the most popular Ale in England, doesn't seem to have been a thing in the USA. Probably just breweries bigging up their Ales.

Amsdell's XX has about the same gravity as a London X Ale of 1900, though the bitterness is a bit lower. (Refer back to 1899 Barclay Perkins X for a full comparison. I can't be arsed to do it for you.)

The grist has the same ingredients as usual as Amsdell. Except there's also a little black malt, presumably for colour. It doesn't specify where it was added, so it could have been in the copper. Where it would have added more colour than in the mash. What was added in the copper was 20 lbs of salt. Which is slightly less than an eighth of an ounce for a recipe of the size below.

1900 Amsdell Winter XX		
pale malt	8.25 lb	65.32%
grits	4.00 lb	31.67%
black malt	0.05 lb	0.40%
glucose	0.33 lb	2.61%
Cluster 30 mins	2.25 oz	
OG	1056	
FG	1022	
ABV	4.50	
Apparent attenuation	60.71%	
IBU	31	
SRM	6	
Mash at	156° F	
Sparge at	170° F	
Boil time	30 minutes	
pitching temp	58° F	
Yeast	WLP051 California V	

Mini Book Series volume XXX: Let's Brew!

1900 Amsdell Export Scotch

Amsdell brewed a pretty wide range of top-fermenting beers. Including some very British sounding ones. Like Scotch Ale.

Doubtless it was inspired by exports from Scotland. At one point in the 19th century William McEwan and William Younger exported large quantities of beer to the USA.

So what is particularly distinctive about this beer? It's more lightly hopped than their other beers. And with the addition of caramel (called "color" in the log) it's darker, too. It also has a ridiculously high FG. Which does sort of sound like Scotch Ale.

As with most of Amsdell's beers, this was kräusened (about 18% of the total volume).

1900 Amsdell Export Scotch		
pale malt	8.50 lb	61.42%
grits	2.75 lb	19.87%
glucose	2.50 lb	18.06%
caramel	0.09 lb	0.65%
Cluster 60 mins	1.00 oz	
Cluster 30 mins	0.75 oz	
Cluster dry hops	0.25 oz	
OG	1067	
FG	1035	
ABV	4.23	
Apparent attenuation	47.76%	
IBU	26	
SRM	11	
Mash at	156° F	
Sparge at	170° F	
Boil time	60 minutes	
pitching temp	58° F	
Yeast	WLP051 California V	

1900 Amsdell Special Still

There must have been something unusual about this beer. Because the brewing record is covered in red.

What does the name mean? I think it signifies a beer that wasn't highly carbonated like some American Ales. Which were filled into asks under such pressure that they could be served without any external gas. This is also a type of Stock Ale, as half of it was filled into a vat. Presumably to be left to mature for several months.

It has the standard ingredients, common all Amsdell's beers: pale malt, grits and glucose. Though rather less of the latter, in this case.

1900 Amsdell Special Still		
pale malt	9.25 lb	66.07%
grits	3.75 lb	26.79%
glucose	1.00 lb	7.14%
Cluster 60 mins	1.50 oz	
Cluster 30 mins	1.25 oz	
Cluster dry hops	0.375 oz	
OG	1064	
FG	1021	
ABV	5.69	
Apparent attenuation	67.19%	
IBU	41	
SRM	4	
Mash at	158° F	
Sparge at	170° F	
Boil time	60 minutes	
pitching temp	56° F	
Yeast	WLP051 California V	

1900 Amsdell Light XXX Stock Ale

Another Amsdell Stock Ale. One which, other than a slightly lower hopping rate and a bit more sugar, is pretty much identical to Special Still.

You may have noticed that Amsdell produced a lot of quite similar Ales. I'm scratching my head a bit trying to make out what the difference between some of them is. The one thing that isn't the same with this one is that it wasn't vatted.

1900 Amsdell Light XXX Stock Ale		
pale malt	9.75 lb	70.91%
grits	2.50 lb	18.18%
glucose	1.50 lb	10.91%
Cluster 60 mins	1.25 oz	
Cluster 30 mins	1.25 oz	
Cluster dry hops	0.375 oz	
OG	1064	
FG	1021	
ABV	5.69	
Apparent attenuation	67.19%	
IBU	37	
SRM	4	
Mash at	156° F	
Sparge at	170° F	
Boil time	60 minutes	
pitching temp	56° F	
Yeast	WLP051 California V	

Mini Book Series volume XXX: Let's Brew!

1901 Amsdell Polar

Two things strike me about Amsdell: the brewed several very similar beers, they had some good names for their beers.

Why this should be called Polar, I've no idea. It's not as if it was a beer designed for the Arctic. You'd expect a beer like that to be much stronger. This looks pretty much like a London X Ale, except it doesn't contain any dark sugar. Compare it with the 1899 Barclay Perkins X Ale earlier in this book.

One thing that sets Amsdell's beers apart from English ones are the very short boil times. 90 minutes was about as short as they got in England at this time. That and the fact that they brewed all their beer single gyle.

1901 Amsdell Polar		
pale malt	8.25 lb	68.75%
grits	2.75 lb	22.92%
glucose	1.00 lb	8.33%
Cluster 60 mins	1.25 oz	
Cluster 30 mins	1.25 oz	
Cluster dry hops	0.25 oz	
OG	1054	
FG	1019	
ABV	4.63	
Apparent attenuation	64.81%	
IBU	39	
SRM	4	
Mash at	157° F	
Sparge at	170° F	
Boil time	60 minutes	
pitching temp	58° F	
Yeast	WLP051 California V	

1901 Amsdell XX

What's the difference between XX and Polar? Not very much.

There's a tad more glucose in XX. But other than that, the gravity and hopping are near identical. So why have I included this beer? Because it was Amsdell's bread and butter beer, of which they brewed much more than anything else in their range. It's a classic Albany Ale. I could leave that out, could I?

1901 Amsdell XX		
pale malt	7.25 lb	65.91%
grits	2.50 lb	22.73%
glucose	1.25 lb	11.36%
Cluster 60 mins	1.25 oz	
Cluster 30 mins	1.25 oz	
Cluster dry hops	0.375 oz	
OG	1053	
FG	1016	
ABV	4.89	
Apparent attenuation	69.81%	
IBU	40	
SRM	4	
Mash at	156° F	
Sparge at	170° F	
Boil time	60 minutes	
pitching temp	58° F	
Yeast	WLP051 California V	

1901 Amsdell Diamond Stock

No confusion about how Diamond differs from the other Amsdell beers. It's stronger and more heavily hopped. Which is what you would expect of a Stock Ale.

The ingredients are the same as most of Amsdell's beers: pale malt, grits and glucose. How different did their beers taste from each other? There must have been a fair amount of similarity. Especially as they would have been using the same yeast in everything.

Being a Stock Ale, I'd assume that this would have been aged for a while before sale. It doesn't specifically mention it being vatted in the brewing record, but I suspect that it was.

1901 Amsdell Diamond Stock		
pale malt	12.00 lb	68.57%
grits	3.75 lb	21.43%
glucose	1.75 lb	10.00%
Cluster 60 mins	2.50 oz	
Cluster 30 mins	2.50 oz	
Cluster dry hops	0.50 oz	
OG	1082	
FG	1028	
ABV	7.14	
Apparent attenuation	65.85%	
IBU	65	
SRM	5	
Mash at	158° F	
Sparge at	170° F	
Boil time	60 minutes	
pitching temp	56° F	
Yeast	WLP051 California V	

Mini Book Series volume XXX: Let's Brew!

1901 Amsdell Sth Porter

What's a Porter and what's a Stout? I'd usually say that Stout is a stronger version of Porter. Yet this Amsdell Porter is stronger than Labatt's Brown Stout. I long ago abandoned a search for any sort of consistency in beer naming. There isn't any.

Unlike all Amsdell's other beers, their Porter contains no grits. Instead there's rather a lot of black malt. Combined with quite heavy hopping, that must have made for quite a bitter beer.

The real FG would have been lower than indicated as this beer was vatted. My guess would be 6 to 12 months ageing, which would have knocked the FG down to around 1020°.

1901 Amsdell Sth Porter		
pale malt	11.00 lb	69.84%
black malt	2.00 lb	12.70%
glucose	2.75 lb	17.46%
Cluster 60 mins	2.25 oz	
Cluster 30 mins	2.25 oz	
Cluster dry hops	0.50 oz	
OG	1074	
FG	1025	
ABV	6.48	
Apparent attenuation	66.22%	
IBU	62	
SRM	46	
Mash at	158° F	
Sparge at	170° F	
Boil time	60 minutes	
pitching temp	56° F	
Yeast	WLP051 California V	

1904 Amsdell XX

Just for fun, here's a slightly later Amsdell XX.

It's not so much different to the 1901 version. A little stronger and a little hoppier. Plus it contains a little black malt and some syrup. So the recipe is a fair bit more complicated, though it does still contain the standard pale malt, grits and glucose.

1904 Amsdell XX		
pale malt 6 row	8.50 lb	70.10%
Black malt	0.125 lb	1.03%
Glucose	0.75 lb	6.19%
Syrup	0.25 lb	2.06%
grits	2.50 lb	20.62%
Cluster 90 min	2.00 oz	
Cluster 30 min	1.00 oz	
OG	1055	
FG	1016	
ABV	5.16	
Apparent attenuation	70.91%	
IBU	55	
SRM	9	
Mash at	158° F	
Sparge at	160° F	
Boil time	60 minutes	
pitching temp	60° F	
Yeast	Wyeast 1099 Whitbread Ale	

Index

18th century, 186
19th century, 12, 70, 85, 124, 166
20th century, 42, 60, 88, 124, 129, 181, 209
4d Ale, 15
54/-, 129
60/-, 129, 130
70/-, 129, 130
80/-, 129, 130
AK, 70, 107
Ale, 15, 41, 42, 43, 45, 51, 52, 53, 57, 60, 61, 62, 63, 64, 71, 72, 73, 74, 77, 78, 79, 81, 83, 85, 108, 109, 110, 111, 112, 113, 129, 130, 143, 167, 187, 205, 206, 207, 208, 209, 210, 214, 215, 277, 278, 283
amber malt, 11, 15, 133, 134, 186, 187
Amsterdam, 2, 9, 10
Australia, 113
Barclay Perkins, 11, 40, 63, 80, 112, 124, 186, 205
barley, 46, 71, 125, 256
Bass, 112, 113, 124, 129, 256
Bass Charrington, 129
Bavaria, 228
Bavarian, 229
Beasley, 112
Bernard, 76
Best Mild, 40, 45, 46
Bitter, 40, 45, 56, 68, 70, 72, 76, 78, 82, 88, 89, 107, 112, 125, 256, 281
black malt, 11, 45, 84, 88, 89, 142, 143, 167, 179, 186, 187, 209, 210

Bohemia, 228
Bohemian, 228
bottled beer, 40, 52, 76, 109, 110, 111, 124, 142, 179, 183, 208, 209
bottled Stout, 142, 181
British beer, 56, 60
Brown Ale, 15, 78, 80, 110, 111, 205, 277, 281, 282, 283
Brown Beer, 61
brown malt, 11, 46, 63, 142, 166, 180, 182, 184, 186
Brown Stout, 142
BSt, 186
Burton, 206, 207, 208, 209, 256, 277, 282
Burton Ale, 206, 207, 282
Californian, 12
CAMRA, 43, 281
caramel, 15, 39, 40, 42, 45, 56, 60, 63, 73, 76, 82, 84, 124, 130, 133, 134, 166, 179, 183, 205, 207, 208, 277, 278, 281, 282
cask, 43, 51, 56, 64, 70, 111, 281
Charrington, 112
Chiswell Street, 125, 142, 181
Cluster, 12, 38, 39, 51, 53, 60, 63
Country, 107
Courage, 112, 129
crystal malt, 15, 39, 43, 44, 45, 64, 72, 78, 79, 84, 124, 125, 134, 167, 205, 210, 214, 215, 277, 282
Czech, 179
Dark Mild, 56, 78, 205,

214
decoction, 228, 229, 230
Dickmeisch, 227
Dickscheit, 230
double decoction, 230
draught Stout, 179
Dry Stout, 166
Dublin, 181
Edinburgh, 129, 130, 187
Edinburgh Ale, 130, 187
England, 107, 124, 129, 130, 186
Export, 112, 129, 130, 181
Extra Stout, 181, 182, 183
finings, 281
flaked barley, 42, 46, 71, 125, 143, 206
flaked oats, 46, 125
Free Mash Tun Act, 56
Fuggle, 277
Fuggles, 12, 15, 38, 39, 40, 41, 42, 44, 45, 46, 51, 53, 56, 57, 60, 63, 64, 68, 71, 72, 74, 77, 79, 84, 88, 89, 108, 113, 124, 125, 133, 134, 143, 167, 180, 182, 184, 205, 206, 207, 208, 209, 210, 214, 215, 278, 282, 283, 284
Germany, 230
glucose, 42, 45, 71, 72, 110, 113, 206, 210
Gold Label, 211
Golden Pride, 208
Golding Varieties, 125
Goldings, 12, 40, 44, 45, 56, 62, 64, 68, 72, 74, 77, 79, 80, 81, 82, 83, 84, 88, 89, 108, 109,

312

110, 113, 124, 125, 130, 133, 184, 187, 205, 207, 208, 209, 211, 215, 277, 278, 283
Goldings Varieties, 207, 208
Good Beer Guide, 68, 214
Government Ale, 15
Guinness, 133, 166, 181, 256
Holland, 2
hops, 11, 38, 43, 44, 45, 56, 60, 61, 68, 70, 84, 88, 89, 109, 110, 113, 124, 125, 129, 130, 133, 142, 179, 205, 207, 209, 214, 215, 230, 277, 283
invert sugar, 39, 40, 44, 46, 60, 63, 64, 73, 74, 77, 79, 108, 124, 125, 182, 210, 277, 284
IPA, 61, 70, 80, 81, 124, 125, 129, 205, 283
Ireland, 179
Irish Stout, 186
John Keeling, 281
keg, 64, 76, 125
KKKK, 205
Kulmbach, 229
Leeds, 52, 76
Light Ale, 73, 78, 109, 110, 111
Light Mild, 73, 76
London, 39, 42, 43, 45, 46, 51, 60, 61, 70, 72, 80, 88, 89, 107, 113, 124, 129, 142, 166, 179, 181, 186, 205, 206, 208, 209, 210, 211, 256, 278
London Metropolitan Archive, 80, 113, 129, 181

London Porter, 61, 142, 186
London Stout, 179, 186
LP, 70, 72
MA, 57, 282
MA malt, 57, 282
Mackeson, 84, 142, 166, 181, 183, 184
malt, 11, 227, 228, 230
Malt, 53, 182, 184
Mann, 112
Mann Crossman, 112
McEwan, 130
Midlands, 73, 166
Mild, 11, 15, 38, 39, 40, 42, 43, 45, 46, 51, 52, 56, 57, 60, 61, 63, 64, 76, 78, 80, 107, 129, 130, 205, 206, 208, 214, 256, 277, 281, 283
Mild Ale, 43, 208, 283
mild malt, 15, 51, 53, 62, 64, 108, 134, 166, 167, 180, 182, 183, 184, 214, 215, 281
Munich, 227
No.2 invert, 72, 183, 278
No.3 invert, 15, 78, 166, 278, 283
Oatmeal Stout, 179
oats, 46, 179, 180
Old Ale, 61, 205, 208, 214
PA, 57, 61, 68, 70, 71, 72, 107, 108, 110, 124, 125, 128, 129, 130, 214, 215, 283
PA malt, 57, 108, 110, 124, 125, 215
Pale Ale, 11, 70, 72, 75, 80, 82, 109, 110, 111, 112, 113, 129, 130, 133, 142, 166, 186, 214, 283

pale malt, 11, 39, 40, 41, 42, 44, 45, 46, 51, 53, 60, 63, 68, 71, 72, 73, 74, 76, 77, 78, 79, 80, 81, 83, 84, 88, 89, 109, 113, 125, 130, 143, 166, 167, 180, 182, 183, 187, 205, 206, 207, 208, 210, 211, 277, 278, 284
parti-gyle, 52, 73, 129, 181, 183, 206, 208, 214, 277
parti-gyled, 52, 73, 129, 181, 183, 206, 214
parti-gyling, 181, 208, 214
Pilsner Urquell, 109
Porter, 11, 61, 63, 107, 142, 179, 181, 186
roast barley, 281, 282
Robert Younger, 129, 130
Running, 186
S, 78, 179
Saaz, 179, 180, 182, 187
Schönfeld, 230
Scotch Ale, 61
Scotland, 107, 129, 186
Scottish Ale, 186
Sheepscar, 51
Small Beer, 227
SS, 179, 186
SSS, 179
Stout, 45, 46, 61, 63, 80, 84, 110, 111, 129, 133, 142, 166, 167, 179, 180, 181, 183, 184, 186, 209, 256, 281
Strong Ale, 80, 107, 110, 186, 205, 208, 209, 211
sugar, 11, 15, 38, 39, 42, 43, 44, 45, 46, 51, 52, 53, 56, 57, 60, 63, 68,

71, 72, 76, 80, 84, 88, 107, 108, 109, 110, 113, 124, 125, 130, 134, 142, 167, 179, 180, 183, 184, 207, 208, 209, 210, 211, 214, 215, 277, 283
Tetley, 51, 52, 53, 112
triple decoction, 230
Truman, 112, 113, 142, 186
underlet, 42, 72, 88
Usher, 281
Wales, 107
Watney, 72, 112, 129, 281
Wenlock, 112
wheat, 38, 39, 73, 74, 76, 77, 84
Whitbread, 56, 61, 62, 63, 64, 71, 72, 73, 76, 80, 82, 84, 112, 113, 124, 125, 128, 129, 130, 142, 179, 180, 181, 182, 183, 184, 186, 283, 284
Whitbread Gravity Book, 72, 82
William Younger, 179, 186, 187
WW I, 15, 38, 40, 43, 64, 73, 84, 107, 124, 125, 130, 133, 142, 166, 179, 181, 183, 205, 207, 283
WW II, 15, 38, 40, 43, 64, 73, 107, 124, 125, 130, 133, 142, 166, 179, 181, 183, 205, 207, 283
X, 42, 52, 60, 61, 62, 64, 70, 205, 206, 208, 277
X Ale, 42, 60, 64, 70, 206, 277
XK, 63, 70
XX, 15, 39, 43, 44, 60, 61, 63, 281
XXX, 40, 41, 56, 57, 60, 107, 205, 214
XXXX, 60, 214
XXXXX, 214
Yorkshire, 51, 53, 73, 76
Younger, 40, 112, 129, 186, 187

www.ingramcontent.com/pod-product-compliance
Lightning Source LLC
Chambersburg PA
CBHW051038160426
43193CB00010B/983